LIBERAL UTILITARIANISM
AND APPLIED ETHICS

SOCIAL ETHICS AND POLICY
Edited by Anthony Dyson and John Harris
Centre for Social Ethics and Policy,
University of Manchester

LIBERAL
UTILITARIANISM
AND APPLIED
ETHICS

Matti Häyry

London and New York

First published 1994
by Routledge
11 New Fetter Lane, London EC4P 4EE

Simultaneously published in the USA and Canada
by Routledge
29 West 35th Street, New York, NY 10001

© 1994 Matti Häyry

Typeset in Garamond by
Computerset, Harmondsworth, Middlesex
Printed and bound in Great Britain by
T.J. Press (Padstow) Ltd, Padstow, Cornwall

Printed on acid free paper

British Library Cataloguing in Publication Data
A catalogue record for this book is available from the British Library

Library of Congress Cataloging in Publication Data
Häyry, Matti.
Liberal utilitarianism and applied ethics/Matti Häyry.
p. cm.–(Social ethics and policy series)
Includes bibliographical references and index.
1. Utilitarianism. I. Title. II. Series.
B843.H38   1994
171'.5–dc20   94–345
ISBN 0–415–07785–0

To all my friends

CONTENTS

PREFACE

The idea of writing this book came to me on the 13th of December, 1990, at approximately 10 o'clock in the evening. A few hours earlier I had publicly defended my doctoral dissertation at the University of Helsinki, and I was now having dinner with Timo Airaksinen, who had supervised my work, John Harris, who had examined it, and Heta Häyry, who had defended her own dissertation in November. During the starters, the conversation turned to my thesis, which was on health care ethics, and to the fact that in my defence I had rejected moral absolutism in certain medical matters. Halfway through the main course, Timo and John tried to convince me that my line of argument was skewed, and that it would inevitably lead to full-fledged ethical relativism, anarchy and chaos. I disagreed with them, of course, but did not quite know how to justify my position. It was not until the dessert had been served that the answer, and the idea of preparing this book, hit me.

I have been convinced that the main ideas of utilitarianism are sound since I read my very first book on moral philosophy, G.E. Moore's *Ethics*, in April 1982. I could not see then, and still cannot see today, how it could be my duty to act in ways which do not produce the maximum of net good. I was forced to defend my view on several occasions during the academic year 1987–8, when Heta, I and a colleague of ours, Heikki Kannisto, frequently sat up long nights discussing the pros and cons of various ethical theories. To keep the arguments flowing, we often assumed fixed roles. Usually Heta defended a liberal view, Heikki advocated virtue ethics and I upheld the utilitarian theory. In the course of these discussions I gradually learned that there are corollaries to the traditional utilitarian principles which make the doctrine intuitively unacceptable to many people. I did not, however, give up my conviction that there must be a form of utilitarianism which can be defended against the intuitionist critiques. Eventually, in 1989, Heta and I put our heads together and came up with the first formulation of liberal utilitarianism.

I had, however, started writing my dissertation in 1985, that is, before I had any ideas concerning the liberal version of utilitarianism. Since I mistrusted deontological moral theories even more than the classical utilitarian doctrine, I had to assume a more general theoretical approach. My solution was to rely on the methods of applied ethics as I understood them. The view presented in the thesis was that certain medical decisions and health care policies can be justified only by appeals to the principles of consistency and intuitive acceptability. The problem with this solution is, as pointed out by John and Timo, that it appears to endorse complete ethical relativism, and to undermine the objective basis of morality. But appearances are, I believe, deceptive here. What my critics failed to see, and what I failed to emphasize in my dissertation, is that appeals to logic and emotion in difficult cases like abortion, euthanasia and the allocation of scarce medical resources do not necessarily rule out appeals to more fundamental ethical principles in less controversial situations. The fact that I do not trust traditional ethical theories in contentious issues does not automatically mean that I do not trust them in more clear-cut cases.

We finished our dessert, and over coffee I told John that I intended to write a book on utilitarianism and applied ethics. I described my views on both doctrines, and explained to him how I thought I could, by combining them, alleviate the relativism which was so apparent in my dissertation. John wanted to see a written outline of my ideas, and I sent him the sketch of a book a few months later. In July 1991, Routledge commissioned me, on John's proposal, to write the book for the Social Ethics and Policy Series. I started my work in September 1991, and completed the bulk of the book in May 1993.

I have incurred several debts during the preparation of this book. My warm thanks are due to Timo Airaksinen, John Harris and Heikki Kannisto, who have all in their different ways made my present work possible. Mark Shackleton, Lecturer in English, University of Helsinki, has revised the language of the manuscript, for which I am truly grateful. I also extend my thanks to Mikko

Salmela, who went well beyond the call of duty in providing me with the essential literature on utilitarianism, and to Martti Kuokkanen, Sirkku Hellsten and Marjaana Kopperi, who offered their comments on the completed manuscript. A generous Research Fellowship granted to me by the University of Helsinki has provided my livelihood since June 1985. I acknowledge this support with gratitude.

As always, my greatest debt is to Heta Häyry. Not only did she co-author the first formulation of liberal utilitarianism, she also discussed with me in detail all the arguments presented in the book, and suggested numerous useful corrections and amendments. Even more importantly, she has once again provided me with the emotional support and intellectual responses which alone can turn the strenuous marathon of preparing a philosophical book into the pleasurable country walk we all would like it to be.

I dedicate this book, following the example of the cinematic figure of Henry Chinaski, to all my friends.

Matti Häyry
November 1993

INTRODUCTION

The social ethics and social policy of modern welfare states are based on principles and ideals introduced and developed by the utilitarian philosophers of the eighteenth and nineteenth centuries. General well-being and equality among individuals have been focal to legal and social reforms since the rise of classical utilitarianism in Britain, and reformist movements ranging from liberalism to socialism have recognized the status of these values as goals of good government. Furthermore, the economic doctrines employed in today's West mainly descend from the views put forward by the nineteenth-century advocates of the principle of utility. It can, in fact, be reasonably argued that modern societies cannot be fully comprehended without understanding the nature and evolution of the utilitarian theories which constitute their ethical core.

Public decision-making has in the majority of twentieth-century Western countries been founded on roughly utilitarian ideals, that is, on the idea that the happiness of society at large outweighs the happiness of a few privileged individuals. This axiom can be supplemented by the concept of a society as an organic whole, in which case those who employ the maxim can end up supporting various versions of collectivism and totalitarianism. But when the utilitarian principles are combined with the credos of individualism, the ensuing theory will most likely be critical towards collectivist and totalitarian pressures. Moral theorists who place their trust in rights and duties rather than in the notion of the good have sometimes believed that utility calculations are automatically hostile towards the interests of individuals, but this belief is mistaken. Utilitarianism in its original form is capable of respecting the well-being of particular individuals to a degree which is quite compatible

1

with the respect granted to autonomous persons by rights-based and duty-based moralities.

It is, admittedly, true that if a holistic interpretation is given to the principle of general well-being, the pursuit of an abstract common good can lead to violations of the rights of individuals and minorities. It is also true that the utilitarian way of thinking which prevailed in England at the turn of the twentieth century seems to have provided British philosophers with no tools to criticize the growth of totalitarianism in the European continent. It was only after the traditional branch of moral philosophy now known as practical or applied ethics began to re-emerge in the 1960s that the plight of individuals in the hands of unjust governments was recognized by academic philosophers. Even then, the philosophers in question founded their judgements on the concepts of liberty and rights rather than on the notion of utility. The American pioneers of applied ethics especially believed that it is more effective to challenge, for instance, racial, ethnic or gender-related discrimination by direct appeals to human rights and civil liberties than by indirect references to the greatest general good.

It would, however, be an error to think that applied ethics could be understood, let alone practised, in a purely non-utilitarian framework. The philosophical study of real-life moral issues has been profoundly influenced by the methods and ideals of utilitarianism. The majority of applied philosophers believe, as do all utilitarians, that ethical decision-making must be based on reliable data concerning the consequences of alternative actions. There are normative ethical theories which do not recognize the significance of the outcomes of human deeds, but these theories either fail to define unequivocally the rights and duties of moral agents in difficult situations, or condone courses of action which are intuitively and emotionally unacceptable. Those philosophers who have set out to solve practical moral problems by the methods of applied ethics can argue with utilitarian theorists that they have devised a fully comprehensive model of normative decision-making.

Despite the newfound interest in practical issues, and despite the obvious link between applied ethics and the utilitarian way of thinking, many contemporary moral philosophers regard utilitarianism as an uninteresting and immoral doctrine. The rejection of the theory is frequently based on the conviction that considerations of utility in ethics necessarily lead to cold pseudo-scientific calculations and to gross violations of liberty and justice. According to persistent philosophical folklore, utilitarians are always prepared to sacrifice their families and friends for the sake of benefiting total strangers, and to frame and inflict harm on innocent passers-by in order to further the general good of society. Consistent utilitarians are also supposed to prefer, under certain circumstances, the dumbly pleasurable life of an oyster to the more demanding lives of culturally refined human beings. In addition, policies based on utility measures are believed to be, by nature, totalitarian and insensitive to any demands for autonomy, justice and fairness.

There are, indeed, versions of utilitarianism which do warrant these counterintuitive conclusions. The main target of legitimate criticism is the doctrine of classical utilitarianism, formulated at the turn of the nineteenth century by Jeremy Bentham, who in many respects can be seen as the founder of modern utilitarianism. At the core of Bentham's classical doctrine there are three principles which are widely held to be focal to all forms of utilitarianism. The first of these, the greatest happiness principle, states that all human efforts ought to be aimed at maximizing happiness and minimizing suffering in the world. The second, hedonistic principle spells out the classical utilitarian theory of value by defining happiness as the pleasure, or absence of pain, of sentient living beings, and suffering as the pain, or absence of pleasure. The third principle, the principle of impartiality, requires that the pleasures and pains of all sentient beings ought to be taken equally into account when decisions are made. The classical utilitarian calculus does not permit any favouritism or privileges based on mutual feelings, family relationships, shared nationalities or the like.

Taken together, the three principles of classical utilitarianism give rise to a theory which may demand that we sacrifice those we love, or act in unjust ways in the name of the common good. But fortunately for the defenders of utilitarianism, the classical doctrine is not the only feasible version of the theory. Even Bentham, the alleged author of the view, can in fact be dissociated from some of its most incriminating elements. The same observation applies to his predecessors and, to variable degrees, to his successors. Theoretically speaking, it should not be by any means impossible to develop qualified principles which do not lead to the dubious conclusions that undermine the credibility of the classical view.

My first aim in this book is to show how the conventional

twentieth-century understanding of the history of utilitarianism is inadequate, and how a more careful reading can bring to the fore interesting facts concerning the early development of the doctrine. In Chapter 1 I undertake to prove that, contrary to popular philosophical belief, classical Benthamite utilitarianism cannot be seen as the original formulation of the utilitarian view. Bentham's work was, as a matter of fact, preceded by over a century of British moral thought in which the concepts of happiness, pleasure and universal impartiality had been central. Although Bentham attributed the invention of these principles to the continental philosophers Cesare Beccaria and Claude-Adrien Helvétius, the basic tenets of utilitarianism had been introduced and developed within the British tradition by English, Irish and Scottish writers, including, most notably, John Locke, George Berkeley and David Hume. A detailed examination of the works of these and other British moralists clearly shows that the historical reconstruction of utilitarianism is not dependent on the relatively narrow views expressed by the proponents of the classical doctrine.

The significance of the historical introduction presented in chapter 1 is twofold. On the one hand, it serves to refute the deep-rooted notion that modern versions of utilitarianism ought closely to resemble Bentham's theory. A common argument against those utilitarian theories which evade the problems of the classical view is that they are not sufficiently Benthamite, and therefore not genuinely utilitarian. The historical survey shows that this objection is misdirected. On the other hand, the chronicle of early utilitarianism also reveals the sources of many criticisms which have been levelled at the doctrine. The account makes it possible to see that the majority of these critiques have already been recognized, and duly countered, by the utilitarian theorists of the eighteenth century.

My second aim in this book is to analyse and assess the strengths and weaknesses of the most important forms of classical and modern utilitarianism. There are four questions which the proponents of the utilitarian doctrine should be able to answer in order to prove that their views are legitimate, but which continue to puzzle them. The first two questions concern the normative and axiological bases of the creed. On what grounds can it be argued that the morality of actions should be defined exclusively in terms of the greatest general happiness? And what exactly is meant by the term 'happiness' in the formula? The third question bears on the application of the utilitarian principle in practice. Some theorists argue that the moral rightness of each particular action should be assessed separately by referring to its actual or expected consequences. Others, in turn, maintain that the utilitarian criterion should be applied to rules instead of individual actions. Rules are, according to the latter view, justifiable if their existence or observance produces the greatest general good, while singular actions are morally right only if they conform to legitimate rules.

These questions regarding the normative, axiological and practical aspects of utilitarianism can, as I endeavour to show in Chapter 2, probably be answered with relative ease by contemporary proponents of the doctrine. But the fourth question, which concerns equality and justice, is more difficult to deal with. Most utilitarian theories seem to demand that we seek to promote the greatest general good even in situations where our efforts inevitably violate some traditional precepts of justice. There are cases in which the solution offered by utilitarianism is, in the last analysis, more sensible than the alternatives suggested by conventional moralities and deontological ethical theories. But there are also cases in which it is impossible to defend the classical utilitarian position against charges of injustice. The sacrifice of an innocent individual in the name of the greater general good is a perfect example. Even if the overall well-being of individuals in a community were considerably enhanced by publicly executing an innocent person, the sacrifice would be firmly condemned by the considered judgements of moral persons as well as by traditional theories of justice. Those who profess the utilitarian creed have not, however, been able to accommodate the fundamental moral intuitions which underlie the condemnation, nor have they been able to deny convincingly their ethical relevance.

The findings of Chapters 1 and 2 make it both possible and necessary to revise the essentially Benthamite principles of contemporary utilitarianism. My third aim in this book is to work out an ethical theory which preserves the sound parts of utilitarian thinking while rejecting the elements which make it unacceptable to most reasonable people. The revised theory, which I call liberal utilitarianism, is introduced and developed in Chapter 3. According to this view, the universal well-being of sentient beings can be employed to define the moral rightness of actions only insofar as the actions in question do not threaten to frustrate the basic needs of individuals or groups. The restriction of the theory to cases which do not involve serious conflicts of interest guarantees that the problems regarding utility and justice do not arise. On the other hand, of course, the limitation also exposes liberal utilitarianism to the objection that it leaves many important real-life moral questions unanswered.

My fourth, and final, aim in the book is to formulate a set of general principles which can be employed in ethical decision-making when the precepts of liberal utilitarianism do not apply. In Chapter 4 I argue that the required guides can be found by examining the methods of applied ethics. The point of these methods, when the discipline is not understood as the mechanical application of ready-made ethical theories, is to justify moral choices by appeals to logic and shared emotions. The proposed methodology is centred on the idea that the doctrines and views behind ethical decisions can be falsified by showing that they are conceptually or logically inconsistent or incoherent, and further tested by observing the intuitive responses provoked in individuals and groups by their application to reality.

Since it is quite possible that shared emotions differ ethnically, nationally, culturally and socially, the solutions offered by applied ethicists may differ from one group or place to another. This does not imply that the validity of moral judgements would depend entirely on the opinions of the people who pass them. Given that the ideals of liberal utilitarianism are intuitively acceptable to all moral persons, as I argue in Chapter 3, the rights and duties defined by that creed rise above all culturally determined criticism. In addition, particular ethical problems can be tackled by appeals to principles which are widely held in many different societies. There are, however, also moral dilemmas which cannot be untangled by referring to universally or cross-culturally held opinions. My analysis in Chapter 4 indicates that there are no absolute, unequivocally valid answers to these problems. But moral philosophers should, nonetheless, continue to seek and to set forth solutions which are likely to survive the tests of logical consistency and intuitive acceptability.

This book explores the foundations of utilitarianism and, at the same time, the theoretical basis of social ethics and policy in modern Western welfare states. The discussions here are not extended to particular social issues, nor do they provide individuals with foolproof answers to specific moral problems. These important matters cannot be studied properly without a thorough understanding of the general principles underlying ethical decision-making in real-life situations. It is my aim in the following chapters to contribute to such understanding by examining the historical and contemporary forms of utilitarianism, and by putting forward an ethical theory which combines the methods of applied ethics and the ideals of universal equality and well-being.

1

UTILITARIANISM AND THE BRITISH TRADITION

The classical utilitarianism presented in introductory courses of moral philosophy is usually said to derive from the work of Jeremy Bentham and John Stuart Mill. The original statement of the utilitarian doctrine is attributed to Bentham's *An Introduction to the Principles of Morals and Legislation* (1789), which is thought to centre on the following three principles:

1 *The greatest happiness principle.*
  An act, omission, rule, law, policy or reform is the right one if and only if it produces, or can be reasonably expected to produce, at least as much happiness as any other alternative which is open to the agent or decision-maker at the time of the choice.

2 *The hedonistic principle.*
  'Happiness' means the pleasure and absence of pain of sentient living beings. The qualities of different kinds of pleasure and pain are irrelevant to the happiness calculation – the only variables to be considered are the intensity, duration, probability, closeness, continuity and purity of the pleasures and pains in question, and the number of individuals who experience them.

3 *The principle of impartiality.*
  In the happiness calculation, the pleasures and pains of each sentient living being shall be weighed equally: the relationship of the individual in question with the agent or decision-maker or primary beneficiary or burden-bearer for the chosen course of action or inaction shall not increase or decrease the value to be attached to its or her or his experiences.

Mill's contribution to classical utilitarianism is normally taken to

8

be twofold. On the one hand, he amended the utilitarian axiology by stating that the quality of pleasures and pains should, contrary to Bentham's view, play a definite role in the happiness calculation. Mill's oft-quoted words on the matter in *Utilitarianism* (1861) are: 'It is better to be a human being dissatisfied than a pig satisfied; better to be Socrates dissatisfied than a fool satisfied.'[1] On the other hand, Mill also tried to soften the harsh paternalism implied by Bentham's theory by stating that legal regulations should not be extended to people's private affairs. As he put the matter in *On Liberty* (1859): 'The only part of the conduct of any one, for which he is amenable to society, is that which concerns others. In the part which merely concerns himself, his independence is, of right, absolute.'[2] With the addition of these two elements to the Benthamite teaching, classical utilitarianism is supposed to have reached its most complete expression.

This view of utilitarianism is, however, oversimplified and problematic on many accounts – as, of course, most introductory summaries tend to be. To begin with, although Bentham presumably accepted the three principles mentioned above, it is less than obvious that he could be regarded as their author. The greatest happiness principle, which Bentham himself seems to have found in the later eighteenth-century writings of Cesare Beccaria and Claude-Adrien Helvétius,[3] was first formulated by Francis Hutcheson as early as 1725: '[T]hat action is best, which procures the greatest happiness for the greatest numbers.'[4] As for the hedonistic principle, Bentham was hardly the first to hold that the only intrinsic good is pleasure and the only intrinsic evil is pain. Hedonism has been one of the major theories of value at least since Epicurus (341–270BC).[5] Besides, although Bentham explicitly founded his axiology on the balance of pleasure over pain, he also stated that 'pleasure' in the context of ethics is equal to benefit, advantage, utility and good.[6] These equations confuse the ultimate basis of his theory. And even the status of impartiality in Bentham's theory is uncertain. Mill referred to the slogan 'everybody to count for one, nobody for more than one' as Bentham's dictum,[7] but no unambiguous formulation of this principle can be found in the original works. On the contrary, there are passages in Bentham's writings which are clearly directed against absolute impartiality between individuals.[8]

Granted that Bentham was not the first to employ the principles of happiness, pleasure and impartiality, defenders of the orthodox textbook view could argue that he was at least the first to combine these three principles into a unified doctrine. But this, as already noticed by Mill, was not the case.[9] Throughout the eighteenth century, religious conservatism had been defended by obviously utilitarian arguments, although the name of the doctrine had not yet been invented. And William Godwin, rather than Bentham, was the first secular utilitarian to gain wide recognition for his radical application of the three principles.[10]

Similar remarks apply to Mill's amendments to the classical doctrine. The importance of the quality of pleasures in utility calculations was evident to most eighteenth-century utilitarians, and respect towards people's private affairs can be found in the seventeenth-century writings of John Locke. From the historical viewpoint, Mill's authorship of these ideas is questionable. Even more seriously, however, there are theoretical discrepancies in the amended doctrine which cannot be accounted for within the orthodox view. First, it is impossible to accept both Bentham's hedonistic theory of value and Mill's alterations to it, since the two axiologies are mutually incompatible. One cannot, at the same time, state that qualitative factors must and must not be taken into account in utility calculations. Second, it is equally impossible to combine absolute impartiality with the non-regulation of private affairs by law. Strict impartiality in legislation would entail, among other things, that individuals ought to be protected against their own potentially harmful choices, whereas respect for privacy would lead to the rejection of such authoritarian forms of control.

What these remarks amount to is that there is in fact no original and privileged form of utilitarianism which could be exclusively attributed to the joint work of Bentham and Mill. Both historical considerations and theoretical reflections seem to support this conclusion. For the sake of convenience, the name 'classical utilitarianism' can be employed to refer to the straightforward application of the principles of happiness, pleasure and impartiality as these were understood by Bentham. But Mill's amendments to the Benthamite theory should not be regarded as alternative or additional features of the classical view. The accurate description is, rather, that new forms of utilitarianism emerge when the Millian alterations are assumed. On the one hand, Mill's axiological remarks give rise to a theory which has been called in the literature 'ideal utilitarianism'. This theory rejects crude hedonism and instead emphasizes the value of knowledge, virtue, cultural achievement and human perfection in general. Mill's respect for individual freedom, on the other hand, brings about a view which can be called 'liberal utilitarianism'. This latter view stresses the importance of protecting people's privacy against the authoritarian implications of absolute impartiality.

THE HISTORICAL FORMS OF UTILITARIANISM

Even granted that Mill's amendments cannot be reconciled with Bentham's views, it can still be argued that the classical doctrine constitutes the original and privileged form of utilitarianism. The argument for this view rests upon an assumption which I have already rejected, although parenthetically, namely that Bentham was indeed the first to profess utilitarian ideals. If the assumption were tenable, all later developments of the doctrine could perhaps be ignored as distorted and inferior versions of the classical view.

But as I have noted above, the assumption is not tenable. At least three types of utilitarianism, or, to employ Henry Sidgwick's term,[11] 'universalistic hedonism', can be distinguished within the British tradition preceding Bentham. These three views are psychological utilitarianism, theological utilitarianism and radical utilitarianism.

Psychological utilitarianism states that human beings either inherently are, or can be educated to be, universally benevolent towards their fellow beings. Bishop Richard Cumberland in his critique of Thomas Hobbes was one of the first to express this view,[12] and the theory was further developed by Anthony Ashley Cooper (3rd Earl of Shaftesbury),[13] Francis Hutcheson[14] and David Hume.[15]

Psychological considerations are also relevant to the development of utilitarianism in an indirect way. The associationist school of psychology, set in motion by John Locke[16] and established by David Hartley[17] and James Mill,[18] cleared the path for secular theories of ethics by arguing that the so-called 'moral intuitions' which constitute the basis of most traditional moralities are not innate ideas planted into people's minds by God or Nature. According to the associationist view of Locke, for instance, 'innate moral ideas' are no more than perverted combinations of primary ideas which before

11

the 'association' have no empirical or logical connection with each other.

Theological utilitarianism assumes that human beings are by nature egoistic, and can only be motivated into doing something by threats of punishment and promises of reward. It is the existence of a benevolent and almighty God, who by religious sanctions regulates our lives, that makes it in fact rational for every human being to act benevolently towards others. Bishop George Berkeley opted for this view in a sermon on 'passive obedience',[19] and it was held in one form or another by, for instance, John Gay,[20] John Brown,[21] Abraham Tucker,[22] William Paley[23] and James Fitzjames Stephen.[24]

Radical utilitarianism, finally, is the application of the requirements of altruism and benevolence to reforms in legislation and in political life. The theoretical foundation of this doctrine varied from descriptive altruism to psychological egoism, but the central position was invariably occupied by the three principles attributed to Bentham at the beginning of this chapter. The first acknowledged proponent of radical utilitarianism was William Godwin, whose uncompromising applications of the utilitarian calculus gave the view the bad name it still has in many quarters.[25] Other proponents of the theory included Jeremy Bentham, James Mill and John Stuart Mill.

Let us examine these types of utilitarianism one by one in their proper historical context.

UNIVERSAL ALTRUISM

The first version of British utilitarianism, descriptive universal altruism, emerged during the late seventeenth century as a reaction against the moral, social and political thought of Thomas Hobbes.[26] In his work, Hobbes was the first to bridge the gap between self-interest and virtue, which had become an acute problem for Western ethics by his time. In Greek philosophy there had been no gap between people's own good and their morality, since personal happiness had been seen as one of the qualities of a virtuous individual, and virtue had been seen as an ingredient of true happiness. But Christianity had rejected this view, and claimed instead that worldly pleasures and joys ought to be abandoned in the name of morality. The difficulty with the Christian doctrine was, as shown in the early sixteenth century by Niccolò Macchiavelli[27] and

Thomas More,[28] that its application seemed to produce disastrous results both at the level of government and at the level of everyday life. Moralities which emphasize the absolute nature of virtues but fail to recognize people's need to further their own best interest often fail to move people to right action.

Hobbes bridged the gap between self-interest and morality by distinguishing between the descriptive (physiological) causes of human behaviour and the normative (prudential) reasons which ought to guide it.[29] From the physiological viewpoint, all human beings are, according to Hobbes, motivated only by their own short-term self-interest. People try to stay alive, and they try to obtain as much power as possible over other people. But since the universal and uncontrolled urge for power can only lead to widespread violence and chaos – to what Hobbes called the state of nature[30] – rational human beings who care about their own long-term well-being cannot tolerate 'natural' behaviour in other people. This is why it would be prudential for them to enter a contract, or act as if they had entered a contract, which prevents individuals from violating the basic rights of other individuals. Granted that the contract could be enforced, it would guarantee unity and peace within the nation, and security among its population.[31] Egoism and self-interest, moderated by reason and prudence, are the basic forces which, according to Hobbes, ought to make people respect each other's rights and liberties in a civilized society.

The psychological egoism of Hobbes' theory was widely rejected by his contemporaries. Among the first to attack his views were Ralph Cudworth, Henry More and Samuel Clarke – the first two members of the seventeenth-century philosophico-religious group called the Cambridge Platonists. The group denied the relevance of human desires and religious revelation in ethics, and stressed the primacy of reason in judgements concerning right and wrong. Cudworth asserted that moral truths are similar to mathematical truths in two respects: they are both objective truths, and they can both be grasped intuitively by human reason.[32] Cudworth's intuitionist ideas were then employed by More, who argued – among other things – that the moral truth of universal altruism is self-evident. More's statement of the view is simple and appealing: 'If it be good that one man should be supplied with the means of living well and happily, it is mathematically certain that it is doubly good that two should be so supplied, and so on.'[33] Whatever the difficulties of this view, it does offer an alternative way of filling the gap between self-interest and morality. If moral choices are guided by reason, as Cudworth and More believed, the evil effects of egoism can be avoided by purely intellectual processes, without having to resort to contracts dictated by mutual distrust and the universal fear of death.

Clarke accepted the ideas of Cudworth and More, but he also added to them an axiom of equity, or impartiality. In the spirit of the Christian Golden Rule, he wrote: 'Whatever I judge reasonable or unreasonable for another to do for me; that, by the same judgement, I declare reasonable or unreasonable, that I in the like case should do for him.'[34] Granted that people would like other people to act benevolently towards them, Clarke's axiom points in the same direction as More's moral arithmetic: in the direction of universal altruism. In their opposition to Hobbes, the Cambridge Platonists came close to becoming the first utilitarian moral philosophers. The fact that they have, however, escaped the label is primarily due to their rigid commitment to intuitionism. Although Cudworth, More and Clarke did count the principles of benevolence and equity among their ethical axioms, the ultimate criterion of moral goodness for them was conformity to reason, not universal altruism.

The first philosopher to devise a distinctly utilitarian view of morality was Richard Cumberland, a dissenting member of the Cambridge Platonists and, later on, the Bishop of Peterborough. In his book *De Legibus Naturae* (1672) Cumberland introduced and defended two points which became central to British moral thinking during the subsequent century. The first point was normative. Cumberland maintained, and with greater consistency than the orthodox Cambridge Platonists, that the general good of humankind ought to guide all human action. This view, a rudimentary statement of the principle of happiness, became so widely accepted among eighteenth-century British moralists that almost all secular theories of ethics from that period can in one way or another be linked with the development of utilitarianism. Cumberland's second point, in turn, was descriptive. He argued against Hobbes' view that people do, as a matter of empirical fact, act benevolently towards each other even without contracts and coercion. It is this second notion that makes Cumberland the founder of psychological utilitarianism, or descriptive universal altruism.

Both Cumberland and his followers tended to take the normative principle of benevolence for granted. But it is not always clear what they mean by benevolent action, since their axiologies are, more often than not, ambiguous or even self-contradictory. Cumberland's theory of value is a case in point. Throughout *De Legibus Naturae* he discusses general good as if it were definable in terms of happiness and psychological pleasure. Every now and then, however, he stresses that pure hedonism is unacceptable, and that the only ultimate good is human perfection. This interplay of hedonism and ideal utilitarianism is also visible in most eighteenth-century theories of universal altruism.

The primary concern for Cumberland and his followers was, however, to explain the empirical point concerning human benevolence. Actions which are motivated by self-centred considerations do not present problems for either scientists or philosophers: we all know from experience that our own interests often move us to action. But assuming that we are sometimes also motivated by other people's interests, how can this other-regarding frame of mind be explained? What are the biological, psychological or social mechanisms which make people behave altruistically?

Cumberland's answer to these questions was threefold.[35] First, he claimed that on purely physiological grounds benevolent individuals can be said to be healthier and happier than individuals who disregard the interests of others. When people notice this, they voluntarily try to behave in an altruistic manner. Second, he assumed that the biological attraction human beings have toward members of the opposite sex gradually transforms into sympathy toward one's own offspring and, ultimately, toward other people as well. Third, Cumberland also believed that when certain actions are iterated, egoistic and altruistic motives may become mixed. People can, for instance, begin to contribute to various charities because they personally enjoy the idea of helping others. But it is by no means uncommon that people continue to give alms even if their original enthusiasm has long since worn out. In these cases their initially egoistic motives have, according to Cumberland's theory, turned into altruistic ones.

Cumberland's views on the causes of altruism may be less than convincing, but he was the first to assert that the phenomenon of benevolence needs to be explained. His work on descriptive universal altruism was taken up during the eighteenth century by two representatives of an apparently antagonistic school of ethics, namely the moral sense theorists Anthony Ashley Cooper – better known as Shaftesbury – and Francis Hutcheson. For both Shaftesbury and Hutcheson, the only criterion of virtue should be, theoretically speaking, the moral sense with which according to them every human being is endowed. The fact of the matter is, however, that they also recognized both the normative and the descriptive principles of altruism introduced by Cumberland.

Shaftesbury, in his work *Characteristics of Men, Manners, Opinions, Times* (1711), defended descriptive altruism by attacking Hobbes' view concerning the 'naturalness' of egoism. Shaftesbury noted that when human beings are hypothetically transferred to the original state of nature, as in Hobbes' theory, they lose in the process many qualities which at the present time are as 'natural' to them as the animal characteristics of their ancestors. Granted that people are egoistic, their actual behaviour depends on the environment in which they live. Individual human beings cannot survive – let alone obtain power – outside of organized societies, and this is why prudent individuals recognize the fact that their own good fundamentally coincides with the good of their society as a whole. Thus social life, according to Shaftesbury, makes altruism indistinguishable from rational egoism. In his own words, 'the question would not be, Who loved himself, or Who not? but Who loved and served himself the rightest, and after the truest manner?'[36] Shaftesbury's argument is, in short, that people are altruistic because they are egoistic and because their own best interest will be furthered best by furthering the interests of other members of society.

Hutcheson in his defence of descriptive altruism relied more directly on the faculty of moral sense.[37] He argued that human beings are inherently equipped with a tendency to approve only benevolence in moral agents. This tendency, according to Hutcheson, can be attributed to our common faculty of moral sense, without which we would always favour actions that benefit ourselves. The fact that people are often benevolent towards each other indicates that the moral sense exists, and the existence of the moral sense explains actual benevolence and altruism.

As regards the normative doctrine of altruism, Hutcheson was the first to formulate with precision the utilitarian principle of happiness. In the second volume of *An Inquiry into the Original of our Ideas of Beauty and Virtue* (1725) he wrote:

> In comparing the moral qualities of actions . . . we are led by
> our moral sense of virtue to judge thus; . . . that the virtue is

in a compound ratio of the *quantity* of good, and *number* of enjoyers. In the same manner, the moral evil, or vice, is as the degree of misery, and number of sufferers; so that *that action is best*, which procures the *greatest happiness* for the *greatest numbers*; and *that worst*, which, in *like manner*, occasions *misery*.[38]

In the light of this citation, and in the light of his acceptance of hedonism[39] and impartiality,[40] Hutcheson could almost be portrayed as the founder of 'classical' utilitarianism – only the reference to 'our moral sense of virtue' would be problematical. But a few less-quoted lines by Hutcheson reveal the complexity of his view. After considering acts which have both advantageous and pernicious consequences he writes:

[But] the moral importance of characters, or dignity of persons may compensate numbers; as may also the degrees of happiness and misery: for to procure an inconsiderable good to many, but an immense evil to few, may be evil; and an immense good to few, may preponderate a small evil to many.[41]

The harsh classical tones of the first quotation are softened in the second by elements of ideal utilitarianism and by a rejection of the victimization of minorities. But the qualifications are not unambiguously beneficial to Hutcheson's theory. If the moral importance of characters, or the dignity of persons, is allowed to enter moral calculations, hedonism must be abandoned. And if a great evil to a small number of people cannot be compensated by small benefits to a large number of people, then strict impartiality must be rejected. In fact, the qualifications make Hutcheson's theory rather similar to the traditional textbook view of utilitarianism criticized at the outset of this chapter.

Although Hutcheson introduced the first precise formulation of the greatest happiness principle, he was himself not a full-fledged normative utilitarian. Like Cumberland and Shaftesbury, he believed that human beings are naturally benevolent towards each other. This descriptive altruism he explained by an appeal to our shared faculty of moral sense. But as regards the moral status of actions, Hutcheson asserted that a complex calculus involving the abilities of the agents as well as the material good produced is required.[42] The consequences of actions do not by themselves provide a criterion for their moral goodness.

Hutcheson's lucid statement of the normative principle of universal altruism was closely followed by the profoundest exposition yet given of descriptive psychological utilitarianism, by David Hume.[43] Hume is perhaps best known in ethics for his reliance on the sentiments of humankind in judging the morality of actions. Hume emphasized the practical nature of morality, and he argued that neither reason nor the alleged faculty of moral sense can in real life move human beings to action. What genuinely motivates us are our feelings of moral approbation and disapprobation, which in their turn are psychologically determined by the perceived utility, or universal beneficence, of actions. According to Hume's theory, humankind tends to have favourable feelings towards actions which are believed to produce the greatest amount of happiness, and to resent actions which are believed to produce suffering and misery.[44]

But granted that human beings are motivated by their own happiness, why should they be moved by the happiness of others? In his major ethical works A Treatise of Human Nature (1739-40) and An Enquiry Concerning the Principles of Morals (1751) Hume presented three arguments and explanations for the descriptive altruism of humankind.[45]

First, he argued that egoism and self-love are not necessarily incompatible with mild benevolence and love of others. It may be true that individual human beings are not perfectly benevolent in their mutual dealings, but they are not perfectly malevolent either. Some people do help others even at some cost to themselves, and most of us help others if it does not require any sacrifices. Moreover, moderately benevolent behaviour is usually considered quite sane, acceptable and human. But when it comes to purely malevolent action, the situation is drastically different. We do not expect that rational individuals deliberately inflict harm on others unless they have been forced to it by exceptional circumstances. Purely malevolent behaviour is regarded as inexplicable and unnatural. In this sense, average human beings can be described as mildly benevolent.[46]

Second, in his early theory Hume also argued that the psychological principle of association makes individuals sensitive to each other's suffering and joy. Hume believed that all people are alike as to the feelings and operations of the mind: if one mind forms a link between certain ideas, then it is safe to infer that a similar link also exists in all other minds. These links between ideas, or 'associations', are according to Hume's view reflexive. If the idea of roses reminds us of their smell, then the idea of the smell of roses reminds us of the flowers themselves. When these observations are applied to the symptoms of suffering and joy, the result is what Hume called the principle of sympathy. Every time we hear or see symptoms of pain in another person's voice or behaviour, our minds pass from the idea of the symptoms of pain to the idea of its causes, thereby making us experience precisely what the other person is experiencing.[47] In his later theory Hume apparently recognized the fact that the idea of another person's pain is less intense than the idea of one's own pain.[48] But he remained loyal to the view that sympathy makes us feel, albeit perhaps more dimly, the pleasures and pains of others.

Third, Hume's final argument is that the admittedly limited natural impulses of benevolence and sympathy are fortified in real life by the use of language in social interaction. In order to survive and flourish people need to communicate with each other, and in order to communicate with each other they need to have a common language. In this common language people and situations ought to be described, as a rule, from the viewpoint of a disinterested observer, since the universal confinement to personal points of view would make human discourse cumbersome, and often impossible. Hume argued that terms indicating social praise and blame especially should refer to qualities which are relevant to members of society in general. His own empirical claim was that persons and actions are, in all cultures, called virtuous if they tend to further general utility, and vicious if they tend to hinder it. This linguistic distinction, Hume further maintained, intensifies our inborn inclination to prefer benevolence and sympathy to malevolence and indifference.[49]

There are two points in Hume's account of universal altruism which make it both theoretically interesting and historically important. On the one hand, Hume was the first to distinguish clearly between the normative and descriptive versions of the altruistic doctrine.[50] His own utilitarianism may have been, in theory, open to normative as well as descriptive interpretations,[51] but there can be no doubt about the fact that Hume himself strongly emphasized the empirical side of the study of ethics. This made him one of the precursors of modern social sciences. On the other hand, Hume's account of universal altruism is also important because it is closely connected with the development of empiricist psychology in Britain and on the European continent. The theory of associations which Hume revived and reinterpreted became quite popular during the latter half of the eighteenth century, and proponents of different types of utilitarianism founded their views on the principles of association. In France and Italy, Hume's influence can be seen in the theories of Claude-Adrien Helvétius and Cesare Beccaria. In British psychology, the associationist school rapidly assumed a dominant position which it maintained until the rise of introspectionism and Gestalt psychology in the late nineteenth century.

ASSOCIATIONISM

The concept of association was introduced in England by John Locke, who in his book *An Essay Concerning Human Understanding* (1690) defended an empiricist theory of knowledge. Locke argued that all our ideas are obtained by experience, either externally by the senses or internally by reflection.[52] The ideas received by sensation and reflection are simple and unmixed, but the human mind has the ability to combine these simple ideas into new complex ones.[53] Locke's own examples of simple ideas include the sensations of yellow, heat, soft and bitter, and the sensations and reflections of pleasure and pain.[54]

According to Locke, simple ideas can be joined together by two different mental operations, by tracing correspondences and by association. This is how he describes these categories:

> [1] Some of our ideas have a natural correspondence and connexion one with another; it is the office and excellency of our reason to trace these, and hold them together in that union and correspondence which is founded in their peculiar beings.
> [2] Besides this, there is another connexion of ideas wholly owing to chance or custom: ideas, that in themselves are not at all of kin, come to be so united in some men's minds that it is very hard to separate them, they always keep company, and the one no sooner at any time comes into the understanding but its associate appears with it.[55]

Locke's distinction implies that the capacity to associate ideas – the second category defined in the quotation – is an unnatural, irra-

tional and pathological function of the human mind. It is this operation, also called 'madness' by Locke, that is responsible for our
belief in such imaginary entities as goblins, sprites, bearded gods sit-
ting on clouds and infallible human beings.[56] The association of
ideas is the source of most of our unreasonableness and prejudice.

Locke's views concerning the human mind can be used in two
ways to support utilitarianism.[57] First, his theory of associations provides by itself a critique against all ethical doctrines which are based
on the idea of 'inborn moral intuitions'. Such intuitions, according
to Locke, are no more than associated sets of simple ideas, that is,
random combinations of naturally unconnected sensations and
reflections joined together by education or habit. Granted that
Locke's view is correct, ethical theories which rely upon moral intuitions are false from the beginning, and they ought to be rejected.
This rejection, in its turn, would support all moral views which
emphasize the natural foundation of ethical norms and values.[58]

Second, however, Locke's theory can also be applied more directly
to back utilitarian ethics. This application, which involves the
redefinition of associations, was anticipated by John Gay[59] – to
whom I shall return in my account of theological utilitarianism –
and worked out in detail by David Hartley.[60]

During the eighteenth century, the concept of association was
extended, contrary to the distinction made by Locke, to include
natural as well as perverted combinations of primary ideas. David
Hartley in his *Observations on Man, his Frame, his Duty, and his
Expectations* (1749) introduced this new extension of the concept by
giving the following definition of the principle of association:

> Any sensations A, B, C, etc., by being associated with one
> another a sufficient number of times, get such a power over
> the corresponding ideas, a, b, c, etc., that any one of the sen-
> sations, A, when impressed alone, shall be able to excite in the
> mind b, c, etc., the ideas of the rest.[61]

The core of the mechanism here is that all combinations of ideas are
formed by association. Simple ideas of sensation are joined together
into complex ideas, and any part of the complex idea can evoke in
the mind any other part of it. The only natural correspondence
which prevails is that between sensations and ideas – all connections
between ideas are regarded by Hartley as equally artificial or equally
natural.

Hartley's theory of action was based on the associationist view of knowledge, and on a detailed account concerning what he called intellectual pleasures and pains.[62] According to Hartley's view, the ideas of intellectual pleasure and intellectual pain are the ultimate sources, or springs, of human action. If the consequences of an action are associated in an individual's mind with intellectual pleasure, the individual desires to perform the action. Similarly, if the consequences of an action are associated with intellectual pain, the individual tries to avert performing it. In a sense, this view makes Hartley a proponent of egoistic hedonism. But his definition of the relevant pleasures and pains alters the situation considerably.

Hartley enumerated six classes of intellectual pleasures and pains which he considered important in human decision-making. These are the pleasures and pains (1) of imagination, (2) of ambition, (3) of self-interest, (4) of sympathy, (5) of theopathy and (6) of the moral sense. These 'intellectual affections', as Hartley also called the springs of action, form a hierarchy in which the pleasures and pains of imagination hold the lowest position, and the affections of the moral sense the highest. There are, however, numerous reciprocal influences between the classes, and this, according to Hartley, makes the analysis of our motives exceedingly complicated. There is, in fact, only one unambiguous conclusion that Hartley himself draws from the theory, namely the partly descriptive, partly normative assertion that all human beings prefer – or ought to prefer – the joys of sympathy (4) to other motives.[63]

Hartley's argument for the priority of sympathy proceeds in two stages. First, as regards the comparison of sympathy with imagination (1), ambition (2) and self-interest (3), the hierarchical structure of the view can be directly applied. One of the tenets of Hartley's system is that the higher affections are partly created and generated by the lower pleasures and pains. Subsequently, the passions which rank low on the scale are always included in those passions which rank higher. The pleasures and pains of sensation,[64] imagination, ambition and self-interest are, therefore, included in the affections of sympathy, and need not be taken independently into account in prudential or moral calculations.[65] When applied specifically to self-interest, this view implies that when we conscientiously fulfil the requirements of sympathy, divine law and moral sense, our rational self-interest will be automatically furthered in the process.[66]

The second stage is more problematical. Since both theopathy (5)

and the moral sense (6) exceed sympathy in the hierarchy of intellectual affections, Hartley was forced to claim that the precepts of
all three converge in real life. He argued for this view by an appeal
to the consequences of human behaviour. In his opinion, actions
guided by popular religious considerations as well as actions dictated by the moral sense produce the best possible consequences in
terms of general happiness. The same result would, in Hartley's
view, follow from the practice of unlimited sympathy towards other
people.[67]

The universal altruism implied by Hartley's theory resembles the
views put forward a few decades before him by Shaftesbury. These
two moralists did, of course, share an interest in the alleged faculty
of moral sense in the human mind. But more importantly, they
both explained or justified universal altruism by arguing that individuals themselves will be benefited by apparently altruistic action.
In Shaftesbury's theory, the individual's good was connected with
the good of society by the fact that human beings cannot survive
and function without the support of human community. Hartley's
more psychological view stated that sympathy, benevolence and
altruism are in the individual's own best interest since they produce
more (intellectual) pleasure than any other alternative. Both seemed
to agree on the credo that people are led to altruistic behaviour by
rationally egoistic considerations.

In the development of associationism, Hartley was followed by
two Anglican clergymen, Abraham Tucker and William Paley, who
shared his interest in psychology but who did not share his belief in
the universal altruism of humankind.[68] From the viewpoint of associationism, the more important and more interesting of the
theorists was Tucker, who by introducing the concepts of 'train' and
'translation' provided a link between Locke's original ideas and the
later psychological theory of James Mill.

The first three parts of Tucker's seven-volume work *The Light of
Nature Pursued* (1768) marked a return of the Lockean spirit to the
treatment of associations. Tucker believed that ideas are often
arranged by the laws of association into long chains of thought
which he called 'trains'. This occurs when curiosity or need prompts
us to track repeatedly, and always in the same order, a chain of ideas
which leads to an important conviction or ideal.[69] The correctness
of the conviction or ideal depends, of course, on the acceptability of
the steps leading to it. But the more frequently the process is repeated,

the more probable it becomes that parts of the train are dropped out and forgotten. In the end, the conviction or ideal evokes in the mind only the judgement of its being true, quite independently of any real proof. Tucker thought that this process, which he called 'translation', explains the emergence of the so-called self-evident truths in metaphysics and in morality.[70]

Tucker did not, however, condemn all allegedly self-evident ideas as incorrect or perverse, as Locke had done. He only pointed out that their apparent self-evidence is an illusion, based on the fact that the original justification is no longer available to the attending mind. Convictions cannot be regarded as genuine and rational unless the individuals holding them can mentally reproduce the trains of thought which lead to the relevant conclusions.[71] By this observation Tucker anticipated the converse view, professed by James Mill a few decades later, that the human mind immediately recognizes the truth of conclusions which have been deduced by sound inferences from valid premises.[72]

One of the most important applications of Tucker's theory is axiological. He argued, against the view presented by Hartley, that there are no qualitative differences between types of pleasure and pain. The affections called by Hartley 'higher intellectual pleasures' are in fact ordinary pleasures of sensation which are, by long-forgotten chains, associated with the ideas of sympathy, fear of God or the moral sense. These affections may actually be more enjoyable than the 'lower' pleasures of the intellect but this, according to Tucker, can be explained in terms of quantity rather than quality.[73] When the supposedly qualitative distinctions between positive experiences happen to indicate genuine differences, the reason is that the pleasures associated with virtuous behaviour are more abundant, more intense or more permanent than mere sensory joys.

Tucker's reliance on simple quantitative hedonism made visible the tension which even before his time had persisted within all 'associationist utilitarian' theories of human action. On the one hand, the utilitarianism of the theories implies that universal happiness should be regarded as the ultimate criterion of moral goodness: people ought to act so as to maximize general utility. On the other hand, however, the associationism of the views suggests that most human beings do not, as a matter of psychological fact, behave altruistically unless certain specific conceptual or empirical conditions prevail. Assuming that both views are correct, associationist utilitarians are faced with a difficult question concerning human motivation here. If individuals naturally pursue only their own personal interests, why should they act morally? An explanation or a justification is urgently needed in order to bridge the gap between morality and reality, between norm and action.

James Mill, whose book *Analysis of the Phenomena of the Human Mind* (1829) contained one of the most uncompromising expositions of associationist utilitarianism, answered the question of motivation by emphasizing the significance of moral education.[74] Mill followed Locke in stating that all our beliefs, attitudes and convictions are combinations of simple ideas which have been acquired by the senses. The mind of a newborn baby is like a dark room, and the senses are the only windows through which knowledge concerning the external world enters the mind. During the first formative years of our lives, we are susceptible to any impressions imposed upon us by our physical and social environment. These early impressions create images and associations which become permanent elements of our characters. This is why education is extremely important. It is the teacher's task to control the flow of sensory impressions in a way that encourages the child to assume only good and useful traits of character. These good and useful traits of character are defined by Mill in terms of universal benevolence and altruism. Individuals ought to perform actions which promote the general happiness of humankind, and their characters can be judged as good and virtuous if they, as a rule, do what they ought to do. Proper moral education is the device that fills the gap between normative and descriptive utilitarianism.

Early moral education can, however, fail to impress upon individuals utilitarian ideals. Mill believed that even in these cases people can be morally improved by education. Although he did maintain that early impressions have a permanent influence on the human mind, he also argued that false convictions and bad ideals can be eradicated by providing individuals with accurate information concerning the foundation of the beliefs. Human reason cannot hold on to opinions or attitudes if it is shown that the opinions and attitudes in question are based on irrational or perverted inferences, or on disconnected trains of ideas. Truth, Mill asserted, forces itself into the centre of the consciousness, and sweeps aside erroneous ideals and convictions.

Mill's view concerning truth and its mental effect shaped both his political theory and his theory of value. In politics, he believed in free speech and wide representation, at least partly because he thought that these institutions would guarantee the truthfulness of public life and political decisions.[75] When a large number of people freely discuss the options available in matters that concern all, it is probable that the truth eventually comes to the fore and becomes universally accepted. In axiology, Mill's belief in the pervasiveness of truth turned his supposedly hedonistic view into a kind of intellectual asceticism. Individuals who have been adequately educated in the utilitarian way of thinking do not aim in their choices at the general satisfaction of the low animal pleasures of the body.[76] Rather, the happiness that they try to maximize must be defined by referring to the deliberate approval of emotionally stable and well-informed (male) adult human beings. Here Mill, himself a Scotsman, came close to the 'impartial spectator' or 'ideal observer' theories professed by notable Scottish philosophers like Adam Smith and David Hume.[77]

THEOLOGICAL UTILITARIANISM

The second main version of British utilitarianism, theological utilitarianism, can be seen as a clericalist reaction to the apparent downfall of descriptive universal altruism. Theological utilitarians assumed from the beginning the pessimistic psychological view that individual human beings are motivated only by their own self-interest and self-love. They did share, however, the normative belief held by the universal altruists that people ought to act benevolently and altruistically towards each other. This set of premises raised the associationist question concerning moral motivation, answered by James Mill in terms of education. Theological utilitarians responded to the tension by placing their trust in the existence of a benevolent and omnipotent God.

The founder of theological utilitarianism was George Berkeley, the Bishop of Cloyne, who is better known in the history of philosophy for his immaterialism. In his sermons on *Passive Obedience* (1712) Berkeley attacked the view expressed by Shaftesbury, according to which people are led to altruistic action by the moral sense that we all naturally share.[78] Berkeley's own conviction was that the inborn egoism of humankind is too strong to be counteracted by human efforts or by human faculties. The only way to make universal altruism attractive to egoistic individuals was, in his view, to introduce an external force which can direct our lives with absolute sovereignty. This external force he found in God.[79]

Berkeley believed, like Hobbes before him, that human beings originally act only from motives which are connected with their own immediate desires and aversions. Since people have learned, however, that suspension often multiplies the pleasures to come, prudence moderates their short-term egoism and makes them sensitive to the needs of those from whom they can be expected to benefit in the future. Berkeley employed an extension of this model – an extension which involves the introduction of God to ethics – to prove that universal altruism is the best and in the long run the most prudential policy overall.

One of the abilities of God, who according to Berkeley is a complete and perfect being, is the power to decide whether individual human beings spend eternity in happiness or in misery. This divine power annuls all ordinary prudential calculations based on earthly pleasures and pains: eternal happiness and eternal misery override, by definition, all temporal experiences. It would be redundant to try to maximize the joys of this world when God's will can always reverse the ultimate balance in the next. In the light of these considerations there are only two relatively simple questions which are important to prudence and to morality. These are: What is God's will? and How can we obey God's will, once we know what it is?

As for the first question, Berkeley deduced two useful points from the premise concerning God's complete nature. First, since God is perfectly good, he[80] cannot wish anything evil to happen. Second, since God already has every good and desirable quality that one can think of, he cannot wish anything for himself. When these two points are combined, the result is a utilitarian view: a benevolent and omnipotent God must be a descriptive universal altruist who wills the greatest possible happiness of his entire creation.

As regards the second question, Berkeley noted that there are two ways in which God's utilitarian will can be obeyed. On the one hand, people can constantly scrutinize every option they have in order to find out which courses of action produce the maximum of general happiness. Berkeley presented three arguments against this solution. First, due to natural limitations in our knowledge and understanding, we can never foresee all the consequences of our actions. Second, even if we could foresee all the consequences of our actions, their assessment would be too time-consuming to be practicable. Third, the evaluation of action alternatives would in this model have to be based on probabilities rather than certainties, and probabilities cannot in Berkeley's view provide a proper foundation for ethics.

On the other hand, we can avoid all these problems by examining more carefully the theological side of the issue. Given that God is wise and powerful, can we assume that he has left us without adequate guidance in this important matter? Berkeley's answer to this question is firmly in the negative. According to his theory, God has in his Ten Commandments given us the rules that we must follow if we wish to maximize general utility. It is not our prerogative to question these rules, or to seek alternatives to them. Although it may sometimes appear that the greatest happiness will be poorly served by actions which conform to these rules, passive obedience is the only option morally open to humankind.[81]

Berkeley's implicit reliance on God's will may seem to undermine the utilitarianism of his theory. There are, however, two facts which favour the utilitarian interpretation that I have assumed. First, genuinely theistic doctrines are founded on the belief that God can arbitrarily choose the criteria for right and wrong, good and evil. Berkeley did not condone this view. Instead, he defined the will of God in utilitarian terms, thereby making it theoretically possible to anticipate God's will by studying the consequences of human actions. Second, although absolute conformity to rules may be alien to utilitarian thinking, attempts have been made during the twentieth century to develop doctrines which would combine rules and utility. These doctrines are often referred to as 'rule utilitarianism'. As a precursor of these views, Berkeley deserves to be counted among the early utilitarians.

Berkeley was followed during the eighteenth century by a succession of theological moralists who stressed in their theories God's benevolence, conformity to rules and the desirability of the *status quo* in social life and politics. The most important developments within this version of normative universal altruism were introduced by John Gay, John Brown, Abraham Tucker and William Paley, whose theories were gradually refined by parallel advances in associationist psychology. Theological utilitarianism went more or less out of fashion at the turn of the nineteenth century, but it was momentarily revived by James Fitzjames Stephen during the 1870s.

John Gay was the first British theorist to work out a detailed account of moral motivation, or – as he himself called it – 'obligation'. In his article 'Preliminary dissertation concerning the fundamental principle of virtue or morality' (1731) Gay defined virtue in a way which was characteristic not only of his own theory but of the entire theological utilitarian tradition before and after him:

> Virtue is the conformity to a rule, directing all actions of all rational creatures with respect to each other's happiness; to which conformity every one in all cases is obliged: and every one that does so conform, is or ought to be approved of, esteemed and loved for so doing.[82]

There are three elements in this definition which Gay himself thought important. First, virtue and morality can only be connected with actions which increase or decrease the happiness of other people. Actions which increase or decrease the agent's own happiness are not moral or immoral but prudent or imprudent. Similarly, actions which are directly related to the love or fear of God are religious rather than virtuous.[83] Second, virtuous action deserves approbation and praise, while vicious conduct merits disapprobation and blame. And third, actions cannot be regarded as genuinely virtuous unless the agent is 'completely obliged' – i.e. has a compelling motive – to perform them. It is the specification of the third point that was Gay's original contribution to theological utilitarianism.

Gay's definition of obligation is based on the assumption that only self-interest ultimately moves people to action. According to him, 'obligation is the necessity of doing or omitting any action in order to be happy'.[84] It follows from the definition that the core of obligations is always prudential: individuals are not bound to do anything which is not in the end beneficial to themselves. Gay considered four sources from which the binding benefit or harm can originate.[85] First, *natural* obligation arises from the consequences of our actions in our inanimate environment. If we feel obliged not to leap from fifth-floor windows because we know that physical injury will causally follow, the obligation is natural. Second, *virtuous* (or moral) obligation is related to the esteem of our fellow creatures. We may, for instance, feel bound to jump out of the window despite the danger if that is the only way to remove dangerous explosives from a crowded room. Third, *civil* obligation can be derived from the rules of law. If we hesitate to jump from high places, the hesitation may be intensified by laws prohibiting suicidal acts. Fourth and finally, *religious* obligation derives from the authority of God.

Gay went on to examine the relative forces of these four types of obligation, and concluded that the only source of complete obligation is the religious one, the authority of God. As he put the matter:

> God only can in all cases make a man happy or miserable: and therefore, since we are *always* obliged to that conformity called virtue, it is evident that the immediate rule or criterion of it is the will of God.[86]

Gay, then, followed Berkeley in asserting that God's will and his rules constitute the only binding and immediate criterion of morality. Although Gay also agreed with Berkeley that God in his infinite benevolence must be a utilitarian, he explicitly denied the possibility that virtue could be found directly from calculations concerning general happiness and misery. The general happiness of humankind does not directly move individuals to action in cases where their own interests are at stake. God's will is the only force which can create complete obligations to perform or forgo actions.[87]

Gay's ideas were taken up two decades later by John Brown, who in his *Essays on the Characteristics* (1751) defended the theological utilitarian view, and especially the definition of virtue as universal altruism.[88] Brown argued that in the history of humankind virtue, or morality, has always been ultimately understood in terms of the greatest public happiness. There may be attitudes and actions which have been regarded as morally good in themselves, but even those attitudes and actions inevitably lose their moral goodness if it can be shown that they undermine general happiness. Acts of dishonesty committed for the sake of one's own child are, according to Brown, a case in point. On the other hand, there are also actions which are commonly seen as intrinsically evil, but which are condoned when they promote the greatest happiness. Brown's example is the legal execution of notorious criminals.[89]

Brown was followed in his line of thought by Abraham Tucker, whose contribution to theological utilitarianism was an explicit principle of justice, or equality.[90] Tucker believed that all the happiness in the world is stored in a limited common stock which is administered by God. One of God's attributes, according to Tucker, is 'equity', and God's equity guarantees that happiness will in the end be distributed equally among human beings, regardless of their relative merits and deserts. This equal distribution of happiness occurs at three stages. First, for reasons known only to God, some people are provided with happiness already in this life, while others are left to suffer. Second, however, immediately after death this imbalance is corrected by meting out happiness to those who have lived in misery, and misery to those who have lived in happiness. Third, after this period of purgatory, the remaining happiness in the 'bank of the universe' will be equally distributed among humans.[91]

Brown's moral sociology and Tucker's theological views may be found less than convincing, but both theorists cleared, in their own ways, the path for the principle of impartiality, which in time became an essential part of radical utilitarianism. Tucker focused attention on the fact that those individuals who control the lives of others – gods, legislators and others like them – have a duty to treat all their subjects equally. Favouritism and partiality cannot be accepted in ideal morality or politics. Brown, in his turn, extended this same precept to everyday interaction between ordinary citizens. His example concerning lies for the sake of one's own child conveyed the message that it is always morally condemnable to promote the lesser happiness of one individual at the expense of the greater happiness of many, whatever one's own relationship with the 'one individual' in question may be. Although peripheral to theological utilitarianism as such, these remarks had a considerable impact on the wider tradition of universal altruism, as I shall undertake to show in the next subsection.

The theological version of utilitarianism reached its peak at the end of the eighteenth century, when William Paley's clear and forceful account, *Principles of Moral and Political Philosophy* (1785), was adopted as a textbook at Cambridge University.[92] Paley contributed little of his own to the theories of his predecessors, and he admitted as much. But in his definition of virtue he summarized neatly the most important tenets of theological utilitarianism. According to Paley, virtue equals: '[1] the doing of good to mankind, [2] in obedience of the will of God, and [3] for the sake of everlasting happiness.'[93] This definition, which links together the good of humankind and the agent's personal happiness, does not seem to recognize significant differences between egoism and altruism, self-interest and benevolence. Paley himself noted that the only difference he could see between prudence and morality was that: 'In the one case we consider what we shall gain or lose in the present world; in the other case we consider also what we shall gain or lose in the world to come.'[94] In the end, then, theological utilitarianism regarded human beings as purely egoistic agents who can only be forced into moral action by threats of eternal punishment.[95]

After Paley's success had blown over, the theological version of universal altruism became obsolete and gave way to intuitionist ethics and secular utilitarian views. A belated appeal to eternal sanctions was made in the latter half of the nineteenth century by James Fitzjames Stephen, who in his book *Liberty, Equality, Fraternity* (1873) tried to revive some of the central points of the doctrine. Although Stephen rejected the assumption of God's existence, he believed that our minds are immortal, and that vicious conduct in this life inevitably leads to eternal self-condemnation and regret in the next.[96] This line of thinking seems to have gained at least some popularity in Stephen's own time,[97] but its influence on twentieth-century ethics has been virtually non-existent.

RADICAL UTILITARIANISM

The third version of British utilitarianism, radical utilitarianism, differed from its immediate forerunners in four important respects. First, the existence of God, or at least the relevance of God and religion to ethics, was explicitly denied. Second, passive obedience to rules was categorically rejected and, instead, the assessment of individual actions and limited classes of actions was emphasized. Third, radical utilitarians mostly forwent the study of the private moralities of individual human beings, and focused their attention on political life and legislation. Fourth, as a result of the rejection of rules and the emphasis on politics, radical utilitarianism was, from the beginning, a clearly reformist doctrine. Theoretically, however, the view did not offer considerable innovations to the British tradition of universal altruism.

The first radical utilitarian to have become famous for his views was William Godwin, who in his *Enquiry Concerning Political Justice* (1793) defended anarchism on utilitarian grounds. Political theorists have not always regarded Godwin as a utilitarian,[98] probably because his theories were in fashion already before Bentham and his disciples gained wider popularity. But all the principles of 'classical' utilitarianism can be found in Godwin's work as well as in the writings of Bentham and the Mills.[99]

The principle of happiness, or the normative principle of altruism, was stated by Godwin when he discussed virtue in the context of human action. He wrote: 'I would define virtue to be any action or actions of an intelligent being proceeding from kind and benevolent intention and having a tendency to contribute to general happiness.'[100] This definition seems to give two necessary conditions to the morality of actions: first, the motivation behind the actions must be benevolent; and second, the consequences of the actions themselves must be expected to correspond with their underlying motives. The first specification should not be taken too literally. It is true that, according to Godwin's theory, an act or an omission which benefits others cannot be defined as virtuous if the original intention of the agent is evil, and the result thereby accidental.[101] But by referring to the goodness of intentions Godwin did not imply that agents should know which acts and omissions are intrinsically valuable, or worthy of praise regardless of the consequences. Rather, the point he wanted to make was that in order to act virtuously agents have to act in accordance with considered judgements regarding the happiness and misery which are likely to follow from chosen courses of action.[102]

When it comes to the principle of hedonism, Godwin's theory is open to two mutually contradictory interpretations. On the one hand, it is possible that he professed the quantitative version of hedonism which had been previously defended by Tucker and which in the nineteenth century became the hallmark of Benthamite utilitarianism. On the other hand, it is also possible that he followed Hartley and preceded John Stuart Mill in assuming that there are certain qualitative differences between various types of pleasure and pain. In the opening lines of the *Enquiry Concerning Political Justice* Godwin put forward both readings:

> The true object of moral and political disquisition is pleasure or happiness. The primary, or earliest, class of human pleasures is the pleasures of the external senses. In addition to these, man is susceptible of certain secondary pleasures, as the pleasures of intellectual feeling, the pleasures of sympathy, and the pleasures of self-approbation. The secondary pleasures are probably more exquisite than the primary: *Or, at least,* The most desirable state of man is that in which he has access to all

these sources of pleasure, and is in possession of a happiness the most varied and uninterrupted.[103]

If Godwin was right in stating that some pleasures are 'more exquisite' than others, then qualitative factors should definitely be taken into account in calculations of utility. But if he was right in his ensuing formulation in which he stressed the value of diversity, then the interpretation is left open to the suggestion that all pleasures are in themselves qualitatively similar. Those individuals who enjoy the pleasures of intellectual feeling, sympathy and self-approbation are happier than those who do not, but this is true only because they encounter a greater number of pleasurable experiences. When the range of potential pleasures is widened, the flow of desirable mental states becomes more intense and more continuous than it would have been without the extension.[104]

Godwin's most important addition to the theory of universal altruism was his secularized principle of impartiality, or justice. Tucker and Brown had before him stated or implied that morality demands the equal treatment of all human beings. But Tucker had confined his requirement of equity to the divine distribution of pleasure and pain, and Brown had only implicitly founded his remarks on the assumption of equality. Godwin, in his turn, made impartiality the cornerstone of his theory. In the first chapter of his book he stated:

> The true standard of the conduct of one man towards another is justice. Justice is a principle which proposes to itself the production of the greatest sum of pleasure or happiness. Justice requires that I should put myself in the place of an impartial spectator of human concerns, and divest myself of retrospect to my own predilections. Justice is a rule of the utmost universality, and prescribes a specific mode of proceeding, in all affairs by which the happiness of a human being may be affected.[105]

In this passage, Godwin put forward three points which were central to his theory, but which have also excited strong criticism. The core idea of justice, as Godwin understood it, was impartiality. When agents consider the consequences of their actions, they are not, so Godwin argued, entitled to take their own personal preferences into account. On the other hand, justice, as defined in the foregoing quotation, is perfectly compatible with the maximization of general happiness. Human actions are, by definition, just if they can be expected to produce the greatest sum of happiness, regardless of the subsequent distribution of pleasures and pains between individuals. Finally, Godwin asserted that the requirement of justice pervades all human behaviour and all aspects of life. Whenever we plan to do something which may affect human happiness, it is our duty to design our actions in accordance with the demands of justice.

Early critiques of utilitarianism were often directed against the third specification of Godwin's account – the idea that universal benevolence should guide all human actions.[106] On the one hand, it was argued that the Godwinian model would make people unreliable and unpredictable. Virtuous persons in Godwin's sense would not honour contracts or keep confidential secrets if greater utility could be served by other means. On the other hand, the early critics also argued that conscientious utilitarians can never actually do anything. By the time they have calculated all the consequences of all their action alternatives, it will be too late to act on the judgement they have reached. The practical conclusion drawn from these considerations was that it would be a mistake to encourage ordinary citizens to think for themselves about their duties. The stability of social and political life can be more effectively maintained by teaching and enforcing unquestioned obedience to the moral rules set by the clergy.

Another objection can be directed against Godwin's second specification, in which he stated that justice and utility coincide in moral matters. Both popular opinion and philosophical theories of justice contradict this view. Justice, as it is commonly understood, is closely linked with the ideas of fair distribution and due retribution, in other words, with the ideal of giving to everyone what is their due.[107] The principle of utility, in turn, does not recognize the validity of any such ideas. When the value of actions and policies is determined by an appeal to the greatest sum of happiness, no intrinsic importance can be attached to traditional notions of fairness. Defenders of utilitarianism can argue, as John Stuart Mill later did, that the only rational core of the principle of justice is that which is compatible with the promotion of the greatest happiness, and that intuitive views concerning justice are therefore irrelevant to rational morality.[108] But the proponents of traditional doctrines can counter this claim by observing that the 'rational' utilitarian view of justice is rather limited, and poorly reflects many of the finer aspects of moral, social and political life.

The final criticism against Godwin is centred on his rigid application of the principle of impartiality, which shocked his contemporaries and, even in the twentieth century, continues to be one of the main sources of anti-utilitarian feeling among Western philosophers.[109] Godwin argued that since some individuals can be expected to promote general happiness more than others, they ought to be given preference in moral calculations. His own example was that if the palace of Archbishop Fénelon (a known benefactor) were on fire, and we could rescue only one person, either the Archbishop himself or his valet, justice would demand that we choose Fénelon. The reason Godwin gave for this preference was simply that the learned benefactor and reformer would be more useful to other people than the humble valet. This, in itself, would hardly have been striking to Godwin's contemporaries. But he went on to state:

> Suppose the valet had been my brother, my father or my benefactor. This would not alter the truth of the proposition. The life of Fénelon would still be more valuable than that of the valet; and justice, pure, unadulterated justice, would still have preferred that which was most valuable. Justice would have taught me to save Fénelon at the expense of the other.[110]

To the potential counterargument that family, friends and immediate neighbours ought to be preferred to strangers, Godwin replied in a manner that was guaranteed to offend the susceptibilities of his readers:

> What magic is there in the pronoun 'my', that should justify us in overturning the decisions of impartial truth? My brother or my father may be a fool or a profligate, malicious, lying or dishonest. If they be, what consequence is it that they are mine?[111]

By these remarks Godwin established the reputation of secular utilitarianism as an immoral doctrine which demands that we reject our families and friends in order to benefit strangers who are more valuable to humankind.

Family and friendship were not the only institutions that Godwin abandoned in the name of justice and true morality. Gratitude, for instance, was in his view an unnecessary frame of mind which frequently leads us to condone immoral dealings.[112] Suppose that somebody gives me a considerable sum of money. There are two alternative settings in which this transaction can take place, and neither of them leaves room for gratitude. First, the greatest possible happiness may be served by giving the money to me, in which case the other person has a duty to do so. If this is the case, I have no particular reason to be grateful – after all, the other person is only doing what she or he is morally bound to do. Second, it may also be that the greatest happiness could be produced by giving the money to somebody else. In this case, I am not entitled to the money in the first place, and my gratitude would equal being thankful for a gift which I know has been stolen from somebody who needs the item more than I do.

Another traditional institution which Godwin attacked was promise-keeping.[113] According to him, promises do not – and cannot – create any special obligations to individuals. If doing what one has undertaken to do promotes general happiness, then one should do it regardless of the promise. If, on the other hand, happiness will not be maximized by keeping the promise, it should not be kept. These considerations can also be applied to private and collective contracts. Godwin believed that the contracts individuals make with each other should always contain a clause which states that the contract may, if unforeseeable changes occur in the circumstances, be annulled by either party. In political theory, Godwin rejected the idea that social contracts could oblige people to obey the law. The fact that laws are backed up with threats of violence shows, according to Godwin, that collective contracts and promises do not actually guarantee the voluntary obedience of citizens.[114]

The system of legal sanctions based on the idea of retribution was yet another social institution that Godwin criticized.[115] In his view, the only legitimate criterion for punishing people was the maximization of general happiness. Revenge and retaliation for past events which cannot be altered by the sanctions were regarded by him as one of 'the most pernicious exhibitions of an untutored barbarism'.[116] The liberal and humane side of his view was that undisciplined feelings of vengeance were not regarded by him as acceptable motives for legal correction. But there was another aspect in Godwin's theory which was less liberal, and which has been frequently brought to the fore by the critics of utilitarianism. If people can be fined and imprisoned purely for the sake of the general good, as Godwin apparently suggested, then questions of guilt and innocence seem to be irrelevant in the evaluation of punitive policies. The same principles which apply to punishing the guilty also apply to punishing the innocent. Critics of utilitarianism have often seen this inference as a conclusive *reductio ad absurdum* of normative universal altruism.

There are, in fact, two ways in which Godwin's position concerning legal correction can be interpreted. Opponents of utilitarianism naturally prefer the interpretation that Godwin wanted the innocent to suffer: this version, if sound, would provide good grounds for rejecting the theory. But a careful reading of the *Enquiry Concerning Political Justice* shows that Godwin did not condone institutionalized killing, imprisonment or torture in the name of general happiness.[117] He believed, in fact, that people's convictions and ways of life cannot be genuinely altered by legal coercion. Individuals can, of course, be coerced into avoiding criminal and vicious behaviour. But the cost of this forced obedience is that those compelled lose their humanity and turn into servile machines who are guided only by their own self-interest and fear. Godwin argued that individuals like these, law-abiding as they may be, would lack both happiness in their own lives and the ability to promote the greatest happiness of humankind. Consequently, instead of wishing the innocent to suffer at the hands of public authorities, Godwin wanted to abolish the whole punitive system. His argument was not that the innocent should be punished alongside the guilty, but rather that the guilty should be acquitted alongside the innocent.

Godwin's own alternative to legal coercion was a modified acceptance of anarchy.[118] Although he admitted that in a state of nature the security of individuals cannot always be guaranteed, he argued that there are, nonetheless, strong reasons for preferring (occasional) anarchy to (permanent) government. Due to the universal lack of security which prevails in the state of nature, individuals are compelled to think about better ways of organizing their lives. This implies that anarchy is a short-lived phase in political life unless people are mature enough to live together peacefully without state coercion. It also implies that anarchy awakens thought and provokes discussion concerning the best forms of social life. Godwin believed that these features make anarchy infinitely preferable to coercive modes of government, which tend to be self-protective to the point where dissident thinking is suppressed by threats of violence.

Godwin's modified anarchism was closely connected with his views concerning axiology and philosophical anthropology. In his opinion, different kinds of people enjoy different types of happiness, and these different types of happiness can be scaled from the lowest to the highest.[119] The 'scale of happiness' which Godwin himself formed consists of four steps. First, the 'labouring inhabitants of the civilized states of Europe' are happy in the lowest sense of the word. They work all day, drink all evening and sleep all night. They are not subject to absolute poverty or fatal diseases, but their range of ideas is scanty, and they are seldom interested in affairs which have no immediate bearing on their own lives. As Godwin put the matter, these individuals are happier than stones and other inanimate objects, but their oyster-like existence is pitiable and, due to its dominant insensibility, only barely human. Second, persons 'of rank, fortune and dissipation' characteristically enjoy leisure, good food and fine wines. They sleep late, hunt and frequent social gatherings. They are merry and carefree, but they are also ignorant, since they never read or otherwise try to improve themselves. Despite their ignorance, however, they are happier than the peasants, because their lives are socially and sensually richer. Third, persons 'of taste and liberal accomplishments' rise above the first two classes by their aesthetic and intellectual pursuits. They study sciences and practice the arts, and enjoy the pleasures offered by truth and beauty. They also feel that they have done meaningful things in their lives, and know that they will be remembered favourably by posterity. The new range of interests and enjoyments makes them, according to Godwin, considerably happier than the peasants on the one hand and the rich and idle on the other. Fourth, and finally, persons 'of benevolence' outrank members of all the other classes by focusing their attention on the interests of other people instead of pursuing only selfish pleasures. Godwin contended that truth is cold and beauty is barren unless they are subordinated to the greatest happiness of humankind. Benevolent individuals seek the good of their fellow beings, pity their misery and rejoice in their happiness. These disinterested feelings and activities, so Godwin believed, produce the most intense and the most copious pleasures that human beings can experience. The highest level of individual happiness is coincidental with the greatest happiness of the greatest number.

The normative conclusion Godwin drew from these considerations was that it is our duty 'constantly to endeavour to raise each class, and every individual of each class, to a class above it'.[120] Although pleasure is the only good, the ability of individuals to enjoy pleasurable experiences depends on the level of humanity they occupy. This is why peasants should be given the means to become rich and idle, the rich and idle should be provided with the impulse to educate themselves, and the educated should be persuaded to believe that benevolence is preferable to egoism and self-love. All this is, in Godwin's view, possible, as he believed that people can be perpetually improved. It may be the case that the highest perfection can never be reached by all. But this possibility must not deter us from trying to do our best to attain that goal. As Godwin noted, it would 'not be the first time that persons engaged in the indefatigable pursuit of some accomplishment have arrived at an excellence that surpassed their most sanguine expectations'.[121]

The assumptions concerning human improvability and the scale of happiness support Godwin's political and ethical views in two important respects. First, when it is assumed that human beings are capable of becoming universally benevolent and altruistic, Godwin's views on the desirability of anarchism become more acceptable. Granted that coercive institutions may be needed in the immediate future, the development of the human race will eventually render them futile and prepare the ground for voluntary co-operation and orderly anarchy. Second, the improvability of humankind also provides an answer to the question of motivation which haunted all eighteenth-century utilitarian theories. By denying the relevance of God in ethics, Godwin rejected the solution of his theological predecessors: he did not believe that people can be driven to genuine benevolence by threats of divine retribution in the afterlife. Instead, he assumed that the inevitable improvement of human beings makes them naturally susceptible to altruistic ideas. The majority of people may be egoistic at the present, but the ideals of the enlightened minority will gradually alter the situation. In the end, all humans will act altruistically towards each other simply because they know that benevolence is the key to their own happiness as well as to the happiness of others.

Godwin's answer to the impending question of motivation was not particularly original. The idea that individuals can be improved by education had been introduced a century earlier by Locke, and it had been developed by Hartley, Hume and the theological utilitarians. Moreover, associationism had by the latter part of the eighteenth century become influential in continental Europe, where authors like Helvétius and Condorcet founded their work on various versions of the theory.[122] Godwin derived most of his psychological views from these sources.

From the viewpoint of Godwin's own ethics and politics, the associationist answer to the question of motivation is problematical. Even granting that disinterested benevolence leads to the greatest personal happiness, the difficulty is to explain how the members of the 'lower classes' can be made to understand the truth of this fact. Labouring peasants, wealthy idlers and educated aesthetes are, by definition, unmoved by the happiness and misery of others. This probably implies that these individuals cannot be converted to altruism by simply telling them that benevolence would make them happier. They cannot be coerced into altruism, either, since Godwin's own principles deny that people's attitudes or convictions could be genuinely altered by the use of force or by threats of violence. Future generations can, of course, become naturally benevolent, given that they are educated by the enlightened minority. But why should members of the other classes allow their children to be taught by the anarcho-progressive dissenters? Godwin's theory does not provide prudential peasants, idlers or aesthetes with compelling grounds to become benevolent, nor with good reasons to let their offspring be brought up in the enlightened spirit of universal altruism.

Bentham's version of radical utilitarianism was slightly superior to Godwin's theory when it came to reconciling the tension between descriptive egoism and normative altruism. Bentham believed that people are, on the whole, motivated only by self-interest, and that they must in certain cases be coerced into taking other people's interests into account. Even in those cases, however, reasonable individuals understand the legitimate role of the principle of happiness in social life. They realize that the regulations which restrict their own actions restrict the actions of all agents equally. They also realize that they are themselves greatly benefited by the constraints which are imposed upon the self-interested actions of others. Given these premises, reasonable individuals accept laws which are based on the principle of happiness, despite the fact that these laws occasionally prevent them from pursuing their own personal interests.[123]

The Benthamite view concerning moral motivation is rather ingenious, although by no means conclusive. There are, no doubt, individuals and groups who can control others by cunning or by force, and who do not need the protection provided by the legal system.[124] But these individuals and groups most probably form a minority of the members of any given society, and the theoretical problem presented by them is, in terms of democracy, less grave than the problem presented by Godwin's 'lower class' majority. Bentham's rejection of anarchy and human perfectibility clearly strengthened the foundation of his normative views. The same rejection implied, however, that his theory became politically less radical than Godwin's anarcho-optimistic doctrine. Bentham defended the view that changes are necessary and desirable in social and political life, but he believed that these changes can best be brought about by reforming the legislative and judicial institutions, not by abolishing them entirely. Legal coercion and force, which Godwin saw as barbarous remnants of our violent past, were regarded by Bentham as acceptable and efficient instruments of social progress.[125]

This comparison between Godwin's anarchism and Bentham's reformism completes my survey of the various forms of British universal altruism. My main claim in this chapter has been that the 'classical' form of utilitarianism, normally attributed to Jeremy Bentham and John Stuart Mill, is in no sense the first, nor theoretically the most interesting, historical version of the doctrine. The 'Benthamite' principles of happiness, hedonism and impartiality had been defended in one form or another by an array of British philosophers, scholars and clergymen before Bentham and Mill. The remarks made by Mill concerning the quality of pleasures and the primacy of freedom had also been anticipated by seventeenth- and eighteenth-century theorists. The only feature which clearly distinguished Bentham and Mill from the tradition preceding them was their practical success. Many legal reforms in England and in other countries during the nineteenth century were initiated and inspired by the Benthamite 'philosophical radicals'. The wide political influence of Bentham and Mill made them the most important utilitarian reformers of all time. But even political success and popular appeal fail to make the doctrines of Bentham and Mill theoretically original or unique within the British tradition.

2

THE DEVELOPMENT OF
MODERN UTILITARIANISM

At the outset of the preceding chapter I defined the three axioms which are generally thought to sum up and mark off Jeremy Bentham's 'classical utilitarianism', namely the principles of happiness, hedonism and impartiality. Bentham praised the continental philosophers Cesare Beccaria and Claude-Adrien Helvétius for inventing these principles, as he seems to have been all but unaware of the fact that similar ideals had occupied a central role in British moral philosophy since the seventeenth century. Bentham's possible lack of historical knowledge did not, however, alienate him from the theories of his countrymen. The basic elements of his 'classical' doctrine[1] have been derived – albeit indirectly – from the eighteenth-century psychological and theological versions of utilitarianism, or 'universal altruism'. And although a certain lack of sophistication occasionally marks Bentham's views on ethics,[2] he managed to place himself clearly within the British tradition of normative altruism.

John Stuart Mill, who was better acquainted with the history of philosophy than Bentham, favoured the teachings of psychological utilitarians, and rejected explicitly the theological version of the view professed by William Paley.[3] It was probably Mill's sensitivity to psychological considerations, combined with his openness to the ideals of Romanticism, that produced his basic axiological deviation from the Benthamite doctrine. While Bentham had held the view that all pleasures are in themselves equally valuable, Mill argued, following David Hartley and William Godwin, that certain 'higher' pleasures should be given priority in moral calculations.[4] The intelligent, educated and conscientious pleasures of noble human beings are, according to Mill, intrinsically preferable to the lower bodily pleasures of fools, dunces and rascals.

Mill's axiological departure from classical teaching had a marked influence on his normative views concerning law and social policy. If all pleasures are equal, as Bentham suggested, the greatest happiness could, in theory at least, be achieved by totalitarian laws and large-scale brainwashing. Aldous Huxley's imaginary Brave New World, in which all people are kept content by a combination of invisible force and psychoactive drugs, would provide the model of an ideal utilitarian society.[5] But if Mill's point concerning the quality of pleasures is taken into account, the situation is drastically altered. The recreational joys which are available to the inhabitants of Huxley's world are clearly inferior pleasures which do not maximize happiness in the 'higher' Millian sense. Any actual or prospective society in which at least some people can experience nobler pleasures would, according to Mill's view, be preferable to Huxley's dystopia. The most desirable form of society would, of course, be the one in which the enjoyment of noble happiness is extended to the greatest possible number of individuals.[6]

Mill believed that the laws of an ideal society should enforce the qualitative principle of happiness by forgoing all unnecessary interventions into people's affairs. According to Mill, the only proper function of the law is to prevent individuals from inflicting harm on each other. In matters which concern mainly or solely themselves, individuals should be left free to make their own choices and their own mistakes.[7] Mill admitted that restrictive societies have sometimes been able to produce a handful of noble and distinguished individuals. But he argued that the moral and intellectual development of ordinary citizens, which he considered more important, necessarily requires liberty in all self-regarding matters.[8] People cannot be coerced into experiencing noble pleasures. This goal can be achieved only by promoting their personal autonomy and self-determination.[9]

Mill's ethical legacy was, then, twofold. On the one hand, he argued that qualitative differences between various types of pleasure ought to be accounted for in the utilitarian calculus. On the other hand, he also maintained that the best means to take qualitative differences properly into account would be to exclude self-regarding behaviour from the scope of legislation and social policy. The latter view was fervently criticized by James Fitzjames Stephen in his polemical book *Liberty, Equality, Fraternity* (1873), which was published in the year of Mill's death.[10] On the whole, however, Mill's utilitarian defence of liberal principles was ignored in favour of the ongoing debate concerning the hedonistic theory of value.[11]

Critics of Bentham and James Mill repeatedly claimed that utilitarians are forced, by their doctrine, into indifference towards the 'higher' pleasures of imagination and taste.[12] The qualitative hedonism of John Stuart Mill evaded this criticism but invited two novel accusations. John Grote in his *Examination of the Utilitarian Philosophy* (1870) argued that Mill's supposedly qualitative differences between pleasures are in fact quantitative: by stating that certain pleasures are higher than others, we are simply asserting that there are experiences which are more pleasurable than the rest.[13] Any other interpretation would be internally inconsistent.[14] F.H. Bradley reinforced the attack against hedonism in his *Ethical Studies* (1876) by maintaining that happiness, conceived as pleasure, cannot be the end of human action, since the direct pursuit of pleasure is always self-defeating.[15]

The line of criticism employed by Grote reached its peak in 1902, when Ernest Albee in *A History of English Utilitarianism* conceded that 'there is perfect agreement . . . among competent critics, of whatever ethical convictions, as to the inconsistency of [Mill's qualitative] view with his general hedonistic position'.[16] Bradley's line of argument, in its turn, was completed by G.E. Moore, who in his *Principia Ethica* (1903) asserted that what is valuable cannot be defined in terms of natural qualities at all.[17]

Moore's exposure of what he called the 'naturalistic fallacy' in ethics overshadowed the development of moral philosophy throughout the first half of the twentieth century, and reduced the once vigorous normative discipline into a linguistic game.[18] Moore's non-naturalism, which was closely followed by other 'meta-ethical' doctrines such as emotivism and prescriptivism, did not primarily state what is good, or what people ought to do, but defined what words like 'good' and 'ought' mean. It was not until the 1950s that analytical philosophers could again address normative questions without fear of disrepute. By that time, the chain of universal altruism had been broken, and Western scholars had learned to regard utilitarianism as the paradigm of failure in moral theory.

THE BASIC QUESTIONS OF MODERN UTILITARIANISM

Due to the gap in the tradition, late twentieth-century utilitarianism is in many respects quite unlike the doctrines professed by Bentham and Mill. One striking feature is the diversity of views which are supposed to pass as utilitarian. J.J.C. Smart's hedonistic act-utilitarianism is very different from R.B. Brandt's ideal rule-utilitarianism, and both differ markedly from R.M. Hare's two-level preference-utilitarianism which is theoretically based on universal prescriptivism.[19] In fact, there are so many different versions of the utilitarian theory today that it would be pointless to try to reiterate them all.[20] A better way to approach the central issues of modern utilitarianism is to review some of the basic questions which have to be answered by all utilitarians.

One focal question concerns the justification of the principle of greatest happiness. The Cambridge Platonists of the seventeenth century believed that reason compels us to pursue the greatest general happiness. The psychological utilitarians of the eighteenth century maintained that the original or acquired benevolence of human beings makes them universally altruistic towards each other. And Bentham stated that people should be compelled to adopt utilitarianism through legal prohibitions. But on what grounds can a modern utilitarian claim that the moral rightness of actions depends on the amount of happiness, or good, that the actions produce? Answers to this question provide a link between traditional forms of universal altruism and present-day utilitarianism.

Another important question is the definition of happiness, or good. Early proponents of universal altruism often combined simple hedonism with a belief in the intrinsic value of human perfection. Gradually the inconsistency of this combined position became obvious, and by the middle of the eighteenth century scholars had learned to state clearly which definition of happiness they preferred. Moore's non-naturalism broke the tradition of British hedonism at the turn of the century, but some modern-day utilitarians have reintroduced the doctrine. Other theorists, however, have abandoned pleasure as the ultimate goal of action, and replaced it with welfare, preferences or the satisfaction of rational desires.

The single most heated issue within the reborn utilitarian school of the 1950s and 1960s was whether or not rules and regulations can have an independent status in the theory. Act-utilitarians, who supposedly followed Bentham and Mill, argued that the rightness of actions must always be assessed by reference to the consequences of the actions themselves. Rules and regulations can be followed in everyday life for the sake of mental economy, but genuine moral choices must be based on the consequences of particular actions. Rule-utilitarians, in turn, focused their attention on certain arguably immoral choices which they thought act-utilitarians must condone. Their claim was that the only way to avoid these immoralities is to proceed indirectly, and to recognize the need for absolute ethical rules in real life. According to rule-utilitarianism, the morality of rules and regulations can be assessed by direct appeals to the greatest happiness principle. The morality of particular actions, however, depends entirely on their conformity to legitimate rules. An attempt to save the best parts of both act- and rule-utilitarianism was made by R.M. Hare in his theory concerning the two levels of moral thinking.

Modern utilitarianism has not been greeted with enthusiasm in all quarters. In addition to the questions of defining and justifying the principles of happiness and pleasure,[21] there are several interconnected problems which allegedly arise from the use of the principle of impartiality. Those who profess egalitarian ideals have noted that indifference concerning the subjects of pleasure and pain makes utilitarian calculations insensitive to questions of distribution and distributive justice.[22] Strict liberals maintain that utilitarian theories, due to their insistence on perfect impartiality, do not recognize the essential distinctness of persons.[23] Virtue ethicists argue that impartiality leaves no room for friendship, gratitude or family feeling. And philosophers who believe in vengeance and retribution rather than in the prevention of future crime and suffering by legal correction criticize utilitarian theories for their supposed tendency to punish the innocent as well as the guilty. At the core of all these anti-utilitarian arguments is the fear that utilitarianism may force individuals to sacrifice something that belongs to them in order to benefit total strangers.

In what follows, I shall study these questions in more detail. I shall begin by considering certain historical and contemporary attempts to justify the principle of happiness. I shall then go on to review the definitions given to the concept of happiness, or good. After an examination of the dispute between act- and rule-utilitarians,

I shall conclude the chapter by describing and assessing some of the most important criticisms presented against modern utilitarianism.

THE GREATEST HAPPINESS PRINCIPLE DEFENDED

One of the perennial tasks of moral philosophy is to justify the 'first principles' upon which all other principles, rules and actions are, or ought to be, based. Some ethical systems, notably common-sense moralities, are pluralistic in this respect, that is, they recognize the validity of several fundamental axioms. The problem with these systems is, however, that when two basic principles yield conflicting practical conclusions, it is often impossible to judge which alternative ought to be preferred. Utilitarianism, in its turn, evades the problem of conflicting moral norms by assuming only one fundamental axiom, the principle of happiness. The formulation given above to classical utilitarianism may seem to imply that the theory recognizes three axioms instead of one. But the so-called principle of hedonism is, in fact, only a definition of happiness, and many utilitarian theorists have argued that impartiality is a conceptual entailment of the central principle of felicity.

Psychological utilitarians believed that people are by nature benevolent, and that their behaviour towards each other is, in the last analysis, always altruistic. This descriptive form of utilitarianism has not been particularly popular among contemporary moral philosophers. On the contrary, the development of the doctrine of socio-biology has led some theorists to argue that human beings, like all other animals, are inherently egoistic or, at the most, only reciprocally or genetically altruistic.[24] But from the viewpoint of normative ethics, an important general criticism can be levelled at both psychological altruism and biological egoism. The fact that people behave in a certain way does not necessarily imply that they ought to behave in that way. Human conduct may or may not be explicable in terms of general happiness, but explanations should not be confused with the justification of fundamental moral principles.

Theological utilitarians, who assumed that human beings are naturally egoistic, defended normative altruism by an appeal to the will of God. According to them, people ought to aim at the general good, because otherwise they will be destined to eternal suffering in the afterlife. Modern moral philosophers may feel queasy about accepting this view for at least two reasons. First, the assumption of a utilitarian God is not likely to receive support from any quarter. Theological ethicists mostly opt for non-consequentialist moral theories, and secular moralists usually deny the relevance of divine influence in ethics. Second, theological utilitarianism does not seem to recognize the autonomy, or overriding nature, of moral considerations in human affairs. Fear of eternal suffering may, no doubt, force individuals into action which can be externally described as altruistic. But it is not obvious that threats of punishment can in any serious sense justify, or legitimize, universal benevolence. Moral rightness is not always reducible to prudential expediency.

The first serious attempts to justify the principle of happiness in terms of morality and conceptual consistency were made by Jeremy Bentham and John Stuart Mill.[25] Bentham's argument for utilitarianism was indirect.[26] He admitted that the greatest happiness principle cannot be supported by deductive proof, but he claimed that all criticisms directed against it can be shown to be inadequate or false. In his opinion, most attacks against the utilitarian doctrine are based on the doctrine itself and challenge the prevailing applications of his principle rather than the principle itself. As regards those critiques which are not essentially utilitarian, Bentham asserted that they are invariably founded on sinister interests, prejudice or caprice.

The idea that even critics of utilitarianism eventually need the principle of happiness to support their own theories is not without appeal. It seems quite natural to think that if virtues, duties and rights are morally important, this is because they tend to increase human happiness by their existence. It is, indeed, difficult to imagine anybody explicitly vindicating virtues, duties or rights which have a confessed tendency to promote, on the whole, misery and suffering.

There are, however, two serious flaws in Bentham's indirect 'proof' of utilitarianism. On the one hand, the truth of negative existential statements cannot be conclusively demonstrated. It may be the case that nobody has to date seen a pink raven, but this does not prove that there are none. Similarly, it may be the case that Bentham had not encountered even prima facie valid alternatives to utilitarianism, but this is probably due to the fact that he did not try very hard to find them. The stock critiques that Bentham directed at what he called the principles of 'asceticism' and of 'sympathy and antipathy' aptly show that he was not deeply-read in moral theory.[27] On the other hand, even if it could be shown that all non-utilitarian doctrines are erroneous, this would not prove that the utilitarian theory is valid. It is perfectly possible that there are no sound first principles in ethics. In that case the scope of Bentham's remarks is reduced to *ad hominem* argumentation against some minor anti-utilitarian credos.

Mill's defence of utilitarianism was more direct than Bentham's.[28] He argued that by studying what individual human beings desire moral philosophers can determine what humankind as a whole should aim at. The outline of his argument is as follows. First, happiness is the only thing that people actually desire as an end. Individuals can, of course, desire other things such as virtue or money, but these, according to Mill, are desired only as parts of, or as a means to, happiness. Second, the fact that all human beings desire happiness (and nothing else) as an end supports the view that each person's happiness is desirable, or good, to that person.[29] Third, since each person's happiness is good to that person, the general happiness is good to the aggregate of all persons. And since the good is what we should aim at, Mill concluded that we should aim at promoting the general happiness of humankind.

Critics of Mill have usually focused their attention on the second and third steps of the above argument.[30] As regards the inference from desire to value, the remark has often been made that the word 'desirable' means 'ought to be desired', not 'can be desired' as Mill's argument seems to presuppose. If this is the correct linguistic account, then Mill can be criticized for proceeding from facts to norms without sufficient conceptual justification. As for the deduction from each person's happiness to the happiness of all, Mill has been accused, probably justly, of committing a gross fallacy of composition. As one commentator has pointed out, it does 'not follow from the fact that each man's dreams are fascinating to him that everyone's dreams are fascinating to everyone'.[31] The same point also applies, *mutatis mutandis*, to desires and desirability. This is not to say that Mill's conclusion is unreasonable. The happiness of all may well be valued by everyone who understands the requirements of morality. But Mill's 'proof' does not lend any support to this view.[32]

Henry Sidgwick in his *Methods of Ethics* (1874) presented the last notable nineteenth-century defence of utilitarianism, or as he called the doctrine, 'universalistic hedonism'.[33] Sidgwick's central idea was that valid moral theories must conform to certain clear and self-evident intuitions which form a coherent whole and which are accepted by all human beings who are capable of combining 'adequate intellectual enlightenment with a serious concern for morality'.[34] According to Sidgwick, there are three fundamental and self-evident intuitions, namely the intuitions of justice, prudence and the universality of goodness. The principle of justice states that 'whatever action any of us judges to be right for himself, he implicitly judges to be right for all similar persons in similar circumstances'.[35] The intuition of prudence, in its turn, asserts that 'one ought to have impartial concern for all parts of one's conscious life'.[36] A prudential person should not, for instance, prefer a smaller present good to a greater future good.[37] And the universality of goodness dictates that rational beings ought to aim at good generally, not at particular aspects of it.[38] Or, as Sidgwick also put the matter, 'the good of any one individual is of no more importance from the point of view of the universe than the good of any other'.[39]

Furnished with these truths, Sidgwick proceeded to analyse and assess the three 'methods of ethics', or moral theories, that he regarded as the most important. The first method, dogmatic intuitionism, states that actions are morally right if they conform to our everyday ideas concerning right and wrong, good and evil. The problem with this approach is that the common-sense intuitions of virtue, right and duty do not always pass the test of coherence, or consistency, which is required of self-evident intuitions. The duties of universal truth-telling and universal promise-keeping, for example, often conflict in real life, and when this occurs, dogmatic intuitionism is unable to resolve the dilemma.

Sidgwick's second method, universalistic hedonism, demands that we aim at promoting the general good. The precepts of this theory, unlike those of intuitionism, do form a coherent whole, and they also conform with the self-evident intuitions of justice, prudence and the universality of good. But these points do not suffice to prove the ultimate superiority of utilitarianism as a moral theory. The same remarks concerning coherence and conformity also apply to Sidgwick's third method, ethical egoism, which is incompatible with universalistic hedonism. According to rational egoism, I must always aim at maximizing my own happiness. The theory does not necessarily violate the principle of justice, since nothing prevents rational egoists from universalizing their view. It is my duty to max-imize my happiness, but it is not anybody else's duty to share my task. Every human being has a moral obligation to promote her or his own good. Similar points apply to the requirement of the uni-versality of good. I can admit that, from the viewpoint of the universe, my good is no more important than anybody else's, but I can still argue, quite reasonably, that from my own point of view my happiness outweighs the happiness of others.

In comparing the three methods, Sidgwick argued that all the central dictates of common-sense intuitionism can be encapsulated by utilitarian principles. Although this does not objectively justify universalistic hedonism, it does provide intuitionists with a good argument in its favour. Following the same logic, Sidgwick also examined the possibility of reconciling egoistic considerations with utilitarian thinking. Eventually, however, he had to admit that unless there is a God who balances the score of happiness in the afterlife, self-interest does not necessarily coincide with the general good. And as we have no self-evident intuitions concerning the exis-tence of an Almighty God, Sidgwick was forced to conclude that ethical egoism and universal altruism are equally rational alterna-tives for individuals who can combine intelligence with serious moral concern.[40]

Assuming that Sidgwick's account was meant as a proof of utili-tarianism, there are three points which render it less than convincing.[41] First, even if the principle of happiness could be justi-fied by appeals to certain self-evident intuitions, this would not prove that general happiness is the foundation of morality. If the utilitarian principle can be supported by the axioms of justice, pru-dence and the universality of good, then these basic axioms, or their presuppositions, constitute the actual first principles. Seen from this angle, Sidgwick's proof must be either invalid or misplaced. Second, the comparison between egoism, altruism and intuitionism does not exhaust the possibilities of ethical theory. Although Sidgwick may have believed that the choice must be made among his own 'meth-ods', there are many other views which are important – for instance, natural rights theories, virtue theories and deontological moralities. All these doctrines cannot be rejected simply by asserting, without argument, that they are no more than variants of dogmatic intu-itionism. Third, a proof of utilitarianism which also recognizes the validity of ethical egoism is not particularly effective. Sidgwick himself concluded that rational individuals have good reasons for choosing benevolence and universal altruism, but that they have equally good reasons for selecting egoism. If this is the case, then there cannot be any conclusive proof for the utilitarian theory.

Sidgwick's work marks the end of classical universal altruism in Britain. The ideals of individualism and liberalism, which had inspired both philosophers and social reformers, were no longer fashionable in Europe, and academic reflection drifted gradually away from practical concerns. Moral philosophers in Oxford and Cambridge pondered the definitions of the right and the good, while the world around them was reshaped by collectivist and totalitarian creeds.

At the turn of the century, G.E. Moore completed an important conceptual conversion which had been initiated already by Mill and Sidgwick and which became the hallmark of modern utilitarianism.[42] Moore replaced the concept of happiness by the concept of good as the first principle of utilitarian ethics, and substituted 'the maximum net sum of good' for 'the greatest happiness of the greatest number' in the utilitarian formula.[43] This axiological shift enabled many new developments in the theory. When the subjective happiness and experiences of individuals ceased to be the only source of value, many objective entities such as justice, virtue and social order became eligible for consideration.[44] The objectivity of values also led many theorists to believe that goodness can be precisely and 'scientifically' measured for socio-political purposes.[45] Eventually, the deletion of 'the greatest number' from the revised principle of utility gave birth to a theoretical monstrosity called 'egoistic utilitarianism'.[46] By inventing this doctrine, contemporary moral philosophers gave final form to a theory which had been criticized in vain by anti-utilitarians since William Godwin's day.

Defences of the modern principle of utility are usually founded on two major premises.[47] First, it is generally assumed that individuals want to maximize the fulfilment or satisfaction of their needs, interests, desires or preferences.[48] Second, it is also assumed that morality and moral judgements are by nature universal, or universalizable. Roughly speaking, this means that moral considerations urge us to do unto others what we would like them to do unto ourselves.[49] Put together, the two premises yield the conclusion that morality, or moral language, demands us to aim at the greatest general satisfaction of needs, interests, desires or preferences. If we fail to act in accordance with the principle of utility, we are either irrational or incapable of grasping the logic of normative concepts.

The problem with this argument is that its second premise can be disputed both on theoretical and practical grounds.[50] On the one hand, linguistic intuitions concerning the nature of morality are deeply ambiguous as well as socially and culturally diversified. It is practically impossible to employ the linguistic approach without committing oneself, at the same time, to ethical relativism – which, however, tends to be abhorred by the majority of today's utilitarian philosophers. On the other hand, even if this commitment could be evaded, the practical deficiency of the second premise would remain. Arguments which purport to demonstrate the validity of a given moral theory cannot, of course, be rejected simply because they fail to persuade the most obstinate critics of the theory. But they can and must be rejected if they do not appeal even to the proponents of the view. This, I think, is the case with the linguistic argument. Individuals who mentally struggle between utilitarianism and self-interest in a real-life situation will hardly be impressed, let alone moved, by the alleged fact that an egoistic choice would reveal their inability to grasp the logic of normative sentences.

Theorists who are less keen on the principle of universality often emphasize the significance of choice in moral matters.[51] According to them, ethical theories do not belong to an absolute and objective reality which exists independently of human individuals and communities. Instead, ethical systems are human-made constructions which can be created, altered and selected either subjectively or intersubjectively. Moral judgements are not, according to the most extreme versions of this view, cognitive statements at all, but mere expressions of approbation or attempts at emotional persuasion. The most notable utilitarian to hold this non-cognitivist view is J.J.C. Smart, who in his book *An Outline of a System of Utilitarian Ethics* (1961) revived the Benthamite doctrine of hedonistic act-utilitarianism.[52] In the opening pages of the book Smart boldly states that it is not his intention to prove the validity of utilitarianism, since this would be impossible. To use his own words, 'ultimate ethical principles seem to lie within the fields of personal decision, persuasion, advice and propaganda' rather than 'within the field of academic philosophy'.[53] But the non-cognitive nature of moral judgements does not prevent Smart from defending utilitarianism by philosophical arguments. His main line of defence in the book

seems to be that there are so few 'conceptually clear and emotionally attractive systems of normative ethics' that if a lucid and
appealing account of utilitarianism can be construed, it will quite
probably be at least prima facie acceptable to all reasonable individuals.[54]

Smart's approach avoids, at least partly, the problems of motivation which proved to be fatal to the linguistic defence of
utilitarianism. Arguments which are based on one's own choice are
likely to be more persuasive than accusations of illogicality. One
cannot convert egoists by saying, 'Your use of moral concepts differs
from that of many important Oxford philosophers.' But one can
perhaps persuade them by saying, 'I have chosen universal altruism
and I am doing fine, why don't you join me?' Ultimately, of course,
it is a matter of empirical fact how people respond to different kinds
of reasoning.

The main disadvantage of the non-cognitivist view is, however, its
affinity to ethical relativism. If personal decisions suffice to justify
moral theories, then there are as many legitimate moralities as there
are intelligible accounts of human conduct. Although Smart may be
right in asserting that there are only a few normative systems which
are both conceptually clear and emotionally attractive, it does not
follow from this that there is only one such system nor that that system must be a variant of utilitarian thinking. What Smart did to
utilitarianism by his analytical clarification can be done – and has
been done – by other philosophers to, for instance, social contract
theories[55] and rights theories.[56] Since, in addition, experience tells us
that human beings are capable of being emotionally attracted to
almost any kind of morality, it seems that Smart's non-cognitivism
does not in the end provide adequate grounds for the universal
acceptance of utilitarianism.

THE VARIETIES OF UTILITY

The next question utilitarian theorists have to address concerns the
definition of happiness. The basic axiological tension between the
'quantitative' and 'qualitative' versions of hedonism is as old as the
tradition of universal altruism itself. The distinction can be traced
back to the work of Richard Cumberland, who in his *De Legibus
Naturae* (1672) designated both natural happiness and moral perfection as the ultimate ends of human action.[57] David Hartley in

1749 was the first to provide a detailed account of the different kinds of pleasure and pain, and he was also the first to argue explicitly that in the formulation of moral judgements higher pleasures and pains ought to count for more than lower ones.[58] Hartley's view was countered two decades later by Abraham Tucker, who maintained that the so-called qualitative differences between pleasures can be explained away by employing the psychological principles of association. The noble pleasures which are said to be higher than others are, according to Tucker, ordinary physiological pleasures of sensation, which are connected with the ideas of sympathy, conscience and moral sense by long and partly subconscious chains of association.[59]

The oscillation between the quantitative and qualitative interpretations of hedonism was continued by the radical utilitarians. William Godwin opted for the view that there are separate levels of happiness, each enjoyed by a specific class of people, and that human happiness can be best promoted by assisting individuals to rise from their present class to the class immediately above it.[60] Bentham, like Tucker before him, believed that all types of pleasure are equally valuable, and that only quantitative factors are relevant in utility calculations. And Mill, in his attempt to reconcile Benthamite teaching with the demands of common-sense morality, reassumed the qualitative position.

Bentham stated the fundamental tenet of his hedonistic axiology in the oft-quoted opening passage of *An Introduction to the Principles of Morals and Legislation*:

> Nature has placed mankind under the governance of two sovereign masters, *pain* and *pleasure*. It is for them alone to point out what we ought to do, as well as to determine what we shall do. On the one hand the standard of right and wrong, on the other the chain of causes and effects, are fastened to their throne.[61]

In another context Bentham expressed the same point in less dramatic tones and in more accurate terms. Whilst discussing the many types of intentionality, and especially the goodness and badness of intentions, he wrote:

> Strictly speaking, nothing can be said to be good or bad, but either in itself; which is the case only with pain or pleasure: or

on account of its effects; which is the case only with things that are the causes or preventives of pain and pleasure.[62]

Although Bentham himself created some conceptual confusion by defining utility as 'that property in any object, whereby it tends to produce benefit, advantage, pleasure, good, or happiness',[63] it is probably safe to presume that his theory of value was essentially hedonistic, and that pleasure and pain were the only intrinsic values he recognized.[64]

Bentham believed that all pleasures in themselves and all pains in themselves are prima facie equally valuable, regardless of their specific type or source.[65] There are, he observed, four major springs from which agreeable and disagreeable experiences usually flow. These sources he called the four 'sanctions'.[66] Physical sanctions cause pleasure and pain without human or superhuman intervention: obedience to the laws of nature tends to benefit individuals, while disobedience tends to inflict harm on them. Political sanctions are defined by legislators, and they are dispensed by judges who act in accordance with the will of the supreme ruling power in the state. Moral, or popular, sanctions emanate from the feelings shared in the community, and they are conveyed by expressions of approval and disapproval. And religious sanctions are allegedly issued by a divine being. But although the origins of any given experience can be traced to one of these four categories, Bentham asserted that pleasures and pains which belong to diverse classes 'differ not ultimately in kind' from each other: according to him, 'the only difference there is among them lies in the circumstances that accompany their production'.[67] The outcome of these considerations is that qualitative factors do not count in the formulation of value judgements in Bentham's ethical system.

As for quantitative factors, Bentham enumerated seven dimensions which ought to be accounted for in the hedonistic calculus. Pleasures and pains in themselves can differ from each other in four respects: with regard to their (1) intensity, (2) duration, (3) certainty or uncertainty, and (4) propinquity or remoteness.[68] Two further dimensions, namely (5) fecundity and (6) purity, are relevant when it comes to the evaluation of actions.[69] By the fecundity of a pleasure or a pain Bentham meant the 'chance it has of being followed by sensations of the same kind' – the pleasure by pleasures and the pain by pains.[70] By purity he meant the absence of additional experiences of the opposite kind. The concluding hedonic dimension, which becomes relevant only if the rated actions affect a number of individuals, is (7) the extent of the pleasure or pain, or the number of people who experience it.[71]

Bentham went on to present a detailed procedure by which the value of pleasures and pains ought to be summed up, multiplied and compared in order to choose the right utilitarian policy or action.[72] It is a matter of some dispute whether Bentham regarded this hedonistic calculus as an actual model of decision-making or merely as a heuristic device. He did admit that people cannot in real life estimate and count every potential pleasure and pain which may be caused by their choices. But he also maintained that the rightness of human decisions can be judged by the extent to which they are sensitive to the seven dimensions of pleasure and pain. Twentieth-century utilitarians, as well as their critics, have generally assumed that Bentham meant his calculus to be taken literally, as the foundation of a new, scientific theory of morality.

Mill's defence of the Epicurean theory of value in *Utilitarianism* (1861) contained a criticism of Bentham's simplified axiology.[73] Mill argued that no Epicurean theory has failed to recognize the fact that intellect, feelings, imagination and moral sentiments produce pleasures which are higher than the pleasures of mere sensation. He admitted that many utilitarians have emphasized the quantitative aspects of hedonism. They have, for instance, maintained that mental pleasures are preferable to bodily pleasures because they are more permanent and less frequently accompanied by pain.[74] But Mill believed that this is only half the truth. He wrote:

> It is quite compatible with the principle of utility to recognize the fact, that some *kinds* of pleasure are more desirable and more valuable than others. It would be absurd that while, in estimating all other things, quality is considered as well as quantity, the estimation of pleasures should be supposed to depend on quantity alone.[75]

By assuming the qualitative interpretation of hedonism Mill countered the critics who had maintained that utilitarianism is unable to accommodate the noble joys of, say, art and philosophy. But he also committed himself to the difficult task of explaining which particular types of pleasure ought to be preferred to others and on what grounds.

As for distinguishing the more desirable experiences from the less desirable, Mill suggested the following test: 'Of two pleasures, if there be one to which all or almost all who have experience of both give a decided preference, irrespective of any feeling of moral obligation to prefer it, that is the more desirable pleasure.'[76] This test, Mill argued, reveals that pleasures which employ the higher mental faculties are universally preferable to pleasures which can be enjoyed by animals and uneducated human beings. Intelligent individuals, if they were given the choice, would not choose to become fools, erudite human beings would not prefer ignorance to learnedness, and altruistic persons would not wish to become selfish. According to Mill, none of these informed preferences ultimately depends on quantitative factors.[77] He noted that those individuals who are foolish, ignorant and egoistic may in fact lead more pleasurable lives and be more content than those who struggle to improve themselves. But contentment should not be mistaken for happiness. As Mill himself put the matter in probably the most quoted passage of *Utilitarianism*:

> It is better to be a human being dissatisfied than a pig satisfied; better to be Socrates dissatisfied than a fool satisfied. And if the fool, or the pig, is of a different opinion, it is because they only know their own side of the question. The other party to the comparison knows both sides.[78]

Mill admitted that many educated individuals who should have 'known both sides' have nonetheless abandoned the more refined joys in the pursuit of transitory bodily pleasures. But he believed that these individuals have not, by the time of the choice, been capable of enjoying noble pleasures any more. Deprivation and discouragement can, according to Mill, easily destroy the tender flower of refinement, leaving the individual unable to relish the finer joys. When this is the case, the choices made by the individual can no longer be regarded as informed or considered.[79]

At least three major criticisms can be levelled at Mill's qualitative hedonism. To begin with, the statement that one mental state is better than another simply by virtue of its higher quality is probably nonsensical from the viewpoint of normative ethics. Consider, for instance, the following dialogue, presented originally by S.C. Patten, between Smith and yourself at a neighbourhood lunch counter:

'Terrible!' says Smith.

'The sandwich?' you ask, leaning forward for a closer look.

'No,' he says, 'the sandwich is O.K. Or at least as good as they go. No, it is the pleasure – the pleasure I'm getting from the sandwich is terrible.'

'Pardon me?'

'What I mean is that compared to the pleasure I got in hearing the symphony last night, the pleasure I'm receiving from eating this sandwich isn't much.'

'Ah I see,' you say with some relief. 'It's that you're not getting *as much* pleasure from eating the sandwich as in hearing the symphony.'

'Oh no. I didn't mean to say that,' Smith says. 'As a matter of fact, though it never occurred to me until now, the pleasurable states I received from the concert last night, taken together, seem pretty much equal in amount with the pleasure I am getting from this sandwich. Still, last night's states of pleasure were better. Much better. Sublime, I'd say.'[80]

As Patten observes, Smith's account of his experiences is unintelligible. Pleasures as sensations simply cannot be compared with each other in terms of better and worse in the way suggested in the passage.

Another objection which is often presented against qualitative hedonism is that the view is intrinsically inconsistent.[81] The core of this objection, first stated in precise detail by G.E. Moore, is the following. According to any type of hedonism, pleasure – and only pleasure – is intrinsically valuable, or good in itself. Assuming that all pleasures share a unique and common property P, it follows from the basic tenet of hedonism that those experiences – and only those experiences – which have property P are good in themselves. It also follows, since nothing else can increase or decrease the value of things, that experiences are more valuable the more they have property P. According to qualitative hedonism, however, there may be 'higher' pleasures which have less property P than certain 'lower' pleasures but which are, nevertheless, intrinsically more valuable. This conflict between the qualitative and the hedonistic elements of the Millian axiology has led a number of utilitarian as well as non-utilitarian philosophers to reject qualitative hedonism as an inconsistent doctrine.[82]

Moore's solution to the axiological problems of utilitarianism was to state that goodness is, in fact, an undefinable, simple quality which cannot be conceptually linked with natural properties or states of affairs.[83] A theorist who defines value in terms of pleasure, need, desire, evolution or any other entity or process which can be perceived by the external senses commits, in Moore's language, the 'naturalistic fallacy'. It may be the case, according to Moore, that pleasure is always a part of what is good. If this is the case, nothing can be truly valued unless it is, among other things, pleasurable. But it does not follow from this that the goodness of an experience or the goodness of a state of affairs could be identified with its pleasantness. It is always possible to ask, as Moore did in his famous open question argument, 'Is pleasure good?' and there are good semantic grounds for believing that this question is not identical with the question, 'Is pleasure pleasant?'[84] The rejection of all forms of naturalism led Moore to accept an axiological version of ethical intuitionism.[85] He did not believe, like Sidgwick and the seventeenth-century Cambridge Platonists before him, that normative moral principles can be divined by intuition. The first principle of utilitarianism, 'It is one's duty to maximize the good', was for him an analytical truth which needed no support from ethical considerations.[86] But Moore thought that the answer to the question 'What is good in itself?' can be found only intuitively. His own intuition, for which he claimed universal validity, was that 'the most valuable things, which we know or can imagine, are certain states of consciousness, which may be roughly described as the pleasures of human intercourse and the enjoyment of beautiful objects'.[87] Moore's aestheticism became rather influential within the intellectual circles of his own day, especially among the members of the so-called Bloomsbury Group, but it was effectively overshadowed by his non-naturalism during the interwar era.[88]

The third objection to Mill's qualitative hedonism can be extended also to Moore's aestheticism, or 'ideal utilitarianism'.[89] Both theorists asserted that certain cultivated joys, such as the pleasures of intellectual debate and aesthetic enjoyment, ought to be preferred to delights which are more typically enjoyed by uneducated individuals. But if this preference is employed to guide practical policies, the result is either paternalistic or elitist. On the one hand, the higher values can be promoted by raising individuals from ignorance and indifference to cultivation and concern. This solution, which was defended in 1793 by William Godwin,[90] can be initially praised for its democratic spirit and egalitarian zeal. But the problem with it is that cultivation, concern, and the higher pleasures are usually defined by a small minority of people, whose values are not necessarily shared by the rest of society. The imposition of the minority's tastes upon the majority would be prima facie condemnable, since it would undermine the personal autonomy of many individuals. On the other hand, it could also be argued that the higher values can be promoted by restricting the scope of morality. The proponents of this solution can claim that it is futile to educate the masses, since ordinary human beings lack the inborn qualities without which it is impossible to appreciate fine arts and refined company. This elitist claim is not supported by psychological or sociological data, and it was not explicitly supported by either Mill or Moore, but it is quite compatible with their doctrines of qualitative hedonism and ideal utilitarianism.

Modern defenders of Mill have argued that the objections against his theory have been based on an interpretation of hedonism which he did not in fact hold.[91] It is possible to regard pleasures and pains as simple mental states which are phenomenally similar to the sensations of cold, light and pressure. Theories which rely on this view are admittedly open to the accusations of nonsensicalness and inconsistency presented above. But Mill's theory of value was obviously more complex. He argued explicitly that contentment should not be confused with happiness, and it is difficult to see how this point could be reconciled with the definition of happiness, or pleasure, as passive sensation. The inconsistency between mental state hedonism and Mill's qualitative view should not be seen as a refutation of his ethics, but rather as a compelling reason to find a better reading for his axiology.

An alternative interpretation of hedonism defines pleasure as the intentional object of desire, or as the satisfaction of desires.[92] This redefinition can be employed to defend utilitarianism against the charges of nonsensicalness and inconsistency. In terms of desire, the dialogue between you and Smith at the neighbourhood lunch counter would have taken a different turn. Smith could have explained, quite simply, that despite the abundance of pleasurable sensations produced by the sandwich, he ranks last night's concert higher in his value system than today's lunch. Moore's objection can also be countered by an appeal to the desire theory. There is no intrinsic contradiction in the view that one group of desires can be preferred to another, even if the latter group is liable to produce a greater number of positive sensations.

A closely related alternative to mental state hedonism is 'preference utilitarianism', which states that value judgements ought to be based on the autonomous choices, or comparative assessments, made by individual human beings.[93] While the desire theory of value has often been regarded as a variant of hedonism, the preference view has generally been granted a more independent status. Choices between two courses of action, or two states of affairs, are the cornerstone of the statistical doctrine called decision theory, which has become an important part of contemporary economics and political science. Many theorists who master the new and allegedly precise methods of evaluation seem to believe that ethical problems can be solved by mathematical analysis and game-theoretical calculation.[94] But this is by no means the case. The fundamental questions of utilitarian ethics and morality can sometimes be clarified by the new methodology, but they can certainly not be solved by its implementation.

One cardinal issue which cannot be resolved by applying decision theory concerns immoral and repugnant desires and preferences. According to the desire and preference versions of utilitarianism, experiences can be assessed and 'higher' and 'lower' pleasures told apart by appeals to people's evaluations and decisions.[95] But the problem with this view is that people's actual choices and decisions can be harmful or offensive to others. There are, for instance, individuals who wish to discriminate against other human beings on racial grounds. If their wishes are fulfilled, other people will be harmed. There are also individuals who desire to live their lives in unproductive idleness or in a delirious state of intoxication. Their desires, although not necessarily harmful to others, can be regarded as repugnant from the viewpoint of those who have chosen a more sociable way of life. But despite the harmful or offensive nature of these wishes, a straightforward desire or preference utilitarian ought to value them as highly as any other choices made by autonomous individuals. No amount of mathematical analysis can dispel this counterintuitive conclusion.[96]

The problem of immoral and repugnant wishes has by no means gone unnoticed within the utilitarian tradition. A solution was already sketched by Mill, who in his account of hedonism stated that higher pleasures can be distinguished from lower ones by examining the considered preferences of informed human beings. Mill's suggestion was that evil desires and indolent tendencies cannot be seriously held by individuals who have also been acquainted with better desires and ways of life. Over a century later this point was taken up and specified by Richard Brandt, who in *A Theory of the Good and the Right* (1979) founded his axiology on the concept of 'rational desire'.[97] According to Brandt, a person's desires are rational if and only if the person has undergone a process which Brandt calls 'cognitive psychotherapy'. In this process the individual's desires are, in Brandt's words, 'maximally influenced by evidence and logic',[98] and the idea is that those desires which survive the process are rational and genuinely desirable, whereas those desires which are extinguished by it are irrational and void of any real positive value.

The validity of the 'informed preference' and 'rational desire' views can, however, be challenged on psychological grounds. The crucial question is whether or not all immoral desires can actually be removed by purely cognitive persuasion. Mill and Brandt obviously assumed that this is the case, but the possibility of what R.M. Hare has called 'pure fanaticism' seems to point in the opposite direction.[99] Pure immoral fanatics, if such a class of people exists, are individuals whose harmful and anti-utilitarian views cannot be altered by information, logic or moral persuasion. The immoral desires held by them are immune to cognitive psychotherapy, which implies that they are also, following Brandt's definition, rational and ethically respectable.

Hare's own response to this criticism is to state that pure immoral fanaticism is conceptually impossible. He identifies two other kinds of fanatic thinking to support this point.[100] First, people can hold immoral views because they are unwilling or unable to think critically about moral matters. If this is the case, the individuals in question belong to the category of impure rather than pure fanatics. The existence – and relative prevalence – of this type of people presents, according to Hare, vast practical problems, but it does not create any theoretical difficulties. The fact that people's illogical and uninformed preferences are also often immoral does not refute the view that their logical and informed preferences are, or would be, moral. Second, even people who are willing and able to think critically about morality could, in theory, stubbornly hold on to some of their pre-critical, seemingly anti-utilitarian preferences. But in that case the preferences must, in the end, be consistent with utilitarian thinking, even if this is not apparent to the pure moral fanatics themselves. This class of misplaced utilitarian integrity is a logical possibility, but Hare believes that members of the class do not actually exist in real life.

The prevalence of impure fanaticism and the logical possibility of stubborn utilitarianism have, in Hare's view, lured many critics into thinking that pure immoral fanatics also exist. But Hare argues that this is not conceptually possible. Pure immoral fanatics would have to be persons who are willing and able to think critically, but who nevertheless fail to consider everybody's preferences equally. This combination is, however, inconsistent, since critical thinking necessarily involves the universalization of one's moral prescriptions, and this operation in its turn inevitably leads to the equal consideration of preferences. Theorists who deny this are linguistically incompetent in ethical matters, that is to say, they are incapable of grasping the true logic of moral concepts.[101]

I have already argued, in the preceding subsection, that appeals to linguistic intuitions are unconvincing. People are not, as a general rule, intimidated by the fact that their use of English deviates from the standards set by philosophers. But whatever the normative foundation of the doctrine, there is another problem which undermines the desire and preference theories of value. This problem is indirectly related to the possibility of pure immoral fanaticism.

All views of 'informed preference' and 'rational desire' are based on the idea that there must be a technique, such as critical thinking or cognitive psychotherapy, which can be employed to extinguish the evil and imprudent wishes of individual human beings. Unfortunately, however, attempts to devise these purifying techniques seem to be faced with a dilemma. On one horn of this dilemma, theorists who assume a non-linguistic approach have to admit that not all evil preferences or desires will be removed in the process. If the conditions of rationality include only factual elements like knowledge, lack of emotional disturbance and the ability to make logical inferences, there will always be strong-minded individuals whose anti-utilitarian wishes can survive the process. The obnoxious implication of this view is that immoral wishes have to be treated, at least initially, with full and unmitigated respect in moral calculations.[102]

On the other horn of the dilemma, theorists who assume the

linguistic approach have to argue that it is logically impossible for immoral wishes to survive the process of critical thinking or cognitive psychotherapy. According to this view, the conditions of rationality must demand that individuals abandon their immoral desires and preferences. But the problem with this solution is that when it is combined with the normative principle of utility, the result is viciously circular. Within the utilitarian tradition, the only legitimate way to assess the morality of actions and convictions is to refer to their tendency to maximize utility. In the preference utilitarian theory, moreover, utility is defined in terms of preference satisfaction. These two premises yield the conclusion that morality is definable only in terms of the maximal satisfaction of preferences. On the other hand, however, the proponents of the 'corrective' theory of value assert that only morally acceptable preferences ought to be accounted for in the utility calculus. This implies that rational or critical preferences both define and are defined by moral goodness in the utilitarian doctrine. The doctrine, in consequence, is undoubtedly circular.

It seems, then, that the traditional experience-centred theories of value fail to support modern utilitarianism. Moral theorists have also developed axiologies which are based on objectively measurable entities such as needs and interests,[103] but these have not been the focus of attention in the bulk of recent utilitarian studies. I shall return to these attempts to define utility in objective terms in the following chapter.

An axiological variant which is closely related to the 'need' and 'interest' approaches is 'negative utilitarianism', which states that it is not the maximization of pleasure but the minimization of pain that counts in the moral assessment of actions.[104] This view, which has never been fully developed, owes its popularity to the sound idea that the elimination of suffering has a certain urgency which is missing from the augmentation of pleasure. But the view, as a whole, is as problematical as the more traditional versions of utilitarianism. Two deficiencies are particularly apparent. First, the possibility of irrational suffering makes negative utilitarians subject to the same type of critique that faces the proponents of the desire and preference views. There may well be persons who are genuinely aggrieved by the fact that other persons are not made to suffer.[105] And if this is the case, negative utilitarianism can be rejected on the same grounds as the 'corrected' desire and preference theories. Second, it can be argued that the most effective way to minimize suffering in the world would be the extinction of all sentient life forms. But nihilist normative conclusions like this are widely regarded as immoral.

ACTS OR RULES?

During the 1950s, 1960s and early 1970s, the choice between act- and rule-utilitarianism was much to the fore in philosophical discussion. Both utilitarian and anti-utilitarian theorists eagerly debated whether the felicific calculus should be applied directly to particular acts, or to the rules according to which particular acts are judged. In the discussion the direct application model was usually seen as the traditional utilitarian solution, and the recourse to rules was regarded as the innovation which can be employed to reform the doctrine.[106]

Contrary to popular belief, the direct application of the hedonic calculus to individual acts was historically preceded by indirect forms of utilitarianism. The eighteenth-century theological moralists George Berkeley, John Gay, John Brown, Abraham Tucker and William Paley believed that although the pursuit of general happiness should ultimately guide all human conduct, individuals cannot be trusted to judge for themselves which acts produce the greatest amount of happiness in particular situations. Lack of knowledge prevents people from foreseeing all the consequences of their actions, and lack of time hinders them from assessing properly even those consequences that they can foresee. This is why utility calculations should be left to the only being in the universe who is omniscient and omnipotent, namely God. The morally right course of action, as far as individual human beings are concerned, is to obey implicitly the rules set by God and handed down to humanity by the clergy.[107]

The direct assessment of individual acts, which was supposedly one of the hallmarks of nineteenth-century utilitarianism, was not in fact among the most prominent features of the 'radical' or 'classical' doctrines. It is, of course, true that the proponents of these views did not condone the 'rule-worship' of their theological predecessors, and that they were prepared to evaluate individual actions on their own merits. William Godwin, for instance, argued that if an agent has to choose between rescuing a known benefactor or one's own father or brother, the right choice can be made only by assessing the impact of the chosen action on the general happiness of humankind.[108] And John Stuart Mill defined utilitarianism as the 'creed which . . . holds that actions are right in proportion as they tend to promote happiness, wrong as they tend to produce the reverse of happiness'.[109] But on the other hand, radical utilitarians did not confine their attention to individual actions. Godwin argued, more or less explicitly, that the greatest happiness can in the end be best promoted only by professing anarchism.[110] Bentham in his work stressed the importance of laws and legislative principles rather than the relevance of individual choices.[111] And James and John Stuart Mill emphasized the primacy of education in moral life. In their theories, the disposition to act in utilitarian ways was at least equally important in comparison with individual acts and their assessment.[112]

The first explicit and exclusive statement of act-utilitarianism can be found in G.E. Moore's ambivalently utilitarian book *Ethics* (1912). Moore believed that: 'a voluntary action is right whenever and only when its total consequences are as good, intrinsically, as any that would have followed from any action which the agent could have done instead.'[113] This view, Moore argued, implies that the moral status of actions can be objectively determined: particular actions cannot be simultaneously both right and wrong, and if they have once been right, they have always been and will always be right. But, as Moore noted, these remarks apply only to particular actions, not to classes of actions. The fact that one instance of murder or adultery has once been morally wrong does not prove that all instances of murder or adultery have been or will be wrong. There cannot be any absolute rules stating once and for all which classes of actions are universally good and which are universally evil, since every particular action must be measured separately, by reference to its own consequences.[114]

During the decades that followed the publication of Moore's book, utilitarianism gradually came into disrepute, and its place in moral theory was occupied by emotivist and intuitionist views. In 1936, however, 'when utilitarianism must have been at its lowest ebb',[115] R.F. Harrod's article 'Utilitarianism revised' offered the doctrine a new lease of life. As far as methodology was concerned, Harrod reintroduced the point, assumed previously by Mill and Sidgwick, that moral theories ought to be evaluated by their ability to explain and arrange everyday ideas and beliefs regarding morality. When he applied this methodological point to utilitarianism, the rejection of rules became acutely problematical.

Focusing his attention on the intuitive prohibition on lying, Harrod wrote:

> The Utilitarian, it would seem, should say, always lie when the probable consequences including the speaker's loss of credit and the possible general loss of confidence in the spoken word involve more happiness than those produced by the truth. If everyone lied in those circumstances and in those circumstances only, all would apparently go well. But as a matter of fact this is not the case.[116]

As Harrod correctly observed, the everyday moral intuitions of the woman or man in the street would not necessarily condone the telling of lies, even if that would produce the best possible consequences in particular situations. Our 'common moral consciousness' seems to prefer the view that there are rules which ought to be obeyed without exception.

Harrod argued that the demands of common sense can best be met by combining utilitarianism with the Kantian ethics of absolute obligation. According to his view, general rules, not particular actions, ought to be assessed by reference to their good and evil consequences. The application of this principle to the practice of lying, for instance, results in the following view:

> A lie is justified when the balance of pain over pleasure is such that, if a lie was told *in all circumstances* when there was no less a balance of pain or loss of pleasure, the harm due to the total loss of confidence did not exceed the sum of harm due to truthfulness *in every case.*[117]

More generally, Harrod stated that the right criterion for the morality of actions is: 'Would this action if done by all in similar relevant circumstances lead to the breakdown of some established method of society for securing its ends?'[118] In Harrod's opinion, this universal principle conforms with our common moral consciousness, and it can therefore be accepted as the basis of ethical theory.

The views expressed in 'Utilitarianism revised' gained some popularity in the philosophical community, and by the beginning of the 1950s there were a number of utilitarian theorists who had assumed both Harrod's methodology and his normative conclusions.[119] But dissenting voices were also heard. The main opponent of the modified, or 'restricted', version of utilitarianism was J.J.C. Smart, who in his writings defended a straightforward, 'extreme' version of hedonistic act-utilitarianism.[120] Smart rejected the view that common sense or ordinary language could provide the foundation of ethics, and argued that philosophers should not address themselves to 'ordinary men' at all but to the 'good hearted and benevolent people' whose immorality is due to mere logical confusion.[121] And these right-minded individuals, Smart maintained, should not be told to obey rules when it is obvious that disobedience would be the best way to promote human happiness.

Smart did not altogether abandon the use of rules in ethical decision-making. He admitted that lack of time, lack of knowledge and lack of impartiality often prevent people from calculating the consequences of their actions, in which case people are forced to resort to experience-based rules of thumb. These rules of thumb are, according to Smart, extremely useful tools in ethical decision-making, but they should not be regarded as moral principles which justify particular actions. He presented the following example to elucidate the point. Suppose that obedience to rule R is known to have the best consequences in 99 per cent of all relevant cases. This knowledge is important for ethical decision-making, since in cases of uncertainty it would obviously be a good strategy to act according to rule R. But what if, in a particular case, we know for certain that the best consequences would be produced by breaking the rule? Would it not, Smart asks, be monstrous to obey the rule, when one knows for sure that disobedience would prevent some avoidable misery?[122]

Proponents of rule-utilitarianism responded to Smart's criticism by arguing that if the utilitarian rules are formulated carefully, and if all possible exceptions are duly taken into account, there will be no untoward consequences which could be avoided by breaking the rules.[123] Justifiable moral principles define precisely the relevant circumstances under which they condemn or condone actions. Only imprecise, and therefore unjustifiable, rules can be legitimately broken.

By the middle of the 1960s, however, rule-utilitarianism came under attack at a more general level. David Lyons in his influential book *Forms and Limits of Utilitarianism* (1965) distinguished two

70

main types of the indirect doctrine and argued that both types can, and must, be rejected. First, 'ideal rule-utilitarianism' holds that actions are right if and only if they conform to such a set of rules that if everybody lived by that set of rules, the general good would be maximally promoted. This principle offers a genuine and substantive alternative to act-utilitarianism, but it is problematical on at least two accounts. One problem is that particular actions which conform to the principle do not always maximize the good. This makes it plausible to argue that the view is not utilitarian at all. The other problem, as Lyons sees the matter, is that the principle does not sufficiently respect our moral intuitions concerning justice and fairness.[124] Second, 'generalized utilitarianism' states that an action is right if and only if actions of the same kind always produce the best consequences in relevantly similar circumstances. The difficulty with this view, according to Lyons, is that it cannot be distinguished from act-utilitarianism. If lying is morally acceptable for Smith today and for Jones tomorrow, the only ultimate 'relevant similarity' between the cases is that both instances of lying produce the greatest possible utility. The rule-utilitarian features which are supposed to define morally right actions in a unique way can be equally well described in act-utilitarian terms.[125]

The debate between act- and rule-utilitarians cooled down gradually, and by the late 1970s the discussion had taken a new turn. Most moral philosophers admitted that both traditional solutions had their difficulties, and the search for a compromise was under way. The rejection of act-utilitarianism was generally based on its alleged inability to guide practical decision-making. The evaluation of all the consequences of one's actions was seen as a complicated process which cannot possibly work in real-life situations. The rejection of rule-utilitarianism, on the other hand, was founded on the fact that rules in themselves do not justify actions in the proper utilitarian sense. Conformity to a set of rules is, in this context, a poor merit for an action which falls short of maximizing general good. Agreement on these points led many theorists to believe that the traditional views must be superseded by a theory which does not rely on the direct calculation of consequences, but which does not legitimize actions by appeals to general rules either.[126]

R.M. Hare in his book *Moral Thinking* (1981) presented a theory which is designed to reconcile the act- and rule-based versions of utilitarianism. Hare's argument is centred on the distinction he makes between two levels of moral thinking and between the principles which ought to be employed at each level.[127] First, there are the 'intuitive' principles which 'are for use in practical moral thinking, especially under conditions of stress'.[128] These moral axioms have to be sufficiently simple to be learned and grasped without extraordinary effort, and sufficiently general to be useful in a variety of real-life situations. Second, there are the 'critical' principles which are 'what would be arrived at by leisured moral thought in completely adequate knowledge of the facts'.[129] Critical moral thinking can be employed to create and revise intuitive principles, to solve conflicts between them and to account for exceptional cases.

Hare believes that the ultimate criterion of morality at the critical level is act-utilitarian: actions are right if and only if they maximize universal preference-satisfaction.[130] But since individuals do not normally have the time, patience or benevolence to think critically, it would be futile and even dangerous to recommend the act-utilitarian maxim for everyday use. Intuitive principles must be simple and general like the norms and prohibitions of ideal rule-utilitarianism. These principles do not in the end justify actions, since obedience to general rules may fail to maximize utility. But they do provide good grounds for practical decision-making.[131] Besides, it is not necessary to hold intuitive ideals which allow too many immoral actions in particular situations. Everyday moral principles can be submitted to the test of critical thinking, and if conformity to intuitive rules leads to actions which would not be condoned by the best critical principles, the intuitive rules should be revised.

Hare's two-level theory of moral thinking is probably the best solution offered to date to the dispute between the act- and rule-based versions of utilitarianism. If the intuitive and critical principles can be kept clearly apart, as Hare suggests, there will be room for both acts and rules in the utilitarian doctrine. Critical principles conform with the precepts of what Lyons called 'generalized utilitarianism', and thus also with the dictates of act-utilitarianism. This is the level at which particular actions and universalized prescriptions are ultimately justified or condemned. Intuitive principles, in their turn, bear a close affinity to the general precepts of 'ideal rule-utilitarianism'. This is the level at which practical decision-making takes place.

But the problem here is, as noted by James Griffin in his essay 'Modern utilitarianism' (1982), that the separation of the two levels is not as clear-cut as Hare would like us to believe.[132] One difficulty is that act-utilitarian calculations cannot be confined to the level of critical thinking. Practical decision-making is often based directly on estimates concerning people's preferences, not on simple intuitive rules which can be easily followed. On the other hand, there are also principles which Hare would classify as 'intuitive' but which cannot be reasonably excluded from critical moral conversation. Griffin mentions three examples: John Rawls' maximin rule, Ronald Dworkin's principle of equal concern and respect and moral requirements of a minimum acceptable level of welfare.[133] These are all non-utilitarian constraints which should, arguably, be weighed against Hare's preference-utilitarianism in the formulation of critical moral principles.

JUSTICE, INTEGRITY AND RIGHTS

The internal difficulties of modern utilitarianism began to alienate Anglo-American philosophers in the late 1960s, and the 1970s saw the revival of many non-utilitarian moral theories.[134] From the viewpoint of these theories, utilitarianism is frequently seen as an immoral doctrine which fails to take virtues and individual rights adequately into account. Some theorists argue that utilitarian policies lead to an unjust distribution of goods in society. Others state that utilitarianism does not recognize the separateness of individual human beings, or the value of their personal integrity. Still others believe that utilitarianism requires unreasonable sacrifices of some members of society.[135] I shall conclude my account of the development of modern utilitarianism by examining these four critiques, and the answers that have been given to them.

The first critique states that utilitarianism wrongly identifies social justice with the maximization of aggregate or average utility. An ideal utilitarian government should always aim at the greatest possible satisfaction of desires or preferences, even if this means vast inequalities in the distribution of goods. But this approach would, in the opinion of a variety of non-utilitarian moralists, lead to gross social injustice and unfairness. Egalitarian theorists, who by definition favour an equal distribution, maintain that individuals have basic needs which ought to be met before less important desires and preferences can be taken into account.[136] Meritorian philosophers believe that merits and deserts, rather than the maximization of utility, should guide the allocation of rewards.[137] And libertarian moralists fear that the maximization of utility may require redistributive measures, which they regard as unfair and unacceptable.[138]

Attempts have been made to reconcile utilitarianism with these challenges by appeals to empirical facts. Egalitarian thinkers have been reminded of the psychological law of diminishing marginal utility. According to this law, when it is applied to the present context, individuals receive more utility from the satisfaction of their basic needs than they receive from the satisfaction of more transitory desires and preferences. An egalitarian distribution of the most basic goods would, so the argument goes, maximize utility and would therefore be recommended by any sensitive type of utilitarianism. Meritorian theorists, in their turn, can be at least partly pacified by the observation that merit and desert, when employed as secondary criteria for the allocation of rewards, would most probably increase industriousness among the population, and eventually lead to the greatest general good. Utilitarianism, then, can not only recognize merit and desert but can also explain why taking them into account is important. Libertarian moralists are, admittedly, more difficult to reassure. For them, maximum liberty from positive constraint, including an absolute right to one's own private property, is an overriding consideration, which cannot be legitimately measured against any public utility. The only way to reconcile classical forms of utilitarianism with libertarian ideals would be to assume that the protected rights to liberty and property actually make people, on aggregate or taking the average, maximally happy.[139] The validity of this assumption would guarantee that libertarian and utilitarian decision-makers ought to agree on the practical, if not on the fundamental, questions concerning legislation and social policy.

But the problem with all these attempts to revise utilitarianism is that they make moral rightness contingent upon empirical facts.[140] If the law of diminishing marginal utility is valid, utilitarian theorists must endorse the equal distribution of basic goods. If rewards according to desert increase productivity, utilitarian ideals support a meritorian system of distribution. And if absolute negative rights are conducive to the greatest general good, conscientious utilitarians should sanction strict liberal policies. On the other hand, however, if the specified conditions are not met, then there are no utilitarian grounds for protecting or enhancing justice. Equality has no value without diminishing marginal utility, merits are important only as instruments of economic efficiency and liberties should be protected only as a means to social welfare. Contrary to these points, proponents of the various anti-utilitarian views can argue that justice and moral rightness should, in fact, be absolute categories, not empirical constructions which can be overridden by historical or socio-economic factors. People and social systems ought to be just, regardless of the consequences in terms of utility and public welfare.

There are two ways in which utilitarian theorists can respond to this challenge. The first way is to argue that one of the classical figures who supported the doctrine, most likely Bentham or Mill, already anticipated the critique, and built in the theory constraints which prevent gross violations of liberty and equality.[141] It can be argued, for instance, that people cannot be truly happy unless their decisions and choices are free and uncoerced. It can also be argued that the personal happiness of one individual depends on the equal happiness of others, and that injustice would therefore always decrease general utility. The second way is to state that whether or not the utilitarian theory was revised by the classical figures, it can certainly be modified now by adding principles which prevent violations of liberty and justice.

Moral theories can, no doubt, be improved both historically and systematically. It cannot be a priori impossible to combine liberty, equality and utility to form a balanced ethical theory – this, in fact, is what I shall attempt to do in the following chapter. But reformers of utilitarianism have not always proceeded with sufficient caution in their task. It is, for instance, fatally easy to lump together all the good and useful principles that one knows, to formulate them in one of the 'exact' mathematical languages used by economists and analytical philosophers, and to claim that the result is a revised and sensitive version of utilitarianism.[142] This strategy is, however, vulnerable to two types of criticism. On the one hand, the moral principles involved are often mutually contradictory, or consistent only in trivial cases. On the other hand, even assuming that the various principles can be adequately prioritized and harmonized, it is not evident that the resulting doctrines should be classified under the heading of utilitarianism. There are limits beyond which utilitarian theories cannot be developed as utilitarian theories, and one of these limits is surely reached when deontological principles are given an independent status in a set of ethical maxims.[143]

The second major critique against utilitarianism states that the view 'fails to take seriously the distinction between persons'.[144] The core of this complaint is that utilitarian thinking draws a false analogy between prudential and moral considerations. All prudential individuals know that it is sometimes wise to choose a small pain now in order to prevent a greater pain in the future. But, in the words of J.J.C. Smart:

> if it is rational for me to choose the pain of a visit to the dentist in order to prevent the pain of toothache, why is it not rational of me to choose a pain for Jones, similar to that of my visit to the dentist, if that is the only way in which I can prevent a pain, equal to that of my toothache, for Robinson?[145]

Smart believed that the argument presented in the passage is sound, and that people who do not accept the minimization of net pain must be hardhearted and immoral.[146] But as John Rawls noted in *A Theory of Justice* (1972), this conclusion is not necessarily consistent with our considered moral judgements. The practice of inflicting harm or pain on one person or one group of persons in order to benefit others does not always seem commendable. Full-fledged utilitarian neutrality in this matter would, in Rawls' opinion, imply that the essential separateness of individuals would be lost and, contrary to the Kantian principle of humanity, human beings would be used as a means to the welfare of others.[147]

The most thoroughgoing response to Rawls has been provided by Derek Parfit, who in his book *Reasons and Persons* (1986) argued that the separateness of individuals is an illusion, based on our false metaphysical beliefs concerning the nature of personal identity. If only we could see, as Parfit suggests, other people as relevantly similar to our own future selves, and our own future selves as relevantly similar to our present selves, the foundation of morality would be completely reformed. Individual human beings who have regarded themselves as centres of their own moral universe would come to understand that all individuals are worthy of the same respect and consideration. What Rawls saw as a false analogy between prudence and morality would become the cornerstone of the new ethic of equal concern.[148]

It is not easy to pick the winner in the confrontation between

Parfit and Rawls. Parfit's complex arguments concerning morality and personal identity are admirable, and his own basic view in all its simplicity is appealing. Many religious leaders since Jesus and Buddha, as well as numerous moral theorists since the early Cambridge Platonists, have opted for this purely altruistic view. On the other hand, however, Rawls clearly has the unadulterated moral feelings of the majority of Westerners on his side. Our views on morality and personal identity may be mistaken, but the fact is that few of us would voluntarily consent to a great deal of suffering in order to benefit total strangers.

The plausibility of the Rawlsian view is, however, contingent upon the relative harms and benefits involved in the transaction in question. Human beings are perhaps not expected to suffer greatly in order to benefit people whom they do not know or care about, but moderate, even considerable, sacrifices for the sake of one's family and friends are often seen as natural and desirable. Similarly, small personal sacrifices which can be expected to prevent great suffering are always condoned, and often required, by our considered moral judgements. The Kantian principle evoked by Rawls cannot, therefore, be employed to defend libertarian views which condemn taxation, social security and public health services as products of coerced labour and forced sacrifices.[149] The sound core of Rawls' argument is that there are limits to the types of intrapersonal and interpersonal trade-off that can be morally or legally enforced.[150] This does not imply that all trade-offs must be rejected because they would have redistributive effects. As far as the considered moral judgements of the majority of Westerners is concerned, utilitarian ideals are in many cases preferable to libertarian moral thinking.

The third major attack against the utilitarian view was launched by Bernard Williams in 'A critique of utilitarianism' (1973). It has always been a part of the utilitarian doctrine that people are held responsible for things that they fail to do as well as for things that they actually do. This notion of 'negative responsibility' follows quite naturally from the classical theory, which states that it is always our duty to bring about the best possible consequences. We are not only responsible for the evil that we actively promote, but also for the evil that we allow to exist and the good that we fail to bring about.[151] Williams, however, argued that negative responsibility is an absurd and immoral notion which ought to be rejected. He based his argument on the point that all fully developed persons have their own commitments and ground projects which they 'take seriously at the deepest level, as what their lives are about', and they have their projects which are 'closely related to their existence and which to a significant degree give meaning to their lives'.[152] Given the existence and personal importance of these commitments, Williams argued that individuals cannot be expected to abandon their own projects every time they learn that greater general utilities would flow from furthering other people's projects. This would be an attack against their 'integrity', and it would transform them from moral individuals to janitors of a universal value system.[153]

But as James Griffin has observed, Williams' critique is either immoral, circular or compatible with utilitarianism.[154] The main question Williams ought to pose to himself is, 'What makes our personal commitments and projects valuable?' The answer cannot be that my projects are valuable because they are mine, or that all commitments which indicate a coherent set of values are good because of their 'wholeness'. I may be a hardened criminal and my coherent life plan may involve harming a number of other people, and if this is the case, Williams can hardly argue that my commitments should be respected. Another possible answer would be that personal commitments are valuable only if they involve a kind of wholeheartedness, which makes the agents virtuous in some indefinable, yet respectable traditional sense. According to this view, virtuous agents differ from ordinary people in that they base their moral decisions upon such tried values as truthfulness and uprightness, and resent the idea of calculating utilities.[155] The problem with this solution is that it makes Williams' critique circular. If 'integrity' is defined as the rejection of utilitarianism, there is little strength in the argument that utilitarian thinking is incompatible with integrity. Finally, integrity can be taken to include generally good and desirable qualities like honesty, fairness and conscientiousness. But if this is the case, it is difficult to see how Williams' argument could be employed to reject utilitarianism. If widespread honesty, fairness and conscientiousness are likely to promote human happiness, utilitarian theorists have no reason to ignore them in moral considerations. On the other hand, if these qualities are likely to promote misery, it is not easy to see in what sense they can be regarded as good and desirable.

The fourth critique against utilitarianism is based on cases where general utility can supposedly be maximized only by sacrificing innocent human beings as scapegoats.[156] The first and still the best illustration of this type of case was presented by H.J. McCloskey in 'A note on utilitarian punishment' (1963). In his note, McCloskey described a situation where the sheriff of a small town has to make a choice between two evils. An outrageous crime has been committed, and certain sections of the community are highly agitated. If the sheriff does not act quickly, hundreds of citizens will die in violent riots. Unfortunately, however, there are no real suspects in the case, and the only way to prevent the rioting would be to frame and execute an innocent person. Utilitarian morality seems to condone, even to demand, the sacrifice, since a greater number of innocent lives would be lost in the riots. But this solution is not, McCloskey argued, consistent with the intuitions and considered moral judgements of reasonable human beings.[157]

Igor Primorac presented in his article 'Utilitarianism and self-sacrifice of the innocent' (1978) an important, although generally overlooked, addition to McCloskey's critique. Given that the sacrifice in question would produce the maximum of net good or the minimum of net evil, modern utilitarianism would not be content with the demand that the sheriff should execute the innocent victim. Consistent utilitarians would also have to maintain that it is the duty of the innocent person to co-operate and submit to the undeserved punishment in order to benefit others.[158] And if the sheriff experiences any difficulties in finding a suitable scapegoat, all those who think that they could meet the criteria ought to volunteer for the role.

There are three interrelated arguments by which defenders of utilitarianism can respond to these challenges.[159] First, it can be argued that the sacrifice of the innocent would not actually maximize utility in the type of situation that McCloskey described. When other people find out that the sheriff has framed and executed an innocent person, confidence and respect for law and order in the community will be weakened, and the consequences will be even more harmful than those of violent rioting. Furthermore, there is the possibility that the moral sensibilities of the sheriff may be blunted by the decision. If this happens, the sheriff may become susceptible to arresting innocent citizens in situations where the action cannot be justified in utilitarian terms.

As McCloskey observed, however, it is not decisive that the sheriff's refusal could produce the best consequences in the particular situation he described in the original note. The example can be revised and altered to meet all possible empirical objections. It can be assumed, for instance, that nobody will ever know about the deed, and that the sheriff's character and dispositions will not be influenced by the decision. And similar remarks can be extended to all other objections which rest on a factual basis. Eventually, of course, it will be difficult to find real-life situations which would fulfil the required criteria, but it is sufficient for the purposes of the critique that the case remains logically and conceptually possible.[160]

The second utilitarian argument is designed to dispute the methodological status of McCloskey's revised example. It is logically possible to devise cases where the sacrifice of the innocent would maximize utility, but the ethical relevance of such hypothetical cases is unclear. If there are no real-life situations in which utilitarian decision-makers could justifiably frame and arrest innocent citizens, it is extremely difficult to evaluate a counterfactual example in which the reverse is the case. The utilitarian doctrine, so the argument goes, is an attempt to provide individuals with solid grounds for real-life ethical decision-making. It is not intended to justify intuitive choices which are made in fantastic and faraway circumstances. Explanations, however, are a different matter. Our intuitive preference, if we have one, for the sheriff's refusal to frame the innocent is probably based on perverted utilitarian reasoning. Taught by our everyday experiences, we simply cannot believe that the sacrifice would maximize utility in any type of case. This subconscious disbelief is what leads us to condemn the sacrifice although we cannot specify the harm upon which our judgement is founded.[161]

Critics of utilitarianism can counter this argument by two remarks. First, although situations where the greatest good coincides with serious intuitive immorality may be rare, they are not always fantastic or merely hypothetical. If the utilities and disutilities of a difficult case are measured, for instance, by the satisfaction and frustration of desires and preferences, it is often easy to point out the utilitarian reasons which support the immoral decision. One could argue, in fact, that what is fantastic in these cases is the ingeniousness by which utilitarian moralists explain away factors which would disprove their calculations. Second, it is no doubt possible in many cases that those who condemn the sacrifice do it on perverted utilitarian grounds. But this is only a reminder for those who employ complex examples, not a refutation of the anti-utilitarian strategy as a whole. Hypothetical cases cannot be expected to refute utilitarianism if all judgements concerning such cases are basically utilitarian. But there are also examples in which the anti-utilitarian condemnation is clearly founded upon other principles, such as the principle of justice.

The third utilitarian argument against McCloskey is based on the distinction made by R.M. Hare between the critical and intuitive levels of moral thinking.[162] Defenders of this argument can readily admit that utilitarianism is sometimes seriously at odds with our common-sense moral intuitions. Within the two-level view, this does not constitute a valid argument against utilitarianism, since the ultimate justification of ethical theories must be derived from critical moral thinking, not from our everyday intuitions concerning right conduct. It is perfectly understandable that according to our intuitive principles the sacrifice of the innocent should be condemned. Common-sense moral thinking is meant to be used in ordinary circumstances, and in any ordinary circumstances the sacrifice would be harmful and gravely immoral. But the conditions of McCloskey's revised example are not ordinary, which is why the case can be adequately judged only at the critical level. The final judgement is, given the extraordinary conditions of the revised case, that the innocent bystander should be framed and executed. The result is counterintuitive, but in an example like this that is only to be expected.

But the two-tier solution is not as unproblematical as its proponents would like to think. The crux of the argument is that utilitarian two-level theorists allow only utilitarian considerations at the critical level of moral thinking. As James Griffin has pointed out, however, this limitation is not necessarily legitimate. There are certain principles of distributive justice which cannot be simply excluded without argument when it comes to critical moral thinking.[163] Furthermore, there are also deeply-rooted convictions concerning individual rights which cannot be summarily dismissed when the nature of first moral principles is discussed. The majority of people resent the idea that innocent human beings should be deliberately framed and executed in order to benefit others. It is, of course, possible that this conviction would under certain extraordinary circumstances be irrational, and unjustifiable. It is also possible that in these cases agents normally resort to skewed utilitarian reasoning to justify the conviction to themselves. But it is not possible to explain this conviction away by asserting that it is based on dog-matic intuition. The resentment people generally feel against the active and direct sacrifice of the innocent is a fact, but it is a fact that ought to be taken into account in critical moral conversation.

My conclusion, then, is that modern utilitarianism has not been able to cope adequately with all the current questions concerning justice and rights. In the following chapter, I shall set out to develop a theory which, I hope, is better equipped to handle these queries. I shall first show how some prominent attempts to solve the problems of justice and rights are liable to put universal altruism into conflict with another set of values, namely freedom and autonomy. These preliminaries will prepare the ground for my own proposal, the theory of liberal utilitarianism.

3

FROM CLASSICAL TO LIBERAL UTILITARIANISM

In the preceding chapters I have established two points which, I believe, are of primary importance to the development of utilitarianism, and to the development of ethical theory in general. The first point is that the 'classical' Benthamite form of utilitarianism is not the first, nor historically the most interesting, version of the traditional British doctrine of universal altruism. The greatest happiness of the greatest number has motivated a number of British moral philosophers who have not always shared Bentham's views concerning the other elements of ethical theory. It is not, therefore, necessary to confine utilitarian studies to the descendants of the 'classical' doctrine. The second point I have established is that twentieth-century versions of utilitarianism, which are predominantly based on Benthamite principles, cannot survive the criticisms levelled at them in contemporary philosophical literature. While certain critical questions can be answered without much difficulty, the fact that the precepts of modern utilitarianism clash with the demands of justice presents a problem which cannot be adequately accounted for within the view. It is not, therefore, profitable any more than necessary to develop the utilitarian theory along the 'classical' lines.

Since it has proved to be both unnecessary and unprofitable to expound and specify those forms of utilitarianism which have been in fashion for the last two centuries, it is obvious that a fresh start is needed. In view of the difficulties experienced by contemporary utilitarians, however, at least three critical points should be considered in the reconstruction of the doctrine. These critical points are related to the normative and axiological aspects of the theory, and to the correct scope of its application.

THE FUNDAMENTAL PROBLEMS OF UTILITARIANISM

The first problem all utilitarians have to tackle concerns the justification and defence of the principles of happiness and impartiality. It has been asked, time and again: 'Why should a person seek the happiness of others?' And universal altruists have invented elaborate answers, which have been based on intellectual, emotional, intuitive, linguistic, psychological and social grounds. Some theorists have stated that since happiness is good, and since more good is obviously better than less good, happiness ought to be maximized. Others have contended that the natural benevolence and sympathy of individuals makes them want to promote the good of others. And still other moralists have argued that the necessities of social life and linguistic interaction force people to accept the principles of universal altruism.[1]

But the difficulty here is that none of these answers seems to be conclusive. Although more good is undeniably better than less, critics of altruism can state that the only intrinsic values they recognize are their own happiness and the happiness of their family and friends. By holding this view they show that neither nature nor society have succeeded in endowing them with universal benevolence or sympathy. They also show, implicitly, that appeals to linguistic intuitions are not likely to convert them. Another possibility for critics of utilitarianism is to deny altogether the primacy of happiness in ethics. It can be argued, instead, that certain moral rules ought to be obeyed for their own sake, or that advertence to common decency is all that individuals need in their ethical decision-making. Unless revised versions of utilitarianism can be made at least as attractive as these alternative moralities, they remain as unconvincing as the classical and modern variants of the view.

An additional difficulty is created by the fact that the principles of happiness and impartiality can sometimes demand that individuals make personal sacrifices to benefit others. The problem is relatively minor as long as the required sacrifices are small, and the agents can be reasonably expected to make them voluntarily. But there are cases in which classical utilitarians also seem to condone major involuntary trade-offs between individuals and groups. The

84

classic example is the sheriff who executes an innocent person in order to forestall violent riots in the community. Revised versions of utilitarianism which unequivocally sanction such extreme trade-offs cannot be credibly defended.

The second problem all utilitarians have to face is axiological. Every attempt to define the value basis of the doctrine has, to date, involved difficulties. To begin with, proponents of the classical view believed that happiness consists of purely subjective experiences like pleasurable sensations. These physiological units of happiness can, according to the Benthamite doctrine, be added, multiplied and compared both intrapersonally and interpersonally. The difficulty here is that value judgements which are based on the comparison of hedonic sensations yield dubious practical conclusions. On the one hand, these judgements can imply that a very long life as an oyster or a shrimp would be preferable to an extremely good human life. Even the most rudimentary sensations can be multiplied indefinitely by expanding the time dimension. On the other hand, the comparison of pleasures also implies that a world with billions of human beings who lead barely tolerable lives would be better than a world in which ten million people lead extremely happy lives. These conclusions have been widely regarded as repugnant.

Many modern defenders of utilitarianism have believed that happiness, or utility, should be defined in terms of rational desires and informed preferences. The main advantage of this view is that at least some of the repugnant implications of the Benthamite view can be avoided. Informed and rational persons do not, presumably, think that the life of an oyster is more desirable than human life. Nor are they expected to think that human lives which are scarcely worth living should be preferred to lives which are superbly enjoyable. But the problem with this modified subjectivism is that people's desires and preferences can be harmful to other people. It can be argued, of course, that rational and well-informed agents do not desire anything which would dwarf the satisfaction of other people's desires. But this argument would presuppose that all rational agents are also morally good. And since moral goodness can be defined only by an appeal to rational desires, the objection would make the desire-utilitarian theory viciously circular.

Some moralists have tried to avoid the problems of hedonism and modified hedonism by defining happiness in terms of certain objective values. Among the values which, according to these moralists, improve the quality of human life are refinement, education, knowledge, taste, sympathy and benevolence. The problems of repugnant and harmful preferences and desires do not arise within this view, as it is assumed that individuals who are well-educated, refined and benevolent do not wish to live as oysters, nor do they wish to inflict harm on innocent third parties. Besides, even if they did, people's actual wishes have no axiological bearing within the objectivistic theory. Actions and policies are right insofar as they make people knowledgeable, sympathetic and benevolent, not insofar as they fulfil their desires or make them content.

The difficulties of the objectivistic view are twofold. First, it is not easy to determine with confidence which values ought to be promoted by human action, and on what grounds. If, for instance, education makes people unhappy in the hedonistic sense, this seems to constitute a prima facie case for excluding education from the list of objective values. Yet those who profess 'ideal' utilitarian views do not always explain how they would counter objections like this. The impartial observer is often left to conclude that the objectivistic axiology is based on mere predilection and prejudice. Second, the practical applications of ideal utilitarianism tend to be either elitist or paternalistic. If the elitist interpretation is assumed, then public policies as well as private charities should be aimed at promoting the well-being of those who are best equipped to absorb refinement and culture. Such a result would, however, reflect rather poorly the basic egalitarian zeal of universal altruism. On the other hand, the paternalistic reading of the view would imply that culture and refinement should be extended to all individuals regardless of their own opinions on the matter. This solution, while in a sense more democratic than the elitist suggestion, can be criticized for the ensuing restrictions of freedom and violations of autonomy.

The third set of problems which is shared by all utilitarians concerns the application of the principles of happiness and equality. Some theorists have argued that the principles ought to be applied directly to particular actions, while others have stated that they should be applied to general rules which, in their turn, govern particular actions. Still others have claimed that while everyday decisions can and must be made in accordance to general rules, difficult choices require act-utilitarian considerations. As for our moral responsibility to act by the principles of happiness and equality, there are moralists who argue that we are accountable for our harmful omissions as well as our harmful acts. Other moralists, in their turn, argue that this view of responsibility would unreasonably extend the scope of our duties. Similar disputes have occurred between those who wish to count the actual consequences of actions and those who wish to focus their attention on foreseeable consequences, between those who would like to promote the sum total of happiness and those who would like to increase average well-being, and between those who believe in the maximization of pleasure and those who believe in the minimization of pain. Any revised version of utilitarianism which is supposed to outdo the classical and contemporary forms of the doctrine ought to present novel solutions to these problems.

In what follows, I shall first sketch an outline of a view I have labelled as 'liberal utilitarianism'.[2] This theory is my own suggested solution to the prevailing problems of universal altruism. In the subsections that follow the outline, I shall then specify the view by answering, one by one, the three sets of questions that utilitarians ought to be able to answer. In the concluding subsection of the chapter, I shall bring together the principles of liberal utilitarianism in their completed form.

THE DERIVATION OF LIBERAL UTILITARIANISM[3]

The simplest way to present the core ideas of liberal utilitarianism is to proceed dialectically, by showing how the interplay of the principles of utility, equality and liberty can be employed to transform the utilitarian doctrine. The principle of utility, which is the basis of all versions of universal altruism, has been discussed in detail in the preceding chapters.[4] I shall begin here by assuming the classical normative formulation of the axiom, which states that the rightful end of all human action is the greatest happiness, or the greatest balance of pleasure over pain, of the greatest number of individuals. The principle of equality, in its turn, is partly accounted for by the emphasis placed on impartiality within the tradition of universal altruism. When everybody is counted as one, and nobody is counted as more than one, the race, gender, age, nationality and social status of individuals do not, in and by themselves, determine the morality or immorality of actions.

The Benthamite ideals of utility and impartiality do not, however, cover all the aspects of equality, let alone the principle of liberty. I shall specify the requirements of these principles in more detail further on in the course of my argument. But some of the basic ideas of liberal, as opposed to classical, utilitarianism can be encapsulated by recalling the American understanding of the doctrine of liberalism. According to *Webster's*, liberalism can be defined as 'a political philosophy based on belief in progress, the essential goodness of man, and the autonomy of the individual and standing for the protection of political and civil liberties'.[5] It is, in fact, the protection of certain human rights and liberties that marks the initial deviation of liberal from classical utilitarianism.

Actions which are based on the Benthamite criterion of moral rightness are, under certain circumstances, bound to violate the integrity of particular individuals. Consider, for instance, the following situation in a Roman amphitheatre.[6] Ten thousand spectators have gathered to see how one non-consenting human being faces a number of hungry lions in the arena. The probable outcome of the performance is that the human performer will suffer serious injuries, the negative value of which will be 9,999 units of pain. The spectators, on the other hand, will achieve one unit of sadistic pleasure each, making the gross positive value of the performance 10,000 units of pleasure. Assuming, first, that the hedonic standing of the lions remains constant; second, that the comparative value of an afternoon without the performance is zero; and third, that the long-term consequences do not tip the balance, the Benthamite utilitarian is forced to say that the performance should be held. But surely the majority of reasonable people would wish to reject a moral theory whose application leads to such inhumane practical conclusions.

One way to forestall this conclusion is to state that only morally acceptable mental states can be taken into account in the hedonistic calculus. In the amphitheatre example, the pleasures of the spectators must be ignored as immoral, and the performance must be cancelled on account of the pain that the human performer would otherwise suffer. This line of argument is, however, problematical. If the immorality of mental states is defined by an appeal to the greatest happiness, which would be the utilitarian view, the solution proves to be circular. The calculation of pleasures is supposed to define moral rightness, and moral rightness is supposed to define the type of pleasures to be accounted for in the calculus. If, on the other hand, the immorality of mental states is defined in terms of rights, duties, virtues or absolute prohibitions, circularity can be avoided, but the theory ceases to be utilitarian.

Another response to the amphitheatre example is to contend that only rational, or rationally acceptable, pleasures or choices count in the utilitarian computation. Proponents of this view cannot, how-ever, define rationality by referring to morality – utilitarian or non-utilitarian – because of the difficulties of the moralistic view. Neither can they link rationality with prudential self-interest, as there are cases in which this solution would lead to counterintuitive results. In the amphitheatre case, for instance, the spectators as well as the human performer desire what is good for them, both imme-diately and in the long run. The performer desires to stay physically intact, and the spectators desire sadistic pleasure. Granted that the satisfaction of sadistic pleasure does not have any untoward side effects, and that the spectators cannot be reasonably expected to share the performer's predicament in the future, prudence does not seem to offer grounds for the rejection of the performance.

The rationality of mental states and mental processes can, how-ever, be defined in a way that allows classical utilitarians to condemn the spectacle in the amphitheatre. Namely, it can be stated that pleasures and choices which are aberrant, abnormal, perverted, sub-standard, unhealthy or unnatural are not rational, and should not, therefore, be included in ethical calculations. Since sadistic pleasures are, by definition, perverted and unnatural, the utility experienced by the spectators at the amphitheatre ought to be ignored, and the performance cancelled for the sake of the suffering of the human performer.

But the difficulty here is that the definition of the irrational as abnormal or perverted rescues the amphitheatre victim at a cost which is too high to be accepted by reasonable people, especially by reasonable people who subscribe to egalitarian or liberal views. If the definition is employed, all pleasures and choices which deviate markedly from the average pleasures and choices of the majority can be defined as irrational, and excluded from the utility calculation. Applied to legislation and social policy, this would mean that the desires and decisions of all minorities could be outlawed. Activities such as philately, gourmet cooking and homosexual courting could be banned simply on the ground that they irritate or offend those who are not themselves involved in these practices.[7] From the liberal viewpoint, the ensuing codes and policies would be far too moralistic to be ethically acceptable.[8]

The definition of the irrational as perverted would, then, imply restrictions on many activities which should not necessarily be constrained. In addition, it also fails to condemn decisions which are widely regarded as unacceptable. A revised version of the amphitheatre example clarifies this point. Suppose that, contrary to the original description, the spectators have reasonable grounds to believe that the performer is not a real human being but a machine which has been designed to make human-like noises and movements when the lions attack it. The pleasure experienced by the spectators in this modified case is not derived from the suffering of the performer, but from the aesthetic enjoyment that the feline choreography evokes. Unbeknown to the spectators, however, the producer of the show, an artist who always strives at perfection, has substituted a live performer for the machine. Assuming that the utilities are similar to those described in the original example, the performance should be held.

Proponents of the Benthamite axiology can counter this line of argument by stating that choices are not rational unless the agents who make them are fully informed regarding the consequences of their actions. In the revised version of the amphitheatre case vital information has been withheld from the spectators, and they are therefore in no position to make rational choices. Their wishes should, consequently, be ignored in ethical decision-making, and the performance ought to be cancelled.

This counterargument is, however, based on an assumption which is not necessarily valid. According to the assumption, the awareness of the human substitute in the lion act would make the spectators change their minds, so that they would vote against the performance. But this is by no means obvious. There are, of course, individuals who do not wish to inflict suffering on other people, and who would, under the circumstances, rather forgo the pleasure of seeing the show. But to presume that all human beings would make this choice is to presume that all human beings are by nature utilitarian, which has never been conclusively proven. Even defenders of the informed-choice axiology have to admit that people may have desires which are obnoxious. Confronted with this fact they can naturally argue that the unaltered wishes of the non-utilitarian spectators are aberrant and unnatural. But this, as I have shown above, does not provide a sufficient reason for ignoring them.

An alternative way to respond to the amphitheatre example is to abandon subjectivism altogether, and to assume the view that happiness, or the good, must be defined in objectively measurable terms. If this route is chosen, the most prominent candidates for the axiological foundation of ethics are the satisfaction and frustration of human needs. It is not necessary at this stage to spell out and defend any detailed view concerning different kinds of need and their mutual relationship. But one basic principle is worth mentioning. In physiological and psychological theories, it is generally assumed that needs can be arranged in a hierarchical order, and that the derivative, or secondary, needs in the hierarchy cannot be satisfied unless the more basic, or primary, needs have already been met. For instance, the full enjoyment of pleasurable experiences is often impossible for those who are not physically healthy. Furthermore, it is most definitely the case that those who are not alive can neither be healthy nor enjoy pleasurable experiences. This seems to imply that, descriptively speaking, survival needs precede health needs, and health needs precede hedonistic needs.

The scientific standing of these remarks may or may not be good, but that is not important. The main point here is that the idea of hierarchical needs provides a promising foundation for an objectivistic axiology. Given that happiness can be defined in terms of human needs, it seems natural to think that the hierarchy of needs is also reflected in the theory of value. The idea is that the satisfaction of more basic needs is more important than the satisfaction of more derivative needs, since it is obvious that, say, survival and physical health are more fundamental to the promotion of human happiness than the enjoyment of momentary pleasures. If, moreover, the hierarchy of needs is interpreted in a lexicographical manner, the normative implication is that no secondary needs ought to be taken into account until all primary needs have first been satisfied.[9]

One point in favour of the axiology based on needs is that it provides a neat solution to the amphitheatre problem. Both in the original example and in the revised case, the health-related needs of the human performer are clearly more basic than the pleasure-related needs of the spectators. Subsequently, the axiological score of the situation is not 10,000 units of pleasure to 9,999 units of pain, although this would be the Benthamite reading, but one unit of health to nothing. The performance, therefore, ought to be cancelled.

The problem with this axiology is, however, that it seems to make utilitarianism completely insensitive to the demands of individual liberty and personal autonomy. It is, no doubt, natural enough to state that the need to keep oneself in good physical condition is, in general, more important than the need to enjoy pleasurable experiences. But since in the utility calculations everybody counts for one and nobody counts for more than one, there cannot be any differences between a person's own needs and the needs of others. What this implies, among other things, is that public authorities have a duty to discourage, through law and social policy, any pleasurable practices that individuals may be inclined to employ, whenever these practices involve health risks to the individuals themselves. Yet it seems that rational adult human beings ought to be entitled to take their own health risks at least in some areas of life.[10]

There are situations in which the rigid paternalism implied by the objectivistic axiology seems reasonably motivated. This is the case, for instance, when the goal of the policy is to prevent young children from using hard drugs. There are also borderline cases in which explicit legal prohibitions have had untoward side effects, but in which health education has proved to be a moderately effective and justifiable tool. Adult alcohol consumption provides an example of this latter type of case. But a strict version of needs-based utilitarianism would imply that all pleasurable practices which involve personal health risks should always be prohibited if they are not aimed at satisfying the more basic needs of the agents themselves or others. If, for instance, the public health authorities of a nation are convinced that the excessive consumption of salt and fat creates health hazards among the population, and that more moderate measures do not alter the situation, it is their duty to implement coercive legislation against the misuse of salt and fat. But surely such laws must be regarded as absurd, if any weight is given to the liberty and self-determination of individuals.

Defenders of the needs-based axiology can try to respond to these remarks by stating that liberty and self-determination can be included in the list of human needs with as much justification as survival, health and the enjoyment of pleasurable experiences. According to their view, the comparison in the salt-and-fat case is not between the basic need for health and the derivative need for culinary pleasure, but rather between the promotion of health and the promotion of the even more fundamental value of individual freedom. But the difficulty with this attempt is that although freedom and autonomy are, no doubt, important, they are by no means sufficiently important to outweigh all other fundamental values. It may be the case that health and self-determination can be regarded as equally basic needs, since equal cases can be made for the supremacy of each of them. There cannot be much self-determination without health, but there cannot be complete health without self-determination, either. But whatever the mutual standing of these two values, survival remains the most fundamental need overall, since neither health nor self-determination can be enjoyed without it. Subsequently, violations of autonomy can always be justified by an appeal to rising mortality rates. If it seems probable that the excessive use of salt and fat have an adverse effect on the average human life span, public authorities are entitled, indeed obliged, to constrain those who would otherwise inflict harm on themselves by keeping an unhealthy diet.

It seems, then, that classical utilitarianism cannot be adequately reconciled with the ideas of liberalism simply by including liberty among the values that ought to be maximized. The only way to amend the Benthamite theory is, in fact, to supplement the doctrine with certain liberal principles. This was the way chosen by John Stuart Mill in *On Liberty*. In his treatment of public coercion and control he wrote: '[T]he only purpose for which power can be rightfully exercised over any member of a civilized community, against his will, is to prevent harm to others. His own good, either physical or moral, is not a sufficient warrant.'[11] A few lines further on in the same paragraph Mill repeated his point in other words:

> The only part of the conduct of any one, for which he is amenable to society, is that which concerns others. In the part that merely concerns himself, his independence is, of right, absolute. Over himself, over his own body and mind, the individual is sovereign.[12]

Mill's basic idea was that human conduct can be divided into two categories: some choices are other-regarding, or concern others, and other choices are self-regarding, or concern only the agents themselves. Mill argued that when the action or inaction of competent adult human beings influences only themselves, they should not be constrained or coerced even if other people think that their conduct is 'foolish, perverse, or wrong'.[13] The same rule also applies to conduct which does in fact influence others, but 'only with their free, voluntary, and undeceived consent and participation'.[14]

Mill's distinction seems to solve the conflict between liberalism and classical utilitarianism. If the principle of utility can be extended only to those acts and omissions which are harmful to other people besides the agents themselves, there are no legitimate grounds for violations of autonomy by legislation and public policy. Public health authorities, for instance, should leave it to the citizens' own discretion whether or not they wish to consume unhealthy amounts of salt and fat. According to this liberal utilitarian view, the maximization of good by social regulation ought to be restricted to cases where human beings inflict harm on their non-consenting fellow beings.

An extreme interpretation of the core ideas of liberal utilitarianism is strict liberalism. This doctrine states that human conduct is other-regarding in the relevant Millian sense only when agents directly inflict harm on other human beings by malevolent or criminally negligent actions. The proponents of the view argue that individuals are perfectly entitled to uphold social structures which are indirectly harmful to others, and they are also entitled to allow avoidable suffering by their inaction. As long as they refrain from directly and actively harming identifiable fellow beings, their conduct is self-regarding and, by definition, rightfully immune from state coercion and social pressure.

From the viewpoint of universal altruism, strict liberalism is an excessively immoral doctrine. Far from advocating the general happiness of humankind, the view condones forms of behaviour which lead to suffering and inequality. Strict liberals argue, for instance, that the redistribution of income by taxation is a form of theft, and that publicly funded schools, hospitals and social security systems ought to be abolished. These judgements are, however, based on a mistaken view concerning the moral importance of omissions and indirect acts. As Mill wrote in *On Liberty*:

A person may cause evil to others not only by his actions but by his inaction, and in either case he is justly accountable to them for the injury. . . . In all things which regard the external relations of the individual, he is *de jure* amenable to those whose interests are concerned, and if need be, to society as their protector.[15]

The point Mill put forward in this passage is one of the cornerstones of universal altruism. According to all genuinely utilitarian theories, human beings are responsible for the consequences of their actions and inactions alike. By rejecting this focal assumption, strict liberals transcend the boundaries of both classical and liberal utilitarianism.

On the other hand, however, it can be argued that the principle of universal responsibility would place an unreasonably heavy burden on moral agents. If individuals are responsible for all the evils that they could eliminate or prevent, they should presumably spend their entire lives in unearthing and eradicating the evils of this world. In other words, it would be their duty to perform actions which are normally thought of as supererogatory, or lying beyond the call of duty. Critics of utilitarianism have maintained that these extended obligations would totally blur the distinction between self-regarding and other-regarding behaviour.

The balance between strict liberalism and universal responsibility can, however, be found by defining self-regarding and other-regarding conduct in terms of hierarchically ordered needs. In the light of the needs-based axiology that I have outlined, acts and omissions can be called self-regarding in two cases – and only in them. First, the conduct of an individual is self-regarding in the sense that is relevant here if it does not, directly nor indirectly, frustrate the need satisfaction of other individuals. Second, even if the conduct of an individual does frustrate the need satisfaction of others, it can be regarded as self-regarding if it is aimed at satisfying the individual's own needs on the same or on a more basic hierarchical level. Other-regarding behaviour, in its turn, is characterized by the absence of these justificatory features. The conduct of an individual is other-regarding in the proper sense if it frustrates the need satisfaction of others at some level, but is not aimed at the need satisfaction of the agents themselves at a similar or more basic level.

In normative terms, the doctrine of liberal utilitarianism states that while agents are licensed to frustrate the needs of others in order to satisfy or to protect their own similar or more basic needs, they are not licensed to frustrate the needs of others to promote their own more derivative needs. This means, for instance, that individuals can legitimately restrict the freedom of others if this is the only way in which they can save their own lives. They can also deprive others of pleasurable experiences, if their own freedom and health are otherwise at stake. They can even claim that they are entitled to defend their lives by sacrificing the lives of others, or their freedom or health by sacrificing the freedom or health of others, although such claims are often in conflict with the equally valid claims of the opposing party. But there is no direct justification for taking another person's life to promote one's own freedom or health, nor for jeopardizing another person's freedom or health to obtain pleasurable experiences.

My suggestion is, then, that an axiology based on a hierarchy of needs, combined with a normative distinction between self-regarding and other-regarding conduct, provides the basis for a tenable version of liberal utilitarianism. In the following subsections, I shall further specify the axiology and scope of the doctrine, and defend its normative foundation against the critiques which are usually levelled at utilitarian theories.

THE JUSTIFICATION OF LIBERAL UTILITARIANISM

According to the liberal utilitarian theory that I have sketched above, the first normative principle of universal altruism can be put in the following form:

A *The greatest need-satisfaction principle.*
   An act, omission, rule, law, policy or reform is the right one if and only if it produces, or can be reasonably expected to produce, at least as much need satisfaction as any other alternative which is open to the agent or decision-maker at the time of the choice.

When the concept of 'right' is given its standard utilitarian interpretation in this formula, the principle dictates that if there is only one right action which is open to the agent, the agent has a duty to perform that action.[16] All other choices would, under such circumstances, be morally wrong, and the public authorities as well as the general public are entitled to prevent individuals from making them, by coercive means if necessary.

Those who question the validity of utilitarianism have argued that the normative principle of universal altruism is theoretically groundless as well as intellectually, conventionally and emotionally unacceptable. As for the first part of the argument, it is indeed obvious that the principle of happiness cannot be justified by an appeal to more fundamental principles. This remark applies, however, to all attempts to formulate first moral principles, since it is one of the defining features of such principles that they cannot be supported by further ethical axioms. As regards the second part of the argument, it is certainly true that there are versions of utilitarianism which do not strike all people as self-evidently valid. But these versions of the doctrine are based on the Benthamite idea of the linear maximization of net pleasure. By disowning the hedonistic axiology of the Benthamite theory, liberal utilitarians can evade the problems that usually face the proponents of the classical view.

The amphitheatre situation described in the preceding subsection is a case in which critics of utilitarianism are justified in arguing that conventional and emotional considerations do not support the classical utilitarian doctrine. Most people presumably resent the idea that it would be our duty to throw an innocent person to the lions in order to satisfy the sadistic desires of other individuals. Liberal utilitarians do not, however, demand the sacrifice of the innocent victim in the example. On the contrary, they state that it would be seriously wrong to produce pleasure at the expense of the performer's suffering. The only situations in which liberal utilitarians sanction major interpersonal trade-offs are cases in which the more basic needs of individuals can be satisfied only by frustrating the less basic needs of other individuals. Lives can be protected at the expense of liberty, health and pleasure, and liberty and health can be protected at the expense of pleasure.

The liberal utilitarian credos concerning different types of need and their satisfaction can be encapsulated in a normative axiom, which supplements the principle of the greatest need satisfaction, as follows:

B *The principle of hierarchical needs.*
    When the need satisfaction produced by various action alternatives is assessed, those needs which are hierarchically at a less basic level shall be considered only if the action alternatives in question do not, or cannot be expected to, produce an effect upon the satisfaction of needs at a more basic level.

By ruling out trade-offs between the different hierarchical levels of need, this principle restores much of the intuitive plausibility of universal altruism.

There are, however, two further objections that can be levelled even at this specified version of utilitarianism. First, it is not always clear that more basic needs ought to be satisfied at the expense of less basic needs. Suppose, for instance, that it would be possible to keep irreversibly comatose persons alive indefinitely by connecting their blood circulation permanently with the circulation of healthy persons whose blood type is compatible with theirs. Since this arrangement would mean that the very basic needs of the comatose could be satisfied by frustrating only some less basic needs of other people, liberal utilitarians would apparently have to condone this practice, even to enforce it by law if necessary. It is difficult to believe, however, that the majority of people would find such a policy appealing.

Second, there are many real-life situations in which the most basic needs of one person or one group of persons can be satisfied only at the expense of sacrificing the most basic needs of another individual or group. Like all forms of universal altruism, liberal utilitarianism seems to dictate that at least in these one-level situations the needs of the many should outweigh the needs of the few, and that greater need satisfaction should always be preferred to smaller. But the rigid application of these principles would lead to clearly counterintuitive results. Suppose, for instance, that a surgeon has five patients who all desperately need organ transplants. One needs a new heart, two lack functioning kidneys, and two need a lung each. Unless they get the organs forthwith, they will die. Suppose, further, that the surgeon could satisfy all these vital needs by cutting up an innocent passer-by, thus obtaining all the required organs.[17] Since more lives could be saved by performing the operation than by forgoing it, the direct maximization of need satisfaction seems to favour the operation. But this solution cannot be expected to receive much support from conventional or emotional considerations.

The liberal utilitarian response to the first objection can be based on a comparison of different types of need. There are at least three kinds of situation which are relevant to the issue. First, in some cases a choice has to be made between saving lives and providing individuals with pleasurable experiences. For instance, uncle Edward may have to decide whether to buy ice cream for his niece Alice or to rescue his niece Bertha from drowning. The liberal utilitarian insistence on rescuing Bertha would hardly be shocking even to the most uncompromising opponents of utilitarianism. Second, sometimes choices have to be made between health and liberty on the one hand and the enjoyment of pleasure on the other. This is the case, for example, when aunt Celia has to make a choice between taking her nephew Frederick to the movies or her nephew George, whose arm has just been broken, to the hospital. The liberal utilitarian solution, which favours George, is not likely to arouse opposition in any quarter. Third, there are cases in which choices have to be made between lives on the one hand and health or freedom on the other. If the potential health hazard is very small or the restriction of liberty brief and innocuous, the life-saving choice may in many cases be widely condoned. But there are also occasions in which the health hazard in question is considerable, or the constraint on individual freedom is severe. If, for instance, one human life could be protected by performing lobotomies on ten thousand possible murderers, the assessment of the situation would not be as clear-cut as the hierarchy of needs seems to imply. The same point applies to the case of the comatose who can only be kept alive by assigning host persons to them.

The moral significance of these remarks is twofold. On the one hand, as the examples involving aunt Celia and uncle Edward show, there are needs, or values, which cannot be meaningfully traded with each other. When, for instance, Alice's ice cream is weighed against Bertha's life, the point is not that the pleasure produced by the ice cream is quantitatively smaller. If this were the case, then there would have to be a finite number of little girls whose desire for ice cream would outbalance Bertha's need to survive. But this, I believe, is not the case. A lexicographical hierarchy of values does exist, and it must be taken seriously into account in normative assessments.

On the other hand, however, it must be admitted that the hierarchy of values, or needs, to be accounted for in ethical judgements requires specification. The examples involving the comatose and the lobotomized show that the need to survive does not always outweigh all other values. When life itself seems to be of little or no value to the individuals themselves, as in the case of the comatose, it does not seem reasonable to sacrifice the liberty of other individuals for the sake of mere biological survival. As for the lobotomy example, the life of the potential murder victim would, no doubt, be as valuable as any other human life. But the point here is that the same judgement also applies to the lives of the possible murderers. Lobotomy is a rather extreme measure in that while the patients most probably survive the operation, their emotional lives can be totally altered or erased. In a sense, then, the choice in this case has to be made between one life and ten thousand lives rather than between one life and ten thousand units of health.

The difficulties concerning the hierarchy of values do not, however, refute the normative principle of universal altruism. When agents have to choose between various action alternatives, the consequences of their actions may or may not be classifiable in terms of the principle of hierarchical needs. But whether or not this is the case is not crucial. Even if it proved impossible to separate needs hierarchically in certain real-life situations, it would hardly be appropriate to blame this failure on the greatest need satisfaction principle. The source of these problems is axiological rather than normative. If the values assessed in ethical calculations have not been clearly defined in the first place, it is not surprising that they cannot be adequately classified and weighed. I shall postpone the more detailed examination of the liberal utilitarian axiology to the following subsection. It should, however, be noted already at this stage that despite its rhetorical appeal, the idea of hierarchically ordered needs, in the rough-and-ready form in which I have presented it so far, probably does not constitute a sufficiently firm value basis for a moral theory.

The second objection against liberal utilitarianism concerns cases where the satisfaction of an individual's needs at a specified level is liable to frustrate the needs of others at the same hierarchical level. The principles regulating the maximization and classification of needs seem to imply that the greater the net satisfaction of needs, the better the chosen course of action or inaction. This maxim is by no means intuitively implausible. Suppose, for instance, that a choice has to be made between curing Dorothy's chronic pneumonia or Henry's acute cold. It seems natural enough to think that Dorothy's health needs would in this case be greater than Henry's, and that she should therefore be treated before, or instead of, him.

But when it comes to choices involving life and death, the maximization rule suddenly appears to lose its intuitive appeal. Although four extra lives could be saved in the transplant surgeon example by cutting up the innocent passer-by and redistributing the vital organs, few people would, presumably, be willing to sanction the operation. Quite the opposite; it is probably safe to assume that all moral theories which condone the involuntary sacrifice would be emphatically rejected by the majority of people. Utilitarianism, of course, is commonly thought of as one of these unhappy theories.

Contrary to popular belief, however, utilitarian theorists do not always have to choose the option which would maximize universal pleasure or the general satisfaction of needs. In the case of conflicting interests or needs at the most basic level, the immoral conclusion can be avoided by adding the following axiom to the liberal utilitarian doctrine:

C *The principle of other-regarding need frustration.*

When the need satisfaction produced by various action alternatives is assessed, the most basic needs of one individual or group shall be considered only if the satisfaction of those needs does not frustrate the needs of others at the same hierarchical level.

This rule implies that it is never right to frustrate an individual's need to survive for the sake of satisfying other people's needs. The legal and social enforcement of the principle would guarantee, among other things, that innocent passers-by would not be seized by overzealous physicians who wish to save their patients at the expense of the lives of others.

The potential problem with this solution is that, in addition to ruling out clearly immoral choices, the principle of other-regarding need frustration seems to prohibit actions which are normally regarded as permissible. Judith Jarvis Thomson has drawn attention to this difficulty by contrasting the case of the transplant surgeon with the following example:

Suppose you are the driver of a trolley. The trolley rounds a bend, and there come into view ahead five track workmen, who have been repairing the track. The track goes through a bit of valley at that point, and the sides are steep, so you must stop the trolley if you are to avoid running the five men down. You step on the brakes, but alas they don't work. Now you suddenly see a spur of track leading off to the right. You can turn the trolley onto it, and thus save the five men on the straight track ahead. Unfortunately, . . . there is one workman on that spur of track. He can no more get off the track in time than the five can, so you will kill him if you turn the trolley

101

onto him. Is it morally permissible for you to turn the trolley?
. . . Everybody to whom I have put this hypothetical case says,
Yes, it is.[18]

The problem here is that both the trolley driver and the surgeon can
save five lives by sacrificing one life. According to the liberal utilitarian doctrine, neither choice is right. But if Thomson is correct,
the most common intuitive response to the examples is that while
the surgeon is not permitted to operate on the innocent passer-by,
the trolley driver is morally permitted, maybe even obliged, to turn
the trolley. It seems, then, that liberal utilitarianism cannot be intuitively accepted by the majority of people.

This impression is, however, delusive. Although the liberal utilitarian theory states that neither the surgeon nor the trolley driver
can make the right decision by trading one life for five, the doctrine
does not maintain that the two cases should be regarded as morally
equivalent. The semantics of utilitarianism implies that actions
which are not right cannot become duties, but the theory also states
that at least some of these actions can be deemed morally permissible if no right alternative exists. It is perfectly possible, for instance,
that the trolley driver should in the end be permitted to turn the
trolley, while the surgeon should be forcibly detained from cutting
up the innocent passer-by. There are many differences between the
two cases, and one or several of them may well be morally relevant.
Consider, for instance, the following disanalogy.[19] Suppose that just
after the driver of the trolley has decided not to turn the vehicle, a
meteorite hits the trolley, smashing it to pieces. The five workmen
on the main track are saved by the accident, and the one workman
on the side track will also survive. On the other hand, however, suppose that just after the surgeon has decided not to operate on the
innocent passer-by, a falling brick hits him, rendering him unconscious for a week. In this case, the five patients are not saved by the
accident. The threat in this case is intrinsic, and cannot be removed
by external operations. Liberal utilitarianism, as defined by the principles of greatest need satisfaction, hierarchical needs and
other-regarding need frustration, is certainly compatible with the
normative conclusion that the trolley driver is permitted to prefer
five lives to one, while the surgeon is not. But in situations like
these, ethical decisions must be based on extra-utilitarian considerations. The nature and scope of such considerations, and their
connection to liberal utilitarianism, will be discussed in more detail

in Chapter 4, where the relationship of ethical theory and practice is focused upon.

Critics of universal altruism might argue that my defence of the doctrine leaves it open to yet another objection, which is as fatal to it as the argument from intuitive unacceptability. The core of the objection is that my account makes liberal utilitarianism incomplete and deficient by admitting that there are important ethical dilemmas which cannot be solved by employing it. But this argument is based on a mistaken view concerning the nature and scope of normative moral theories and their relationship to practical problems. It is true that liberal utilitarianism, as I have described it in the preceding paragraphs, cannot in and by itself be successfully applied to all real-life situations. When the most basic needs of individuals stand in conflict, purely utilitarian considerations do not suffice to yield positive practical prescriptions. But the same remark also holds true with regard to other major moral theories. For instance, Judith Jarvis Thomson, who blames utilitarianism for condoning the sacrifice of the innocent, and advocates, instead, a theory of rights, cannot herself draw a tenable rights-based distinction between the cases of the surgeon and the trolley driver. Since both the passer-by and the one track workman on the siding possess inviolable rights, no argument which is founded exclusively on moral rights can be employed to distinguish normatively between the cases.[20] Similarly, arguments which are based upon the primacy of moral duties fail to provide the solution. Although it is natural to think that human beings have a duty to protect the lives of the five workmen on the main track, it is also, prima facie, natural to concede that the lives of the five patients, the one workman and the passer-by ought to be protected.

My claim, then, is that no general moral theory is capable of solving all the ethical dilemmas that can be created by the interplay of natural forces and human action.[21] Moral theorists can, of course, analyse and assess even the most difficult problems, but they should not be expected to find unequivocal solutions to them by the mechanical application of traditional moral theories. The only way to resolve deep conflicts between the most basic needs is to resort to assumptions which are shared as universally as possible among human beings. It is, for instance, a widely accepted assumption that agents who have voluntarily brought about a difficult conflict situation may be treated differently from casual bystanders. If the five

persons on the main track are gangsters who have chained an innocent sixth person to the side track, the trolley driver's initial decision
should presumably be reversed. Likewise, if the passer-by in the surgeon case has in fact intentionally and malevolently caused the
ailments of the five patients, the immorality of the redistribution of
organs may decrease considerably.

The evaluation of various imaginary and real-life situations falls,
however, outside the scope of theoretical moral philosophy. I shall
postpone the study of these situations until Chapter 4. Meanwhile,
the most important conclusion here is that liberal utilitarianism,
unlike the 'classical' and 'modern' versions of universal altruism, can
be successfully defended against charges of intuitive unacceptability.
My survey has, admittedly, shown that the value basis of the doctrine must be further specified. I shall undertake this specification in
the following subsection. But assuming that the axiological problems can be solved, it is difficult to see why anybody would wish to
contradict a theory which states, essentially, that the basic need satisfaction of individual beings ought to be promoted if this can be
effected without frustrating the like need satisfaction of other individuals.

THE AXIOLOGY OF LIBERAL
UTILITARIANISM

The rough-and-ready theory of value which emerged from my
dialectical derivation of liberal utilitarianism states that what is good
and desirable can be defined, either directly or indirectly, in terms
of hierarchically ordered needs. According to the direct reading, survival ought to be regarded as the most important value overall,
because being alive is a necessary condition for all pursuit of other
valuable goals. Likewise, health and liberty are more desirable than
transitory pleasure, since in many cases disease and constraint make
it impossible for individuals to enjoy pleasurable experiences.
According to the indirect reading, on the other hand, the satisfaction of needs is important only as a means to happiness. The
primary importance of survival is based on the fact that life is,
strictly speaking, the only necessary precondition of felicity. The
satisfaction of other important needs, the needs for health and liberty, also promotes happiness, but the connection is often less
stringent. Individuals have, after all, been known to be happy

despite minor ailments and constraints. The value of pleasure, in its turn, is relatively low in the felicity-based hierarchy of needs. Although happiness has traditionally been defined with reference to contentment and personal experiences, the objectivistic approach is more compatible with a definition of happiness as, say, general well-being, or the good life.

The nature of needs, as well as the link between need satisfaction and happiness, can be clarified by examining certain remarks and distinctions made by Georg Henrik von Wright.[22] All needs, von Wright argues, are instrumental in the sense that their satisfaction in itself is of no intrinsic value. The fact that somebody or something has a particular need can always be presented in the following schematic form: 'A needs x in order to achieve p.' In this formula, A stands for an individual or a group, x symbolizes the content of the need in question, and p refers to an end which may or may not be achieved by satisfying the need. It is, according to von Wright's analysis, conceptually characteristic of needs that their satisfaction is a necessary but not a sufficient condition to the agent's achieving the defined end.

The ends pursued by living beings are divided by von Wright into two categories. On the one hand, there are what he calls 'necessary' ends, the pursuit of which is in some sense natural and normal. These ends include survival, health, well-being and happiness, or, more concisely, survival and a good life. Actions which are aimed against the attainment of necessary ends are in the majority of cases regarded as unnatural or perverted. On the other hand, there are what von Wright calls 'contingent' ends. These include, for instance, new cars, academic degrees and tickets to concerts. Unlike their necessary counterparts, contingent ends are constantly changing. Once individuals have received their first academic degrees, they can set out to achieve other distinctions, but the degree they have already earned has irreversibly ceased to be among their specified goals.

The division of ends into the necessary and the contingent enables von Wright to make a similar distinction among needs. Those needs which are conceptually linked with survival, health, well-being and happiness he labels as necessary. Living beings need things like nutrition and shelter in order to survive and to have a good life. In addition, they also need other constituents of health and well-being in order to flourish. These remarks apply equally well to all living beings: as far as biological factors go, there are no decisive differences between humans, other animals and plants with regard to the fundamentals of our existence. Those needs, in turn, which are linked with goals like new experiences and new cars, can be called contingent. Human beings, for instance, may need new cars and television sets in order to obtain a sense of superiority over other human beings. Contingent needs like this, or desires, are presumably shared by humans and other higher animals, but the ends related to them are not in any meaningful sense pursued by plants.

It seems to me that von Wright's analysis of ends and needs can be directly employed to solve some of the axiological problems of liberal utilitarianism. The basic needs referred to in the doctrine can be defined in terms of necessary ends, and the derivative needs can, in a like manner, be defined with reference to contingent ends. This idea can be expressed in the form of an axiological maxim as follows:

D *The principle of necessary and contingent ends.*
Needs are hierarchically at a more basic level if and only if their satisfaction is conceptually linked with the achievement of necessary ends like survival, health, well-being and happiness. Needs are hierarchically at a less basic level if and only if their satisfaction is conceptually linked only with the achievement of contingent ends.

Two comments should be added to clarify this axiom. First, the list of necessary ends presented here is not intended to be complete. All goals which can be seen as an integral part of a good life can be included in the list which now comprises health, well-being and happiness. Second, there are needs which are primarily directed at the achievement of contingent ends, but which are, however, also conceptually connected with survival or the goodness of life. These apparently derivative needs may, in the last analysis, prove to belong to the category of basic needs.

The principle of necessary and contingent ends has certain definite advantages over the three-tier hierarchy of needs that I have employed so far. While preserving the ordinal ranking of values which is vital to liberal utilitarianism, the principle solves the problems created by the cases of the comatose and the lobotomized. In the first-mentioned case it would be possible to keep irreversibly comatose persons alive by restricting indeterminably and extensively the liberty of other individuals. This example is puzzling to the three-tier hierarchy of needs, since the view implies that survival should always be preferred to health and freedom. The solution dictated by the view, namely the assignment of host persons to the comatose, is counterintuitive. The principle of necessary and contingent ends, in its turn, leaves room for intuitively more acceptable solutions by stating that the liberty of the potential host persons is at least as important an ingredient of a good human life as the survival of the irreversibly comatose.

In the second problematical case a murder could be prevented by performing ten thousand lobotomies. Since lobotomy does not kill individuals, at least not biologically, the three-tier model would recommend, against common sense as well as against the ideals of liberalism, that the foreseeable murder ought to be prevented. But since lobotomy may easily demolish the very foundation of a good human life, namely personal identity, the principle of necessary and contingent ends can be employed to justify a more acceptable solution. If both biological survival and the inviolability of an individual's mental life are regarded as necessary elements of living well, then the liberal utilitarian doctrine does not oblige the public authorities to sacrifice the potential criminals for the sake of the prospective victim.

There are cases in which it is not easy to determine the level of the need satisfaction created by various actions. Suppose, for instance, that uncle Irwin decides to buy a new car, expressly because he wants to feel superior to his neighbours. The motive seems to place his desire well beyond the limits of necessary needs in any real-life circumstances. Suppose, however, that uncle Irwin lives in a community where the feeling of superiority is an essential element of a good human life. The members of this community are not particularly boastful, nor, on the whole, do they see themselves as better than their fellow beings. But they simply cannot develop their personality, or personal identity, unless there is one thing, however small, in which they can feel superior to others. Many individuals in the community have noble character traits or useful skills which they can employ to excel over the others, but uncle Irwin has no such virtues. The purchase of the car is, in fact, the only instance which can provide him with a personal identity and the possibility of a good life. Should it be concluded, then, that uncle Irwin's desire to buy a car is a necessary need and, as such, comparable to the needs of others to stay physically alive?

My answer to this question is indirect. Cases in which it is difficult to define the quality of the expected need satisfaction cannot, I believe, be decisively judged at the level of moral theory. The full appreciation of uncle Irwin's predicament would require data concerning his own previous choices and actions as well as information about the codes and customs of the imaginary society he lives in. But questions concerning the acquirement and interpretation of specialized historical, psychological and sociological data fall within the scope of applied rather than theoretical ethics. I shall return to applied ethics in Chapter 4. The most important observation to be made at this stage is that problems related to the classification of needs do not undermine the validity of the principle of necessary and contingent ends. There may be cases in which survival and the goodness of life cannot be easily defined, but this does not imply that these values could be legitimately ignored in ethical decision-making.

Another difficult question within the needs-based axiology concerns its scope. According to von Wright's view, all living beings have needs which are related to survival and flourishing, and at least all higher animals are prone to have contingent needs, or desires. Thus, for instance, human beings may need education to cope in the modern society, woodpeckers may need forests to survive and tulips may need fertilizer to bloom. But are all these needs equally relevant to morality? If a choice must be made between the basic needs of a human being and a tulip, is the decision-maker confronted with a tragic dilemma? According to the four principles which define the importance and mutual relationship of needs (i.e. principles A-D), the answer to both these questions is in the affirmative. But despite the impending charge of anthropocentrism, the majority of liberal and utilitarian theorists have opted for an ethical distinction between flowers and people.

The most important reason for thinking that tulips do not need fertilizer in the same, morally relevant, sense as human beings need education is that flowers, unlike people, lack the capacity of awareness.[23] Plants cannot consciously register the losses they suffer when their needs are frustrated, yet this very capacity seems to be essential to moral considerations. Although plants as well as human beings can be physically injured, the injury does not seem to imply moral wrongness, nor constitute an ethically meaningful harm, unless it is sensed or observed in some way.[24] This fundamentally humanistic

108

intuition can be incorporated into the theory of liberal utilitarianism by adding the following axiom to the doctrine:

E *The principle of awareness.*
  When the need satisfaction produced by various action alternatives is assessed, the needs of individual beings shall be considered only if the beings in question can consciously anticipate, sense or perceive, directly or indirectly, the loss involved in the frustration of those needs.

Two remarks should be made concerning this principle. First, the axiom does not deny the fact that flowers have needs. What it implies is that these needs are, in and by themselves, morally insignificant. Second, the maxim does not imply that needs are ethically unimportant if their frustration is not consciously and immediately perceived by the individuals who suffer the loss. The awareness concerning the frustration of needs can be indirect, and the capacity to sense the loss is ethically more important than the actual perception which may or may not accompany the privation.

The requirement of awareness can be employed to make two useful distinctions which have been assumed by many utilitarian theorists.[25] The first line can be drawn between sentient beings, that is to say, beings who are responsive to and conscious of their own sense-impressions, and non-sentient beings who are not. According to the principles of liberal utilitarianism, the needs of non-sentient beings do not count in ethical calculations, and it is therefore morally acceptable to use them as means to the well-being of others without any regard to their own good as an end in itself.[26] Non-sentient beings include inanimate objects, plants and animals which lack consciousness. Sentient beings, in their turn, should be treated as ends in themselves, and their needs ought to be fully taken into account in ethical decision-making.

The second distinction can be drawn between those sentient beings who are aware of their own continuity as subjects of mental states, and those sentient beings who are not. Members of the former category, who have been called within the utilitarian tradition persons, include normally developed human beings, chimpanzees, gorillas, orang-utans, dolphins and possibly other intelligent and social animals such as pigs and dogs.[27] Sentient beings who are not persons do not suffer a conscious loss if their lives are terminated, and they do not, therefore, have any intrinsic interest in survival.

Their needs can be frustrated in ways which are morally condemnable, but only when other elements which make up a good life are concerned. It is, for instance, always prima facie wrong to inflict suffering on sentient beings, regardless of their ability to recognize themselves as subjects of mental states. Persons, on the other hand, can also be wronged by terminating their lives. Sentient beings who are aware of themselves as continuing subjects of beliefs, fears, hopes and expectations are capable of valuing their own continued existence, and this capacity can be employed to justify the widely assumed prima facie prohibition against killing persons.

The fact that sentient beings are capable of suffering and persons are capable of valuing their own lives does not, however, imply that individuals should always try to avoid pain or wish to continue their earthly existence. Those living beings who are capable of making self-determined decisions concerning their own fates often voluntarily choose suffering and death rather than immorality, dishonour or boredom. If the individuals making these decisions are reasonably autonomous, and if the actions or inactions flowing from their decisions do not inflict harm on other beings, the ideals of liberalism dictate that the choices in question ought to be respected.[28] This liberal intuition can be incorporated in the theory of liberal utilitarianism by introducing the following principle:

F *The principle of autonomy.*
When the need satisfaction produced by various action alternatives is assessed, need satisfaction which is freely and informedly chosen by autonomous individuals shall be preferred to the need satisfaction of the same individuals which is not.

This maxim does not apply to cases where interpersonal comparisons are required. The welfare of newborn human beings, for example, is within the doctrine more important than the freely chosen cultural pleasures of their parents. As regards intrapersonal comparisons, however, the principle can be employed to weigh needs at all hierarchical levels. If, for instance, individuals autonomously choose to trade their lives for the promotion of their ideological beliefs, that should, according to liberal utilitarianism, be their prerogative.

There are three ways in which need satisfaction can fail to be 'freely and informedly chosen by autonomous individuals' as required by the principle. First, even agents who are capable of autonomous decision-making can drift into situations without making deliberate choices, or by making choices which are based on inadequate information. Second, individuals can be forced or coerced into courses of action or inaction against their own will. Third, many individuals are either temporarily or permanently incapable of autonomous decision-making in the first place.[29] The principle of autonomy states that need satisfaction produced under any of these circumstances should be regarded as axiologically inferior to need satisfaction which is brought about by the agents' own free, informed and autonomous choices.

Autonomy as a capacity to make self-determined decisions can be perceived by autonomous individuals in the same manner as suffering can be experienced by sentient beings and the continuity of one's mental life can be sensed by persons. This observation implies that the value of autonomy to autonomous individuals, as well as the value of non-suffering to sentient beings and survival to persons, can be derived directly from the principle of awareness. But, unlike non-suffering and survival, autonomy is also valuable to certain beings who are not in fact capable of self-determination. The avoidance of physical suffering cannot be important to those beings who do not actually sense pain. Nor can survival in itself be of any intrinsic interest to beings who do not perceive their own existence.[30] But autonomy is an important conceptual element of the happiness of all persons, and it is therefore plausible to state that even persons who do not have the capacity to make self-determined choices would be better off if they did have that ability.[31] The separate principle of autonomy emphasizes the point that in many cases the doctrine of liberal utilitarianism demands that we positively enhance as well as negatively respect the self-determination of other persons.[32]

The most basic values recognized by the axiology of liberal utilitarianism include, obviously, the non-suffering of sentient beings, the survival of persons and the self-determination of autonomous persons. These values are all compatible with the principle of awareness, which occupies a monitoring role in the needs-based axiology. But not every evaluation which passes the test of conscious recognition can be embodied in the liberal utilitarian view. Moral considerations which are independent of principles A–F above are a case in point. Since many persons who are capable of self-determination also possess a highly developed 'moral sense', or an acute perception of what is right and what is wrong, it can be argued that the principle of autonomy should be complemented by an analogous axiom concerning morality. This axiom would state that need satisfaction which is chosen on moral grounds ought to be preferred to need satisfaction which stems from immoral or amoral decisions. But the problem with this suggestion is that there are, potentially, as many different moralities as there are autonomous persons. While individuals can and should, according to the ideals of liberalism, be left alone to make their own mistakes in matters which concern only their own need satisfaction, they cannot be allowed to trade the basic need satisfaction of others for the promotion of their own moral views. Liberal utilitarianism can be more firmly founded on the necessary and basic needs for non-suffering, survival and autonomy than on the particularized ethical intuitions or imperatives of intuitionist and deontological moralities.

ACTS, RULES, CONSEQUENCES AND RESPONSIBILITIES

Assuming that the normative and axiological foundations of liberal utilitarianism are firm, the next set of questions concerns the doctrine's scope of application. There are at least five major queries which must be settled before the doctrine can be put to practical use. First, should the principles of liberal utilitarianism be employed to assess particular acts, or should they be employed to evaluate general rules or universal prescriptions? Second, are individuals responsible for the consequences of their acts and their omissions alike, and if they are, where does their responsibility end? Is it their duty to promote the need satisfaction of others even at the expense of sacrificing their own need satisfaction? Third, when the moral status of human actions is defined, should reference be made to the actual outcome brought about by these actions, or to the expected or foreseeable consequences effected by them? Fourth, given that the axiological premises of liberal utilitarianism are sound, is it more important to promote the sum total of need satisfaction in the world, or the average need satisfaction of individuals taken separately? Fifth, and finally, should liberal utilitarians opt for a negative or a positive version of utilitarianism, that is, should they restrict their attention only to the prevention of evil, or should they advocate the promotion of positively good and desirable things as well?

As regards the first question, counterarguments have been levelled at both the acts-based and the rules-based versions of universal altruism.[33] The main objections against the adherence to acts are twofold. On the one hand, act-utilitarian solutions to certain ethical dilemmas have often been regarded as counterintuitive and immoral. On the other hand, it has been argued since the early eighteenth century that the limitations of human knowledge make it impossible to recognize those acts which will produce the best results in the long run.[34] The primary argument against rule-utilitarianism, in its turn, is that it is not a form of utilitarianism at all. A theory which dictates that moral agents should obey a set of categorical rules whatever the consequences of their obedience in particular cases cannot be properly labelled as consequentialist or utilitarian, but rather as deontological or absolutist.

The remark concerning the limits of human knowledge does not in fact settle the dispute between act- and rule-utilitarians. It is admittedly impossible to foresee all the consequences of particular acts, but it is equally impossible to predict the final outcome of universal rule adherence. I shall return to this objection in my discussion of the advantages and disadvantages of employing either the actual or the expected consequences of human actions as the criterion of their moral rightness. As for the other arguments, it is, I believe, true that rigid adherence to rules cannot be regarded as a form of utilitarianism. Universal altruists may wish to formulate rules of thumb which are designed to facilitate decision-making in real-life situations, but it would be against their most fundamental ideals to contend that exceptions cannot be made to these rules even if the greatest good could be achieved only by deviating from them.

Charges of intuitive immorality and injustice constitute the most popular, and the most tenable, arguments against the 'classical' and 'modern' versions of acts-based universal altruism. There are two main types of moral conflict with regard to which utilitarians have frequently come up with clearly counterintuitive solutions. First, many classical and modern theorists have been forced by their doctrines to claim that innocent persons ought to be sacrificed if this is the best way to promote general utility. And second, a good many universal altruists have explicitly stated that family and friends should never be intrinsically preferred to strangers or enemies in ethical calculations. Those who oppose utilitarianism have pointed out that, according to widespread moral opinion, the first solution is patently unfair and the second proposal blatantly callous.

As I have argued in the preceding subsections, however, liberal utilitarianism is not as vulnerable to these objections as its predecessors and rivals have been. The needs-based liberal version of universal altruism does not state that it would be right to sacrifice one individual in order to promote the need satisfaction of others. The doctrine does not state that the opposite solution would be correct, either. In fact, what the view implies is that in situations where the basic needs of individuals or groups are in conflict, it is impossible to reach morally acceptable decisions merely by comparing utilities. Since this is precisely what the opponents of universal altruism have tried to prove, the most important disagreement between the rival views seems to vanish into thin air.

When it comes to family and friends, liberal utilitarianism does imply that moral agents ought to prefer the basic need satisfaction of strangers to the derivative need satisfaction of their own kin. If uncle Edward, for instance, has to decide between buying ice cream for his niece Alice and rescuing a stranger's life, he should, other things being equal, choose the life-saving alternative. But this kind of disregard towards one's family ties can hardly be regarded as shocking in any ordinary circumstances.[35] In a more controversial scenario, agents can be forced to choose between the basic need satisfaction of strangers and the basic need satisfaction of their family and friends. But this possibility does not constitute an objection against liberal utilitarianism, since the doctrine does not contain elements which would refute the nepotistic, or family-oriented, solution. It is perfectly possible that agents may, for reasons which are not specified in the fundamental principles concerning needs and autonomy, give priority to those whom they know and love. But this is a matter that falls outside the scope of theoretical ethics and within the scope of applied ethics. Immorality and injustice cannot be employed to make a serious theoretical case against needs-based autonomy-respecting act-utilitarianism.

As regards the second question concerning the application of liberal utilitarianism, universal altruists have traditionally held agents responsible for the consequences of their omissions as well as for the consequences of their positive actions. In 1731, John Gay wrote:

> Obligation is the necessity of doing or omitting any action in order to be happy: i.e. when there is such a relation between

an agent and an action that the agent cannot be happy without doing or omitting that action, then the agent is said to be obliged to do or omit that action.[36]

This self-regarding equation of acts and omissions was extended to considerations which concern others by John Stuart Mill, who wrote in 1859:

> There are ... many positive acts for the benefit of others which [an individual] may rightfully be compelled to perform; such as, to give evidence in a court of justice; to bear his fair share in the common defence, or in any other joint work necessary to the interest of the society of which he enjoys the protection; and to perform certain acts of individual beneficence, such as saving a fellow creature's life, or interposing to protect the defenceless against ill-usage, things which whenever it is obviously a man's duty to do, he may rightfully be made responsible to society for not doing.[37]

Many contemporary universal altruists have followed in the footsteps of Gay and Mill, and argued that the distinction between harmful acts and equally harmful omissions is morally irrelevant. If it is wrong to inflict harm on others by doing something which causes harm, it is equally wrong to inflict harm on others by failing to do something which would prevent it.[38]

Opponents of utilitarianism have contended, however, that the obligation to prevent harm cannot be as extensive and as boundless as the doctrine of negative responsibility seems to state. If individuals are held morally responsible for all the harm they could have prevented, they can, ultimately, be blamed for every waking hour which they have not spent improving the living conditions of their fellow beings. As John Harris, himself a champion of the principle of negative responsibility, has put the matter, the doctrine seems to imply 'that a person ought to go on giving to or working for others until he is as badly off as those he is trying to help'.[39] In the opinion of many traditional moralists, and in the opinion of a number of persons in the street, this conclusion is all that is needed to provide a *reductio ad absurdum* for unlimited universal altruism.

There are two lines of argument that the advocates of negative responsibility can employ to counter the suspicions raised by traditional moralists. On the one hand, they can argue that the doctrine does not in fact require the sacrifices referred to by Harris in the quoted passage, at least not at the level of law and social policy. Harmful omissions are difficult to define, and their regulation is liable to produce undesirable side effects. This is why some utilitarians, notably John Stuart Mill, have believed that although acts and omissions are morally symmetrical, the real-life legal and social control of the latter 'requires a much more cautious exercise of compulsion than [the control of] the former'.[40] The application of the principle of negative responsibility is, so the argument goes, a matter of conscience rather than a matter of public policy.

On the other hand, defenders of the negative actions thesis can point out that the sacrifices referred to by Harris do not necessarily refute the doctrine. The morality required by the thesis may be exacting, but this fact cannot in and by itself justify the rejection of the doctrine. The abolition of slavery must have been an exacting experience to the slaveholders of the nineteenth century, but few theorists would argue that the predicament of the masters could have legitimized the *ancien régime*. Besides, even granted that the negative actions thesis is, for the time being, more demanding than the nineteenth-century principles of individual liberty and racial equality, the exactingness of the doctrine can be removed by human choices. This is how John Harris has put these points in his *Violence and Responsibility* (1980):

> The apparent boundlessness of our obligations cannot mean that we do not in fact have these obligations any more than the boundlessness of disease is an argument against the practice of medicine. It is perhaps not so discouraging if we remember that the overwhelming nature of the task would be mitigated dramatically if contemporary morality changed for the better. It would then look neither so hopeless nor so boundless a prospect. If it were shared and respected by all, the obligation not to harm our fellows would be far from boundless for each.[41]

It can be argued, then, that the widespread recognition of negative responsibility would, in the end, set quite tolerable limits to the moral obligations of individual agents.

Liberal utilitarianism answers the questions concerning acts, omissions and the limits of positive and negative responsibility by dividing potential moral obligations into two categories. First, as dictated by the principle of hierarchical needs, individuals do have an obligation to sacrifice their own derivative needs if this is the only way to secure the satisfaction of the most basic needs of others. Individuals should, according to liberal utilitarianism, go on giving to and working for others until the satisfaction of their contingent desires no longer stands in the way of the survival and well-being of others. Second, however, as stated by the principle of other-regarding need frustration, individuals do not have an obligation to sacrifice their own basic needs to further the need satisfaction of others. Self-determined persons are entitled by the principle of autonomy to make such sacrifices, but if they decide to do so, their behaviour should be classified as supererogatory. The liberal version of universal altruism does not require individuals to give to and work for others until they are as badly off as those they are trying to help. This means that the doctrine of negative responsibility does not lead to absurdities in the context of liberal utilitarianism.

The third question concerning the scope of universal altruism is related to ethical ontology and epistemology. Many theorists, including both proponents and opponents of utilitarianism, have contended that according to the doctrine the moral rightness of actions depends only on their actual consequences.[42] J.J.C. Smart, for instance, presents the following example to support the view that what in fact happens as a consequence of an act is more important than what we think might happen:

> For example, a man near Berchtesgaden in 1938 might have jumped into a river and rescued a drowning man, only to find that it was Hitler. He would have done the wrong thing, for he would have saved the world a lot of trouble if he had left Hitler below the surface.[43]

There are also, however, theorists who argue that since we cannot predict with certainty the actual consequences of our actions, we should be content to assess their morality by reference to their probable, or expected or foreseeable consequences.[44] Bertrand Russell defended this view when he wrote:

> There have certainly been some men who have done so much harm it would have been fortunate for the world if their nurses had killed them in infancy. But if their nurses had done so their action would not have been objectively right, because the probability was that it would not have the best effect. Hence

it would seem we must take account of probability in judging of objective rightness.[45]

Liberal utilitarians, as well as others who wish to defend universal altruism, obviously have to make a choice between the two competing and mutually incompatible views concerning the relevance of actual facts and probabilities in ethics.

The main objection against actual consequence utilitarianism is that the doctrine is probably incoherent as a moral theory. As Marcus Singer has argued, even the retrospective, backward-looking morality suggested by Smart in the quoted passage cannot be consistently construed by an appeal to the actual consequences of actions. Since Hitler did not in fact drown in 1938, we do not know what the actual consequences of his death would have been. We do not, therefore, know for certain that leaving him below the surface would have been better for the rest of humanity than rescuing him, as Smart so confidently states.[46]

Advocates of the actual consequence interpretation have argued, in their turn, that morality requires an objective basis which cannot be provided by an appeal to the expected, probable or foreseeable consequences of human action.[47] If the moral rightness of acts and omissions is linked with subjective beliefs and expectations, so the argument goes, morality becomes a matter of personal tastes and opinions. But this objection is by no means conclusive. The objective nature of morality requires, no doubt, that basic values are not defined by reference to individual tastes, and that agents cannot themselves be the ultimate judges of the morality of their actions. These requirements are, however, fulfilled by a liberal utilitarian theory which determines the rightness of acts and omissions by their foreseeable consequences. Although the definition of necessary needs may be a matter of argument and discussion, it is not a matter of personal taste. And although the consequences which can be foreseen by agents vary according to their epistemic abilities and limitations, these faculties and restrictions are matters of objective fact rather than personal choice. What people know, or what they would know if they had taken the trouble to find out, about the consequences of their actions at the time of the choice is in the majority of cases open to objective verification and evaluation.

An independent argument which supports the foreseeable consequence version of universal altruism is based on the intuition that individuals should not be morally required to do what they cannot do. It would be either nonsensical or unfair to blame the innately blind for not seeing, or the innately deaf for not hearing. Likewise, it would be senseless to hold agents responsible for the unforesee-able consequences of their actions. Yet this is what Smart and other actual consequence utilitarians are forced to do. By asserting that the man who rescued Hitler acted wrongly they also maintain that he is now morally responsible for events which indirectly resulted from his act but which he could not possibly have foreseen at the time of the choice. In other words, the actual consequence inter-pretation implies that it would have been the man's duty to let his choice be guided by information which he did not have, could not have had and could not have been reasonably held responsible for not having. A reading of universal altruism which recognizes oblig-ations like this is, I think, unintuitive as well as incoherent.

The fourth question regarding the application of utilitarianism centres on the ideal size and quality of the population of the Earth.[48] The classical version of universal altruism defines the population optimum in terms of the greatest sum total of net happiness over individuals and over time. At first glance, the idea of maximizing good in the universe throughout history sounds plausible within the Benthamite view. But there are two types of situation in which the doctrine yields intuitively unacceptable results. First, consider the case of a healthy and happy couple who could, if they so chose, have healthy and happy children whose existence would increase the net balance of pleasure over pain in the world. According to the 'total' view, it would be the duty of the couple to reproduce, and the duty of the public authorities to make certain that they do, by using legal coercion if necessary. This solution may be acceptable to classical utilitarians, but it is certainly not acceptable to anybody who believes in the values of individual liberty and personal autonomy.[49] Second, consider the case of a world dictator who must choose between two future scenarios for humankind. In the first scenario the world's human population will consist of ten million superbly happy individuals, in the second the Earth will be inhabited by a thousand billion human beings whose lives are barely tolerable. If the sum total of happiness is greater in the latter alternative, the total utilitarian dictator ought to choose the world where people's lives are scarcely worth living. This conclusion has in the literature been justly called 'repugnant' and 'repulsive'.[50]

A possible response to the first problem, the predicament of the happy couple, is to stipulate that only beings who already exist before the agent's decision, or will exist independently of it, shall be accounted for in the happiness calculation.[51] If this thesis of prior existence is assumed, the potential happiness of the would-be children becomes irrelevant to morality, and need not be considered in ethical decision-making. As regards law and social policy, the liberal principle of the sanctity of family life can be reinstated.[52] The difficulty with this principle is, however, that its application to certain relevantly similar situations leads to conclusions which many utilitarians would find hard to accept. Consider, for instance, the case of another couple, a couple who wish to have a child of their own, but who know that due to a genetic defect any child they have will live a thoroughly miserable life and die before its second birthday.[53] If family life is seen as inviolable in the sense implied by the thesis of prior existence, the couple should be allowed to have as many suffering children as they want. Since happiness and suffering are usually regarded as symmetrical within the utilitarian view, 'classical' moralists who contend that the first couple have no obligation to produce happy children must also admit that the second couple have no obligation to forgo producing unhappy offspring.[54] I shall return to the assumption of the symmetry between good and evil in the paragraphs on negative and positive utilitarianism below. But assuming that such symmetry prevails, the prior-existence thesis does not offer a conclusive solution to the difficulties of the total version of universal altruism.

As for the second problem, the choice of the ideal population, many theorists have suggested that the decision should be based on the average happiness of individual human beings rather than on the total happiness of the population as a whole.[55] In the example presented above, the recognition of this principle would provide the dictator with good grounds to choose the intuitively more acceptable scenario in which ten million people would live in unclouded happiness. Although this alternative would not maximize the sum total of pleasure over pain in the universe, it would maximize the average well-being of present and future individuals. Unfortunately for 'average' utilitarians, however, this view is as vulnerable to counterexamples as the total view. Suppose that in the world of unlimited blessing happiness is not equally distributed among the inhabitants. While nine million individuals are ten times happier than anybody living today, one million individuals have to settle for a level of happiness which is only nine times higher than ours. If the situation is judged by our present standards, the lives of the relatively unhappy minority are, of course, abundantly worth living. But the average-utilitarian dictator would have to disagree, and to argue that the minority ought to be eliminated in order to optimize the mean felicity of the population.

Liberal utilitarianism counters the difficulties of the classical view by stating that family and population policies cannot be discussed in terms of total or average happiness in the way suggested by modern theorists. The principle of other-regarding need frustration implies that it is always right to satisfy the basic needs of an existing being, provided that the operation does not frustrate the basic needs of others. Non-existent beings who will never come into existence need not be counted in the evaluation, since they do not have and will not have needs which could be satisfied or frustrated.[56] Thus the healthy and happy couple do not have an obligation to procreate, even if their children would contribute to the total or average happiness of the world. On the other hand, however, non-existent beings who will come into existence as a consequence of our actions or independently of them will in the foreseeable future have needs which must be accounted for in ethical decision-making. Since the genetically defective couple are directly responsible for the existence of their suffering child, they are also directly responsible for the child's suffering. Their decision to procreate despite the genetic defect would, therefore, be morally wrong. As for those beings who will exist in the future independently of our actions, we have an obligation to abstain from inflicting harm on them, provided that their protection does not inflict serious harm on other present or future individuals. In situations where the basic needs of present and future individuals are in conflict, the matter should be solved by the methods of applied rather than theoretical ethics.

The liberal utilitarian solution to the dictator's population problem is axiological. It is probably safe to assume that the thousand billion human beings who would lead barely tolerable lives in the repugnant world would be unhappy in the general sense that their necessary needs would not be entirely satisfied. It is also safe to assume that the basic needs of the ten million happy inhabitants of the other world would, in turn, be satisfied. Under these circumstances, a liberal-utilitarian dictator would have no difficulty in making the intuitively acceptable choice, that is, in preferring the small but happy population to the large but unhappy one. According to the principles of liberal utilitarianism, there is no obligation to bring worlds of either type into existence if they do not already exist. But if a choice has to be made between developing our present world in one direction or the other, a limited population which is universally happy should be preferred to an extended population which suffers from the frustration of necessary needs.

The mistake made by both total and average utilitarians is that they tend to assign individuals to desirable experiences rather than desirable experiences to individuals. When, for instance, our duties to future beings are discussed, most modern versions of universal altruism seem to presume that the potential happiness or misery of the beings somehow exists prior to their own existence. The idea, which is never explicitly stated, let alone defended, seems to be that the mental states in question await their subjects in some axiological limbo, from which they are liberated by the arrival of the prospective individuals. By focusing on the needs of beings who already exist or who will inevitably exist, liberal utilitarianism evades the metaphysical absurdities involved in this view, and thereby also the demographic difficulties which undermine both the total and the average versions of the theory.

The fifth question concerning the application of universal altruism centres on the principle of symmetry between pleasure and pain, happiness and suffering. This cornerstone of classical utilitarianism was challenged by Karl Popper, who in *The Open Society and Its Enemies* (1945) wrote:

> In regard to hedonism and utilitarianism, I believe that it is indeed necessary to replace their principle: *maximize pleasure!* by one which is probably more in keeping with the original views of Democritus and Epicurus, more modest, and much more urgent. I mean the rule: *minimize pain!* I believe . . . that it is not only impossible but very dangerous to attempt to maximize the pleasure or the happiness of the people, since such an attempt must lead to totalitarianism.[57]

In the late 1950s and early 1960s Popper's words were taken up, and the discussion animated by his remark gradually gave rise to the doctrine which is often called negative utilitarianism.[58] The negative version of universal altruism states, as suggested by Popper, that morality demands us to relieve suffering but not to promote happiness. The emergence of this view coincided with the more general downfall of utilitarianism in the late 1960s, and the negative form of the theory remained by and large undeveloped. Nonetheless, the idea that the prevention of harm and the removal of suffering are more important to morality than the positive promotion of pleasure and happiness has influenced the views of later theorists who have not altogether deserted the ideals of universal altruism. John Harris, for instance, in *Violence and Responsibility* confines his attention to the prevention of avoidable harm, and Anthony Quinton in his preface to the second edition of *Utilitarian Ethics* makes clear his allegiance to negative rather than positive utilitarianism.[59]

As I have already noted in the preceding chapter, the hedonistic form of negative utilitarianism can be justly criticized for its potential nihilism.[60] If there were no sentient beings, there would be no painful experiences, either. This tautology implies that in our present world, where many beings have to endure considerable suffering, the best negatively hedonistic strategy would be to eliminate all sentient life-forms. The principle suggested by Popper could certainly not be employed to refute such an annihilating solution. As for those negative versions of universal altruism, however, which are based on hierarchical needs, the situation is different. Since many sentient beings recognize in themselves a need to survive and a need to make autonomous choices concerning their own lives, the principles of liberal utilitarianism would not condone the minimization of suffering by minimizing the number of beings who have the capacity to suffer.

Although the liberal version of negative utilitarianism cannot be refuted by charges of nihilism, there are, however, good conceptual as well as axiological grounds for preferring the view that the positive promotion of happiness is also relevant to morality. On the one hand, it should be kept in mind that all needs which are not frustrated are, by definition, satisfied. In an important sense, then, the removal of evil and the promotion of good are inexorably joined together by conceptual bonds. On the other hand, axiological considerations also support the positive interpretation. Assuming that it would be possible to remove suffering without promoting happiness, the negative utilitarian theory would state that moral agents ought to confine their attention to the minimization of evil. But even granting that the removal of pain and misery is more urgent than the promotion of positive happiness, it cannot be denied that it is the latter that provides life with its ultimate value. Beings who do not suffer are, of course, better off than beings who do, but beings who are, in addition, happy fare even better. As far as practical morality is concerned, it is presumably true that the minimization of pain should in the majority of real-life cases be preferred to the maximization of pleasure. Theoretically speaking, however, there are no valid reasons to exclude positive happiness from among the criteria of moral rightness.

THE PRINCIPLES OF LIBERAL UTILITARIANISM

The theory of liberal utilitarianism which has been developed in this chapter can be summed up in two sets of principles. The first set consists of the axioms which concern the normative and axiological basis of the doctrine. These are:

A   *The greatest need-satisfaction principle.*
An act, omission, rule, law, policy or reform is the right one if and only if it produces, or can be reasonably expected to produce, at least as much need satisfaction as any other alternative which is open to the agent or decision-maker at the time of the choice.

B   *The principle of hierarchical needs.*
When the need satisfaction produced by various action alternatives is assessed, those needs which are hierarchically at a less basic level shall be considered only if the action alternatives in question do not, or cannot be expected to, produce an effect upon the satisfaction of needs at a more basic level.

C   *The principle of other-regarding need frustration.*
When the need satisfaction produced by various action alternatives is assessed, the most basic needs of one individual or group shall be considered only if the satisfaction of those needs does not frustrate the needs of others at the same hierarchical level.

D   *The principle of necessary and contingent ends.*
Needs are hierarchically at a more basic level if and only if their satisfaction is conceptually linked with the achievement of nec-

essary ends like survival, health, well-being and happiness. Needs are hierarchically at a less basic level if and only if their satisfaction is conceptually linked only with the achievement of contingent ends.

E *The principle of awareness.*
When the need satisfaction produced by various action alternatives is assessed, the needs of individual beings shall be considered only if the beings in question can consciously anticipate, sense or perceive, directly or indirectly, the loss involved in the frustration of those needs.

F *The principle of autonomy.*
When the need satisfaction produced by various action alternatives is assessed, need satisfaction which is freely and informedly chosen by autonomous individuals shall be preferred to the need satisfaction of the same individuals which is not.

These maxims between themselves define liberal utilitarianism as I understand the doctrine. Different formulations can, of course, be given to the theory. A more concise characterization for textbook use could state, for instance:

LU *The essence of liberal utilitarianism.*
According to liberal utilitarianism, it is always right to maximize the satisfaction of needs, provided that the satisfaction of the more basic needs for survival, health, well-being and happiness is not prevented by the satisfaction of less basic needs, and provided that the basic needs of individuals or groups are not in conflict. The needs to be accounted for must be recognizable to the beings who have them, except in the case of autonomy. In the case of autonomous beings, self-determined need satisfaction is to be preferred to other types of need satisfaction.

This definition, although brief and therefore slightly enigmatic, contains in a compressed form all the elements of liberal utilitarianism. An even shorter formulation will inevitably have to ignore some aspects of the theory, but the following negative formulation could perhaps be helpful in everyday decision-making:

OL *The outline of liberal utilitarianism.*
According to liberal utilitarianism, it is always wrong to

frustrate the basic need satisfaction of beings against their preferences, unless this is the only way to secure the basic need satisfaction of others.

Both LU and OL are compatible with the fundamental principles A–F, and they can be counted as versions of liberal utilitarianism. On the other hand, however, no moral theory which is incompatible with the principles can be legitimately called by that name.

The second set of principles focuses on the application of the doctrine. My findings regarding these matters in the immediately foregoing subsection can be summarized as follows:

G *The principle of act-utilitarianism.*
When the moral rightness of human activities is assessed, acts, rules, policies and reforms shall be regarded as individualized acts.

H *The principle of symmetry between acts and omissions.*
When the moral rightness of human activities is assessed, omissions, or negative acts, shall be regarded as morally equivalent to positive acts.

J *The principle of foreseeable consequences.*
When the moral rightness of human activities is assessed, the assessment shall be based on the foreseeable, not the actual, consequences of actions.

K *The principle of actual or prospective existence.*
When the moral rightness of human activities is assessed, the imagined needs of non-existent beings who will never come into existence shall not be counted.

L *The principle of positive utilitarianism.*
When the moral rightness of human activities is assessed, the promotion of happiness, or the advancement of positive need satisfaction, shall be regarded as equivalent to the removal and prevention of suffering, or the disallowance of need frustration.

The views expressed in these axioms are not necessarily held by all liberal utilitarians. There may be proponents of principles A–F who wish to deny the soundness of one or several of the maxims G–L. If the points I have made in this chapter are valid, then these theorists are wrong. But their views can, nonetheless, be classified under the heading of liberal utilitarianism.

Liberal utilitarianism, as I have defined it, is a stable but minimal moral theory. The stability of the doctrine is based on the fact that it does not demand excessive sacrifices, and it does not therefore lead to the unintuitive conclusions which refute the classical and modern variants of universal altruism. It can be safely inferred that those acts which are condoned by principles A-F are either permissible or obligatory. On the other hand, however, the minimal nature of the theory implies that liberal utilitarianism does not in and by itself provide solutions to all moral dilemmas. Tensions between different axiological convictions and epistemic viewpoints, as well as conflicts between the basic needs of different individuals and groups, are matters which cannot be conclusively solved by the principles of liberal utilitarianism. According to my analysis, these questions fall outside the scope of ethical theory, and should be tackled by other means.

4

ETHICAL THEORY AND PRACTICE

The aim of normative ethics is to provide a plausible and inclusive account of the rights and duties of moral agents and moral patients. General ethical theories like liberal utilitarianism do not, however, in and by themselves describe or prescribe all the rights and duties individual beings possess, or owe to one another. There are, for instance, cases in which it is difficult to distinguish between basic and derivative need satisfaction, and there are circumstances under which the autonomy of individuals and their decisions is hard to determine. Furthermore, the basic needs of various individuals and groups may be in conflict, and if they are, the principles of liberal utilitarianism do not clearly define the rights and duties of the parties involved.

Similar observations can be extended to the more traditional rivals of classical utilitarianism. Natural rights theories often tend to postulate contradictory entitlements which cannot be weighed in terms of the natural rights themselves.[1] The Kantian categorical imperative in its turn tends to sanctify substantive moral principles which are mutually incompatible, and which cannot be reconciled by appeals to the categorical imperative itself.[2] And theological moral doctrines which are based on divine revelation and holy scriptures frequently generate conflicting norms which cannot be resolved by purely scriptural means.[3]

There are also moral theories which are impervious to the conflicts between natural rights and conventional moral principles. Classical Benthamite utilitarianism, for example, states that it is always our duty to maximize pleasure and to minimize pain, whatever the consequences of this policy may be in terms of traditionally defined human rights and obligations. The application of the

Benthamite doctrine leads, however, to normative conclusions which cannot be universally condoned.[4] Another influential nineteenth-century theory which could be employed to harmonize clashing moral norms is existentialism. According to the doctrine, the morality of choices depends only on the authenticity or sincerity of the choices themselves. When authentic agents who act in good faith decide to respect one moral principle rather than another, the decision cannot be disputed on objective moral grounds. But although the problem of conflicting norms could, no doubt, be solved by assuming the existentialist way of thinking, the solution would be undermined by the extreme subjectivism of the view. If an individual decides to act cruelly towards other individuals, the sincerity of the decision can hardly be expected to justify the chosen course of action in any morally relevant sense. Yet this is what the existentialist theory of ethics seems to imply.

The fact that general ethical theories cannot provide inclusive and plausible accounts of the rights and duties of moral agents has led some philosophers to believe that rational moralities should be abandoned altogether and replaced by a deeper understanding of the factual values of the communities we live in.[5] Ethical theories, these philosophers argue, do not in fact promote morality but rather destroy it by substituting empty abstractions for the 'concretely determined ethical existence that was expressed in the local folkways, a form of life that made particular sense to the people living in it'.[6] According to these theorists, the only way to regain our original and vital ability to make spontaneous and, subsequently, valid ethical judgements is to return to the traditional values of the community surrounding us.

The difficulties of this nostalgic communitarian view are apparent. Local folkways which are often discriminatory and oppressive can hardly be regarded as the culmination of the development of morality, and the fact that a certain way of life has made particular sense to a specific group of people does not guarantee its acceptability in more general terms.[7] Furthermore, it is surely not necessary to reject the entire bulk of ethical theory because of the inability of moral philosophers to deal with certain exceptional conflict situations. Provided that the difficult cases can be reliably identified and isolated, traditional moral theories are left with a variety of questions to which they can provide adequate answers.

But these critical remarks aside, the idea of falling back on the deep values of the community in situations of moral conflict is not without its appeal. Decisions which are based on shared values are usually acceptable to most members of the community, and even those individuals who do not themselves sanction the choices can often understand the reasoning behind them. These advantages should not, of course, be overemphasized. The fact that minority members understand the majority's way of thinking does not always mean that they accept it, and even if they did, members of other communities could argue that the prevailing consensus is forced. Besides, some decisions affect individuals outside the community, and these decisions cannot as a rule be justified by the inside values of the group who make the choices. If, however, these limitations can be duly accounted for, shared values and ideals can perhaps be legitimately employed in ethical decision-making when traditional moral theories fail to offer firm solutions.

The branch of knowledge which examines contentious moral, social, legal and political issues in the light of ethical theories and popular attitudes can be called, following current academic usage, 'applied ethics'.[8] The history of applied ethics is at least as long as the history of Western moral philosophy,[9] although the discipline was nearly eradicated during the reign of logical positivism in the first half of the twentieth century. The recovery of normative ethics in the 1950s and 1960s was, however, soon followed by a rapid increase in applied ethical studies, and issues like racism, sexism, nuclear deterrence and famine in the Third World became familiar to Anglo-American moral philosophers.[10] Other practical problems which have drawn the philosopher's attention during the last few decades include abortion, euthanasia, capital punishment, civil disobedience, animal welfare, gene technology, reproductive medicine, the decay of the natural environment and the allocation of scarce medical resources. Extensive studies in many of these fields have led to the creation of subdisciplines like medical ethics, business ethics, research ethics and professional ethics. Work in all these areas is based on the assumption that general ethical theories do not in and by themselves provide a sufficient account of the rights and duties of moral agents and moral patients. If they did, normative ethics could be reduced to the direct and mechanical application of theoretical moral principles to real-life decision-making.

Contemporary philosophers have by no means universally hailed the rise of applied ethics. Many theorists have been sceptical about the usefulness of philosophical ethics in practical decision-making, and some have proceeded to note that the dubious moral expertise taught in courses of applied ethics may lead to positively undesirable results.[11] But while these concerns may in some cases be well taken, it would not be wise to condemn the entire branch of knowledge on account of them. Some philosophers and policy-makers have certainly had exaggerated expectations concerning the function of applied ethics in public life, but if a more restricted role is given to studies in applied moral philosophy, they can easily be seen as a useful and even necessary ingredient of normative ethics.[12]

In the following subsections, I shall undertake to analyse in some detail the relationship between the duties and rights of moral agents and moral patients, and the division of labour between theoretical and applied ethics in the assessment of issues concerning individual morality, social policy, legal regulation and political practices. I shall begin my examination in the first and second subsections by exploring the extent to which liberal utilitarianism can define our rights and obligations. The liberal utilitarian theory, as I have described it in the preceding chapters, primarily answers questions regarding 'right' and 'wrong' as qualities of actions, not queries concerning rights and duties. Some semantic principles are obviously needed to bridge the gap between these two vocabularies. Furthermore, there are particular moral questions which cannot be answered by liberal utilitarians at all, and these questions must be set apart from the ones that can be answered.

In the third subsection I shall go on to study the scope and methods of applied ethics. Most critics and many proponents of practical moral studies have, I believe, held an oversimplified view concerning the nature of these inquiries, and it is my aim to show how a closer scrutiny can lead to a more acceptable picture of applied ethics. In the concluding subsection I shall survey some of the most important ethical principles generated by the combination of liberal utilitarianism and applied ethics.

DUTIES ACCORDING TO LIBERAL UTILITARIANISM

According to liberal utilitarianism, it is always *right* to maximize the satisfaction of needs, provided that the satisfaction of the more basic needs of survival, health, well-being, happiness and autonomy is not prevented by the satisfaction of less basic needs, and provided that the basic needs of individuals are not in conflict.[13] *Mutatis mutandis*, it is always *wrong* not to maximize the satisfaction of needs, if this could be accomplished without frustrating more basic needs and if the basic needs of individuals are not in conflict. But what implications does this doctrine have in terms of duties and rights? A few remarks on the semantics of utilitarianism are needed to elucidate the matter.

Given that the rightness of actions is defined simply by their ability to maximize the good, utilitarian moral theorists have, as a rule, presumed that it is our *duty*, or our *obligation*, to do the right thing. If there is only one right option which is open to the agent at the time of the choice, it is the agent's duty to choose that option. If, on the other hand, there are several right options open to the agent, it is the agent's duty to choose one of them.[14] Moral agents cannot have a duty to choose an option which is not right, or which does not maximize the good.[15] On the contrary, it has been argued that they have a duty not to choose any option which does not fulfil the utilitarian criterion of rightness.

Critics of classical utilitarianism have argued that this division of actions into positive duties, optional duties and negative duties is far too limited. J.O. Urmson has presented the following example to illustrate the point:

> We may imagine a squad of soldiers to be practising the throwing of live hand grenades; a grenade slips from the hand of one of them and rolls to the ground near the squad; one of them sacrifices his life by throwing himself on the grenade and protecting his comrades with his own body.[16]

Assuming that the self-sacrifice of the soldier is both a necessary and a sufficient condition for the survival of the rest of the squad, the soldier's choice is, in classical utilitarian terms, the right one. Urmson, however, goes on to ask:

> But if the soldier had not thrown himself on the grenade would he have failed in his duty? Though clearly he is superior in some way to his comrades, can we possibly say that they failed in their duty by not trying to be the one who sacrificed himself? If he had not done so, could anyone have said to him, 'You ought to have thrown yourself on that grenade?' Could a

superior have decently ordered him to do it? The answer to all these questions is plainly negative.[17]

If Urmson's answer is correct, classical utilitarians must be wrong in presuming that moral agents have an absolute duty to do what is right and to abstain from what is wrong. Although the soldier chooses the right option by sacrificing himself, his heroic action should presumably be regarded as an instance of supererogation rather than an act of duty.

Anthony Quinton has drawn attention to two further cases in which the utilitarian criterion of rightness may lead to unreasonably strict codes of conduct. He writes:

> Ordinary utilitarianism, along with some other moral theories and a lot of religiously inspired moral stock responses, is utopianly altruistic. It implies that in every situation in which action is possible one should choose that possibility which augments the general welfare. That would rule out as morally wrong not only harmless self-indulgences like sitting in the sun, reading for pleasure and non-strenuous walks in the countryside (since in each case one could be working or begging for Oxfam), it would also override most of the altruistic things we do for people to whom we are bound by ties of affection.[18]

The crux of Quinton's critique is that certain actions which are either too trivial to warrant much consideration or too spontaneous to allow any calculation clearly ought to be deemed permissible, or at least excusable, even if they fail to maximize general well-being. If Quinton is right, it cannot be our duty to spend our every waking moment collecting money for charitable purposes, nor can it be our duty to benefit humankind at large at the expense of our families and friends. Individuals who choose to devote their entire lives to charity may sometimes be described as saintly, and their actions may be classified as supererogatory. But if their devotion to humanitarian causes makes them impervious to the needs of those near them, they may also be regarded as hardhearted, unfeeling and even immoral.

One utilitarian response to the critical remarks made by Urmson and Quinton can be based on the distinction between positive duties and optional duties. G.E. Moore, for instance, emphasized in his theory the fact that:

whereas every voluntary action, without exception, must be either right or wrong, it is by no means necessarily true of every voluntary action that it either ought to be done or ought not to be done, – that it either is our duty to do it, or our duty not to do it. On the contrary, cases may occur quite frequently where it is neither our duty to do a particular action, nor yet our duty not to do it. This will occur, whenever, among the alternatives open to us, there are two or more, any one of which would be equally right.[19]

Defenders of utilitarianism could, in theory at least, appeal to this distinction and argue that in the situations described by Urmson and Quinton the options open to each agent are equally right. This would imply that the soldier does not have a duty to sacrifice himself, and that ordinary people are not morally required to devote their entire lives to the advancement of impersonal humanitarian causes.

The options open to the soldier and to the ordinary citizen cannot, however, be judged as equally right within the classical utilitarian framework where the good is defined in terms of pleasurable experiences. Urmson and Quinton, well aware of this fact, both suggest alternative axiologies. Quinton's proposed solution is that duties should be extended only to the prevention of suffering, not to the promotion of positive well-being, utility, welfare, happiness, pleasure or desire satisfaction.[20] Urmson in his turn suggests that duties are 'mainly concerned with the avoidance of intolerable results, while other forms of moral behaviour have more positive aims'.[21] But it can be argued that both these solutions are inadequate. Since the soldier in Urmson's example can, objectively speaking, prevent a great deal of suffering by throwing himself on the grenade, and since the death of the entire squad could well be seen as an intolerable result of his failure to do so, both Quinton's and Urmson's axiologies seem to imply that the self-sacrifice is, after all, the soldier's duty.[22] And this is precisely the conclusion that both philosophers originally set out to criticize.

Urmson averts this undesired conclusion by specifying further the scope of moral obligation. He continues:

[We] may regard the imperatives of duty as prohibiting behaviour that is intolerable if men are to live together in society and demanding the minimum of co-operation toward the same end; that is why we have to treat compliance as compulsory and dereliction as liable to public censure.[23]

This definition presents two new features which set duties apart from other forms of right action. First, duties are linked with the preservation of society in a way that more supererogatory actions are not. Urmson notes that while an army without heroic individuals would be impoverished, an army without general attention to the rules of military law would be useless. Analogously, life in a world without saints and heroes would be poor, but it would not necessarily be brutish and short, as a life would be in a world in which individuals neglect their basic duties.[24] Second, Urmson notes that duties, unlike more supererogatory moral actions, can be justifiably linked with the concepts of punishment and compulsion. John Stuart Mill had already pointed out in *Utilitarianism* that duties can be exacted from individuals like debts,[25] and that people 'do not call anything wrong, unless [they] mean to imply that a person ought to be punished in some way or other for doing it'.[26] Urmson assumed a similar view by stating that while people can, of course, be legitimately coerced into carrying out their duties, it would be a horrifying idea to press individuals to perform acts of heroism.[27]

Urmson's remarks are interesting, but they do not provide a clear, let alone tenable, demarcation line between duties and other types of moral action. It is not always easy to define socially intolerable behaviour, and the fact that duties may be exacted from individuals by social sanctions provides a justification for penal practices rather than a definition of moral obligations. It seems, then, that Urmson, like the classical utilitarians he attacked, finally fails to define the role and function of saintly and heroic actions in ethical theory.

The difficulty with most classical and modern formulations of utilitarianism is that they explain duties in terms of the rightness of actions, and identify the rightness of actions with the linear maximization of general welfare. Liberal utilitarianism escapes the problems of its predecessors by denying the latter connection. According to the liberal version of universal altruism, moral agents have a positive duty to do what is right and a negative duty to abstain from what is wrong. If there are several right action alternatives which are open to the agent, the agent has an optional duty to choose one of these alternatives. But since actions which maximize the good in objective terms are not necessarily right, agents do not always have an obligation to promote the greatest measurable welfare or utility.

The heroic soldier in Urmson's example is a case in point. By sacrificing his own life the soldier can save the lives of many others, a solution which would presumably minimize the overall frustration of basic needs and hence maximize net utility. But since the need frustration of the other soldiers can be prevented only at the expense of the soldier's own basic need satisfaction, the principles of liberal utilitarianism do not automatically rule the self-sacrifice right, much less the soldier's absolute duty. The soldier can, if he so chooses, preclude his own needs from the utility calculation, and favour the self-sacrifice as the objectively most desirable alternative. If he decides to do this, he deems, by his own choice, the self-sacrifice right, and imposes on himself a duty to protect the rest of the squad. But as the soldier does not have the duty unless he imposes it on himself, no other person or group can justifiably force it upon him.

In the examples presented by Quinton, classical utilitarians are bound to prefer the impersonal advancement of charitable causes to the simple joys of life and to the small-scale altruism of family life. Liberal utilitarianism, however, does not state that moral agents should always sacrifice their personal lives in order to benefit those in greater need. It may sometimes be our liberal utilitarian duty to forgo a pleasurable country walk, or to cater to the needs of strangers before considering the wishes of those near us. But if occasional country walks are a part of our concept of a good life, then we cannot totally renounce them without endangering our basic need satisfaction. The episodes that Quinton chooses to call 'harmless self-indulgences' are often indispensable elements of human happiness and well-being, and when they are, they should be taken fully into account in moral calculations. On the other hand, if our efforts to satisfy the needs of those we know and love are distinctly more successful than our more general attempts to promote the good of humanity, it would obviously be a mistake to insist on the latter course of action.

In addition to the conventional duties towards our fellow beings, the principles of liberal utilitarianism give rise to two further categories of obligation that are by no means recognized in all moral theories. First, the objective value of maximum need satisfaction implies that, if we so choose, we can have a self-imposed duty to keep ourselves healthy and happy. The overriding nature of autonomy guarantees that paternalistic interventions by others cannot, as a rule, be justified by appeals to our own good.[28] But if we let our autonomous decisions be guided by the objective constituents of our well-being, we can impose upon ourselves the secular perfectionist duty to maximize our own need satisfaction.[29] Second, the axioms of liberal utilitarianism imply that people who knowingly produce children have special duties towards them. Since children would not exist without their parents, it can be argued that all voluntary mothers and fathers are partly responsible for every instance of need frustration that befalls their children. The unfortunately popular idea that children should always be grateful to their parents is, according to this view, seriously skewed. Before the era of efficient contraceptives children were sometimes seen as uninvited intruders who required undue sacrifices of their parents. In the absence of sex education and contraceptives the view was perhaps not always completely unjustified. But even in those days it would not have made sense to blame children for their own existence, nor to liberate those individuals who actually wanted to procreate of their parental responsibility.

The extra duties that voluntary fathers and mothers have towards their children are, according to liberal utilitarianism, partly analogous to the responsibilities that individuals and families have with regard to their domestic animals, especially in modern urban dwellings. Young children and tame animal companions are equally incapable of satisfying their own basic needs independently of others, and this is why those who have chosen to have them also have a duty to provide for their needs. The most important difference between children and pets in this context is that most human beings gradually develop the capacity to make decisions on their own behalf, and the ability to satisfy their own needs. Domestic animals, who do not in general share these human potentials, must be looked after with equal intensity for their entire lives. But the duties parents have towards their children diminish as the children grow up. Mothers and fathers are responsible for providing a basis upon which a good life can be founded, but once the foundation has been secured and the children have become capable of making their own choices, parents cannot be held responsible for the decisions that their children make.

The duties generated by liberal utilitarianism are summarized and presented in a schematic form in Figure 1.

	Can be legitimately imposed by others	Cannot be legitimately imposed by others
Other-regarding	Duty to do what is right and to abstain from what is wrong.	Autonomously chosen duties of supererogation.
Self-regarding	Duties not to harm oneself by non-autonomous actions.	Autonomously chosen duties of self-perfection.

Figure 1 Duties according to liberal utilitarianism

The obligations defined in the upper left-hand corner of the figure, the other-regarding duties which can be legitimately imposed on individuals by others, form the basis of our moral obligations. Duties which are self-regarding or which exist only if we choose to impose them on ourselves are conditional, or allow for exceptions. The duties parents have toward their children form an interesting subcategory which extends from the domain of supererogation to the sphere of the right and the wrong. The obligation to have children cannot be legitimately imposed on individuals or couples by other people even if the creation of a child would in some sense increase the sum total of happiness in the universe. But once the child has been born, the parental duty to provide for its needs can in many cases be justifiably enforced by others. The particular cases in which people can be made to look after their offspring, and the specific duties which can be imposed on them, are matters which ought to be analysed more thoroughly than space allows here.

RIGHTS ACCORDING TO LIBERAL UTILITARIANISM

Proponents of utilitarianism have traditionally held that moral *rights* can and should be defined by referring to the duties that moral agents do and do not have towards themselves and others.[30] Legal rights can be based on promises, contracts and covenants, and they can often be seen as an independent source of legal duties and obligations.[31] But rights which are supposed to have direct moral relevance must according to the utilitarian doctrine be defined in terms of right and wrong, duty and moral obligation.

138

The most important duty-related rights that liberal utilitarianism grants individuals can be divided into three categories in conformity with the obligations that generate them. The weakest type of a right is a *licence*, or a *permission*. This category can be defined as follows:

> Individual *A* has a moral licence to choose (or to do, to have, to be, to forgo, to avoid or to bring about) *X* if, and only if, *A* has no moral duty not to choose (or to do, to have, to be, to forgo, to avoid or to bring about) *X*.

Depending on the specific nature of the licence in question, the symbol *X* can stand either for an act or an omission, for an object, for a quality or for a state of affairs. The primary case in the utilitarian context is the licence to choose a particular course of action. According to liberal utilitarianism, moral agents have a duty to do what is right and a duty to abstain from what is wrong. It follows logically from these obligations that moral agents are licensed to do what is right and to abstain from what is wrong, since agents cannot have a duty not to perform their duty. The doctrine also states, less trivially, that moral agents are licensed to choose freely between options which cannot be deemed either right or wrong.

The absence of a duty to refrain from specified courses of action has not always been called a 'licence' in the philosophico-legal literature. Wesley Hohfeld in his pioneering work *Fundamental Legal Conceptions* used the word 'privilege', and other theorists have employed terms like 'liberty', 'bare liberty' and 'mere liberty'.[32] The point of Hohfeld's usage is that legal licences are typically restricted to a particular person or a particular group of persons. To say, for instance, that police officers have a right, or a licence, to be out after curfew is to say that they have a privilege which other citizens do not have. The permission that entitles police officers to patrol the streets in the night-time can be regarded as a meaningful right only when other people are under a legal obligation to stay indoors.

As Alan R. White has rightly pointed out, however, the interchangeable use of the words 'licence' and 'privilege' is problematical, and possibly misleading.[33] It is, no doubt, true that many legal licences derive their meaning, or point, from the fact that those who have the licence are in a privileged position as compared to others. But there are licences which are not privileges, and privileges which are not licences. Within the liberal utilitarian theory, for instance,

139

all autonomous persons are morally permitted to pursue their own happiness, given that they do not threaten the happiness of others in the process. As this right, or permission, is universal, it cannot be confined to a privileged few. On the other hand, privileges cannot be restricted to the domain of licences. Every time an individual or a group is singled out for preferential treatment, a privilege is granted to them. Any right and any advantage which can be justifiably circumscribed to a limited number of individuals automatically marks off a moral privilege which is possessed by those individuals.

The use of the word 'liberty' for the absence of a negative duty is potentially even more confusing than the use of the word 'privilege'. To be at liberty to do X means, in ordinary language, to be free, usually free from physical or social constraint, to do X.[34] 'Liberty' in this everyday sense seems to refer primarily to a descriptive quality or state of being. Permissions or licences, on the other hand, are normative entities, which do not necessarily imply that the agents who possess them are free to use them. Although most reasonable moralities would grant that all human beings are licensed to pursue happiness when this can be done without hurting others, hundreds of millions of people all over the world are rendered unable to use this licence effectively by the existence of physical and social obstacles. Furthermore, agents are often at perfect physical and social liberty to commit deeds which are wrong, and which cannot therefore be morally permitted.

In addition to licences, moral agents and moral patients can also possess more demanding rights, which imply duties to other individuals and groups. In the literature these rights have been called 'claim-rights', and they have been traditionally divided into two categories, depending on the nature of the duties attached to them. The instances of the first category, *negative claim-rights*, can be defined as follows:

> Individual A has a negative moral claim-right to choose (or to do, to have, to be, to forgo, to avoid or to bring about) X if, and only if, A has no duty not to choose (or to do, to have, to be, to forgo, to avoid or to bring about) X, *and* other individuals have a duty not to prevent A from choosing (or from doing, having, being, forgoing, avoiding or bringing about) X.

Negative claim-rights, as defined by this formula, can be further divided into active and passive rights in accordance with the specific nature of the *X* in question. Moral agents can have both active rights, that is, rights to act in certain ways without the interference of others, and passive rights, or rights to obtain a certain state without intervention. Moral patients, in turn, can have only passive rights, since they cannot be said to act in the relevant sense, and cannot therefore be granted meaningful rights to act.

The second type of duty-implying rights, *positive claim-rights*, can be defined thus:

> Individual *A* has a positive moral claim-right to choose (or to do, to have, to be, to forgo, to avoid or to bring about) *X* if, and only if, *A* has no duty not to choose (or to do, to have, to be, to forgo, to avoid or to bring about) *X, and* other individuals have a duty to help *A* to choose (or to do, to have, to be, to forgo, to avoid or to bring about) *X.*

Positive claim-rights can also be either active or passive, and the remarks concerning agents and patients made in the above can be extended to this class as well as to the class of negative claim-rights.

The other-regarding duties underlying both negative and positive rights can be owed either by particular individuals or groups, or by moral agents in general. In the former case, the rights in question can be called '*in personam* rights', and in the latter case '*in rem* rights'. In legal contexts, *in personam* rights are typically positive and *in rem* rights negative.[35] My legal right against another person for the repayment of a debt, for instance, is related to the other person's duty to take positive action, whereas my legal right to keep my wallet intact is related to everybody's duty to refrain from robbing me. An exception to this rule is provided by everybody's positive duty to assist accident victims in those countries where Good Samaritan laws have been enacted.[36] But generally, legal rights which are linked with duties to positive assistance are restricted to particular individuals.[37]

The definitions given here to negative and positive claim-rights imply that if an individual has a claim-right to *X*, the individual also automatically has a licence to *X*. Ostensibly, this conclusion follows from the fact that the permission to do or to have *X* is explicitly included in the definitions. But the inclusion is not, in fact, necessary. If person *B* has a liberal utilitarian duty not to prevent person *A* from doing or having *X*, it follows that it must be right for person *A* to do or to have *X*. Furthermore, since moral agents and patients are licensed to do or to have what is right, *A* must have a licence to do or to have *X*. The same analysis also applies, *mutatis mutandis*, to the connection between licences and positive claim-rights.

Granted that the claim-rights possessed by moral agents contain, within the liberal utilitarian framework, licences as their components, the following concise definitions can be given to these rights:

> Agent *A* has a negative right to do or to have *X* if, and only if, other individuals have a duty not to prevent *A* from doing or having *X*. Agent *A* has a positive right to do or to have *X* if, and only if, other individuals have a duty to help *A* to do or to have *X*.

It is a matter of some dispute whether moral patients, as opposed to moral agents, can be said to have claim-rights at all. Since moral patients do not act in any relevant sense, it is natural to contend that they cannot possess active rights, or rights to do what they choose. In addition, however, the foregoing analysis seems to indicate that similar observations can be extended to passive rights, or rights to have one's interests accounted for by others. All claim-rights presuppose that their bearers are licensed to do or to have what they prefer, and this means that in order to have rights, individuals must have no duty not to choose certain courses of action or states of being. But if moral patients do not have any duties to begin with, in what sense can it be said that they have no duty to abstain from a particular option? The absence of negative duties does not in their case seem to imply a morally relevant licence, but rather a lack of evidence for the individual's capacity to possess substantive claim-rights.

From the viewpoint of liberal utilitarianism, the question regarding the rights of moral patients is purely verbal. If an individual or a group of individuals have a duty to provide *A* with *X*, the fact that *A* does or does not have the licence, or the claim-right, to *X* does not add morally decisive features to the situation. Consequently, the question can be settled on pragmatic grounds. The solution which is most amenable to the principles of liberal utilitarianism is to divide individual beings into three categories, and to assert that the question of rights must be solved differently in each category. First, moral agents, or autonomous persons who are aware of their own capacity to make ethical judgements and moral choices, have both active rights to choose courses of action and passive rights to obtain states of being. Second, moral patients, or sentient beings who are not full-blown moral agents, do not have active rights. They can, however, be said to have passive rights, but this statement is founded on linguistic conventions rather than indisputable moral arguments. Third, beings which are not sentient cannot be said to have any rights. Moral agents may have duties to protect certain non-sentient living beings and inanimate objects from harm and damage, but these obligations do not give rise to moral rights which could be attributed to the individuals in question.

Although the status of moral patients as bearers of rights can be questioned, there are good conventional grounds for granting passive claim-rights to these individuals. The opponents of this permissive view usually voice their objections when the possible rights of animals are discussed. They argue, typically, that only human beings can have genuine moral rights, because only human beings can be full moral agents with all the rights and duties implied by that role. But what these theorists tend to forget is that in addition to animals there are also human beings who do not fulfil the criteria of moral agency. Young children, unconscious human beings, the mentally retarded and the senile must often be classified as moral patients rather than moral agents, and it follows from this that if animals are excluded from the sphere of rights-related morality, a similar exclusion should also be extended to these human beings. One natural way to avoid this undesired conclusion is to yield to the view that moral patients as well as moral agents can be said to have rights. (Another way to solve the problem would be to say that while agents can be said to have rights, moral patients can in similar situations be said to have a *case* for the treatment which is specified by the duties of other individuals. Animals and young children could, according to this view, have moral cases, which could be interpreted as the rights of those who cannot themselves claim their due.)

The rights and duties generated by liberal utilitarianism have been summarized in Figure 2.

I have used three different symbols to represent the conceptual connections between the statements presented in the figure. First, an arrow pointing both to the left and to the right stands for the logical connective 'if and only if', and should be read 'if and only if the upper is the case, then the lower is also the case'. Second, an arrow pointing to the right stands for an implication, and should be read

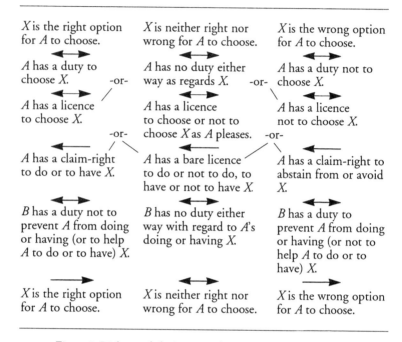

Figure 2 Rights and duties according to liberal utilitarianism

'if the upper is the case, then the lower is also the case'. Third, an arrow pointing to the left symbolizes reverse implication, and should be read 'if the lower is the case, then the upper is also the case'. A line inclined to the left from the word 'or' means that the connective down on the left holds between the lower statement and either one of the upper statements that make up the disjunction. In a similar manner, a line inclined to the right from the word 'or' means that the connective down on the right holds between the lower statement and either one of the upper statements joined by the disjunctive expression.

For the sake of visual economy, I have included three separate norms in the statement regarding bare licences in the centre of the figure (centre column, third up). Agent *A* can have either a bare licence to choose *X*, a bare licence not to choose *X*, or a bare licence to choose or not to choose *X* at will. The first norm is compatible with *A*'s licence to choose *X* or choose at will, the second with *A*'s licence not to choose *X* or choose at will, and the third with *A*'s licence to choose or not to choose *X* as *A* pleases. In all these cases,

B's duties towards *A* with regard to *X* remain the same, that is to say, they are non-existent.

The layout of Figure 2 can, at first glance, emphasize unduly the role of claim-rights and licences in the liberal utilitarian theory of normative ethics. The statements concerning rights occupy a central position in the figure (right and left columns, third up), and all the duties and licences of the agents involved seem to flow from the depicted rights. A closer look at the interconnected norms shows, however, that this impression is deceptive. The only sources from which the rights of agent *A* can be legitimately derived in the figure are in fact agent *B*'s other-regarding duties. It is, admittedly, true that if *A* has a claim-right to do *X*, then *B* (either a specified individual or any passer-by) has a duty not to prevent *A* from doing *X*. But the point of this conceptual truth is that an agent cannot be said to have claim-rights unless other agents can be endowed with the corresponding duties. The inference does not in any way prove that duties could in particular ethical contexts be justifiably derived from pre-existent rights. On the contrary, the normative relationships described in the figure clearly embody the idea that rights, according to liberal utilitarianism, are ultimately derivable from duties. If *B* has a duty not to prevent *A* from doing *X*, then *A* is licensed to do *X*, and *A* can be said to have, by definition, a claim-right to do *X*.

The claim-rights granted to moral agents and moral patients by liberal utilitarianism cannot under any circumstances come into conflict with one another. If it seems that both *A* and *B* have a claim-right to have something which can be granted to only one of them, then neither one can, in the last analysis, be granted the relevant right. Two agents can, no doubt, be licensed to obtain the same unique state of being, as conflicts between licences cause no difficulty for the utilitarian theory. But those individuals who are supposed to have the duties to help or not to prevent the agents in question cannot be obligated to help or to prevent both, since only one of the mutually exclusive alternatives can be right at the time of the choice. An example of the kind of conflict I am referring to is the clash between the interests of the track workmen in Judith Jarvis Thomson's example described in Chapter 3.[38] Both the five workmen on the main track and the one workman on the side track are equally licensed to continue living, but since the driver of the trolley cannot have two mutually exclusive duties simultaneously, none of the workmen can have a liberal utilitarian claim-right to life under the depicted circumstances.

It is not a common feature in normative ethics to deny the existence of conflicts between claim-rights. Philosophers who do not believe in moralities based on the concept of 'a right' have been eager to argue that the inevitable, and frequently unsolvable, clashes between so-called absolute or natural rights can in fact be employed to refute these moralities. Proponents of traditional theories of rights, in their turn, have denied the force of this argument, but not by maintaining that conflicts of rights do not exist. Instead, they have developed several auxiliary theories to explain why the clashes are not fatal to the ethical views they profess.

The solutions which have been offered to the problem of conflicting claim-rights can be very roughly divided into two classes. According to the first, 'orthodox' view, it is the task of moral philosophers to state and to defend a set of rules and principles which can be employed to define all the priorities between rights in potential conflict situations. Moralists who have chosen this strategy have during the last few centuries created ingenious theories of rights, but it is often a matter of considerable controversy whether their arguments have been based on substantive moral distinctions or merely on advanced verbal acrobatics. According to the second, 'eclectic' solution, moral rights are only prima facie valid, and conflicts among them ought to be solved by employing elements from other ethical or philosophical views which are compatible with the chosen theory of rights. This strategy has often been assumed by those who have tried to apply theories of rights to real-life moral, social, legal or political problems and practices.

Although liberal utilitarianism does not recognize conflicts between claim-rights, the doctrine does acknowledge the existence of clashes among moral licences. Since I have asserted, at the beginning of this chapter, that it is the task of normative ethics to give a plausible and, equally importantly, inclusive account of the rights and duties of moral agents and moral patients, these clashes between licences must be solved in one way or another. My own solution, which can presumably be classified as 'eclectic', is to suggest that the moral conflicts left unsettled by liberal utilitarianism can best be solved by using a device called 'applied philosophy' or 'applied ethics'. In the following subsection, I shall endeavour to explain what has been meant and what I believe should be meant by these terms.

THE NATURE AND ROLE OF APPLIED ETHICS[39]

The twentieth-century study of contemporary moral problems, which has, of late, come to be called *applied ethics*, emerged in the 1950s and the 1960s out of the philosopher's frustration in the face of the inability of ethical emotivism, the leading moral doctrine of the time, to judge and to condemn such atrocities as the crimes committed by the Nazis before and during the Second World War. The movement towards normative commitment in philosophy was, in the beginning, distinctly non-British. An early example of the new tendency was provided by the French existentialist Simone de Beauvoir, who shortly after the war published an article entitled 'An eye for an eye', in which she argued, against the general drift of her own pre-war views, that the crimes committed by the Nazis were too abominable to be condoned without severe punishments.[40] This conversion, which later on proved to be permanent,[41] did not lead de Beauvoir to conduct detailed studies in the philosophy of punishment and retaliation. But it did induce her to pay close attention to the issue of justice between different groups of people, and to write *The Second Sex*,[42] the feminist classic which has become a landmark in modern gender studies.[43]

The wider movement towards the study of real-life moral and political issues by philosophical methods was born in the United States during the 1960s, and this movement was from the beginning closely connected with the view that a systematic theory of natural rights should be developed to regulate human actions. This starting point is well reflected in the opening paragraph of Richard Wasserstrom's representative article 'Rights, human rights, and racial discrimination', which was originally published in 1964 in the *Journal of Philosophy*.

> The subject of natural, or human, rights is one that has recently come to enjoy a new-found intellectual and philosophical respectability. This has come about in part, I think, because of a change in philosophical mood – in philosophical attitudes and opinions toward topics in moral and political theory. And this change in mood has been reflected

147

in a renewed interest in the whole subject of rights and duties. In addition, though, this renaissance has been influenced, I believe, by certain events of recent history – notably the horrors of Nazi Germany and the increasingly obvious injustices of racial discrimination in both the United States and Africa. For in each case one of the things that was or is involved is a denial of certain human rights.[44]

In keeping with the spirit of Wasserstrom's observation, the scope of applied ethics in the United States has been confined primarily to those issues which can be analysed by employing the concepts of equality, justice and natural or legal rights. The criticism of racial discrimination, which was the crux of Wasserstrom's article, was soon accompanied by attacks against discrimination based on gender, ethnic origin and sexual orientation. The extension of these discussions to the rights of the unborn, the dying and the medically vulnerable marked the dawn of modern bioethics. The questions of international aid, justifiable warfare and capital punishment have also continually intrigued the bulk of American moralists.[45]

At the beginning of the 1970s British philosophers joined the ongoing discussion which was taking place in American scholarly publications, notably in the newly founded journal *Philosophy & Public Affairs*. Richard M. Hare started this exchange by presenting views on the morality of warfare and abortion.[46] Hare's Australian disciple Peter Singer, who in the early 1970s held a position in Oxford, began by addressing the questions of civil disobedience and international aid, and then went on to instigate a movement for the liberation of animals from the effects of what he called 'speciesism'.[47] And John Harris, another Oxford moral philosopher, distinguished himself by presenting forceful and ingenious arguments against violence by omission, or negative actions.[48]

The Oxford utilitarians headed by Hare, Singer and Harris were not greeted with undivided enthusiasm across the Atlantic. Singer, whose plea for non-human animals can without difficulty be interpreted in terms of natural rights, quickly established his reputation as a pioneer of international applied ethics.[49] But the commitment to universal altruism shared by Hare, Singer and Harris has not gained much transatlantic popularity. Most American moral philosophers had by the early 1970s rejected the formerly popular doctrine of rule-utilitarianism,[50] and they had become convinced that social, political and legal morality should be centred on the rights of the individual rather than on the good of society as a whole. The publication of John Rawls' *A Theory of Justice* in 1972 marked the final breakthrough of this view to the American philosophical consciousness.

The primacy of rights and utility in normative ethics has been occasionally challenged by theorists who believe that virtues and vices rather than entitlements or contentment should form the basis of morality. The idea of Aristotelian virtues was examined by G.H. von Wright in his *The Varieties of Goodness* (1963), and further developed by Peter Geach in his *The Virtues* (1977) and by Philippa Foot in her *Virtues and Vices* (1978). While von Wright and Geach did not proceed to discuss the role of virtues in real-life situations, Foot has applied the views of Aristotle and Thomas Aquinas to the problems of abortion and euthanasia.[51] Her moderately conservative and distinctly anti-utilitarian views have not gone unnoticed in the United States – Foot was, in fact, a member of the editorial board of *Philosophy & Public Affairs* at the time Hare, Singer and Harris published their first contributions in the journal. The predominance of the concept of natural rights has, however, hindered the wider dissemination of virtue ethics in the North American continent, particularly after the publication of Rawls' *magnum opus*.[52]

Another alternative to the normative ethical theories based on rights and utility is the Kantian view that duties and obligations form the core of our moral existence. In Britain, Ruth Chadwick has applied this view successfully to certain difficult questions in medical ethics.[53] Genuinely Kantian approaches have not, however, been prevalent on either side of the Atlantic, perhaps partly due to the confusion created by Rawls, who in his book asserted that his essentially contractarian position can be classified under the heading of Kantian ethics.[54] While this interpretation may in some sense be valid, it ignores the fact that Kant emphasized the primacy of duties rather than the focal position of liberty and individual rights in the regulation of social life.

The publication of *A Theory of Justice* has, paradoxically, also hindered the development of rights-based applied ethics in the United States. The inventive and complex theory put forward by Rawls has during the last two decades bewitched the majority of American moral philosophers, and the result is that they have ceased to pursue applied ethics as an autonomous academic subdiscipline. Some of them have focused their attention on the criticism and development of the views presented by Rawls, and others have set out to find alternative theories of justice and individual rights. These activities are, no doubt, academically respectable, but they belong to the domain of what can be called 'practical philosophy', or the philosophical study of the principles of moral, social and political life, rather than to the sphere of applied ethics, or the philosophical study of contemporary moral, social and political issues.[55] There are also a number of American moralists who have specialized in the application of ethical theories to problematical real-life situations. But insofar as their work consists of the mechanical use of authoritative moral doctrines, it would be more accurate to classify these exercises under the label of 'casuistry' than to regard them as studies in either pure or applied philosophy.[56]

The combination of pure philosophy and casuistry which has for the last two decades passed for applied ethics in North America has naturally been criticized by a number of moral philosophers. One of the most competent critiques against the model has been presented by Arthur Caplan in the context of modern medicine. In his article 'Can applied ethics be effective in health care and should it strive to be?' Caplan enumerates three features which have been regarded as crucial to philosophical medical ethics. First, philosophers are supposed to master the practice of conceptual analysis. By this remark Caplan means that the philosophers' talents, as seen by themselves at least, include the ability to clarify the meanings of words, to detect logical confusions and fallacies and to establish patterns of sound and valid argumentation. Second, it is often assumed, mostly by applied philosophers themselves, that they possess a body of knowledge concerning ethical theories which can be directly brought to bear on real-life moral and social problems. The knowledge in question is twofold. On the one hand, it includes 'a mastery of ethical traditions within philosophy and, perhaps, theology', and on the other hand, it contains 'an understanding of the ways in which moral beliefs and opinions can legitimately be justified through linking them to appropriate moral theories drawn from these traditions'. Third, the ethical expertise of philosophers is sometimes believed to be intensified by the fact that they are disinterested and neutral about the moral events that they examine. Within the context of medicine, for instance, applied philosophers are persons who do not have a vested interest in the kinds of care that is delivered, or in the safety and efficacy of particular procedures. Furthermore, they are also individuals who do not have a political need to align themselves with any person or group within the medical setting. Allegedly, this enables philosophers 'to weigh alternatives and reflect upon policies in ways that those caught up in the system, either as providers or recipients of health care, cannot'.[57]

In his article Caplan argues that the first-mentioned ability is liable to turn philosophers into a conceptual police force, while the second quality is apt to make them technicians applying a bulk of pre-existing information to practical situations. The third feature, in its turn, likens philosophers to the ideal legislators and arbitrators of popular eighteenth-century ethical theories. When these characteristics are put together, and when the philosophers who answer to Caplan's description are put to work, the result is what he calls the 'engineering model of applied ethics'.

Engineering in applied ethics takes the form of so-called deductive-nomological explanations, which have been both defended and criticized during the last few decades in the philosophy of natural and social sciences.[58] The original point of these explanations is that a set of basic premises concerning the laws of nature, together with a quantity of empirical data about the preceding events, can be combined to explain why a certain event did or did not take place at a given point in time. Analogously, the engineering model of applied ethics states that moral laws can be joined with the description of any real-life situation to produce a justification or a refutation for a policy or a course of action about to be taken in that situation. In both cases, it is assumed that the scientific or ethical knowledge in the arbitrator's possession can be applied to real-life situations in an entirely impartial and value-free manner.

Caplan voices three objections against applying the ethical engineering model to everyday work in hospitals and medical centres.[59] First, there is the question of identifying moral problems in clinical surroundings. When applied ethicists are seen as experts in their own field, and only in their own field, it is natural to think that the clinico-ethical problems are selected and introduced to them by medical professionals. But since it is far from obvious that doctors and nurses are capable of competently identifying the moral dilemmas of their profession, important ethical questions may be overlooked by house philosophers who rely on the information given to them by their medical colleagues. Second, if applied ethicists are seen as engineers, they will be expected to solve problems more or less mechanically, on the basis of certain externally determined premises, instead of extending their concern to the validity of those premises. It is, however, often difficult and sometimes impossible to find moral solutions to dilemmas which have been created, or at least aggravated, by political decisions or administrative principles. Third, applied ethicists who work within the health care system are not in fact as impartial as their alleged role as ideal arbitrators would demand. House philosophers, in their white coats and with their personal beepers, are much more likely to identify themselves with physicians and hospital administrators than to side with patients, nurses or visitors in conflict situations. Caplan concludes that since ethical engineering in the clinical setting mostly leads to incomplete analyses and biased recommendations, it would be best if philosophers kept out of hospitals and medical schools.

Caplan's remarks can, I believe, be extended to all fields in which philosophers have been hired to supply moral advice. By assuming the engineering model described by Caplan applied ethicists can, no doubt, create the illusion that their theoretical expertise is useful in such areas as health care provision, business administration, technology assessment, mass media, international policy-formulation and public decision-making. But the role of engineer philosophers within all these areas is either negligible or ethically suspect. Those who employ philosophers do not, as a rule, expect them to pursue relentlessly the moral truth regardless of the consequences of their findings to the employer. The motive for hiring academically educated moralists is, more frequently, a desire to find solid-looking ethical grounds for practices which are prone to arouse opposition among the employees, the clientele or the community at large.

In the light of these observations, it seems clear that the nature and role of applied philosophy and applied ethics ought to be redefined. An alternative to the engineering model can, fortunately, be found in the work of certain British philosophers, notably in Jonathan Glover's pioneering work *Causing Death and Saving Lives*.[60] Glover argued in his book that contemporary moral, social and political issues can be studied systematically by methods which are not unlike those used in scientific research. Moral principles can, according to Glover's view, be falsified by appeals to inconsistency and incoherence, and further tested by observing the responses provoked in various individuals by their application to reality. Glover believed that the logical and conceptual tests of consistency and coherence can objectively establish or refute general moral principles, whereas the role of people's moral responses is, due to the possibilities of manipulation and cultural differences, more problematical. The task of applied ethicists in this model is to develop moral rules and regulations which are maximally acceptable and reasonably applicable to real-life moral issues.

The methodology described by Glover, and employed by many other British applied philosophers besides him, is, I believe, essentially sound and practicable. I would like to argue, however, that popular opinions, or people's moral responses to certain test cases, can be assigned a slightly more prominent role than Glover allows for. The work of applied ethicists can, I think, be divided into two closely related tasks, which both involve the assessment of moral responses as well as the analysis of conceptual coherence and consistency. In what follows, I shall describe these tasks, which I have called (1) *cognitive deprogramming* and (2) *rational reconstruction.*[61]

(1) One of the problems of the engineering model of applied ethics is that those employing it often assume that only philosophers possess knowledge concerning ethical theories. Other professionals are seen as members of hermetic interest groups who are capable of ignoring all moral principles in their struggle for power and benefits. But the fact of the matter is, of course, that physicians and nurses, politicians and administrators, journalists, scientists and business executives do have their codes of ethics and their individual moral beliefs. Depending on their position and background, and on the strength of their varying convictions, professionals may adjust their conduct according to an array of official or unofficial codes and regulations, or they may prefer to observe their own moral values or the moral values of the community in which they live. Whichever framework the professionals choose to assume, however, they are bound to have an ethical stand on the issues that applied ethicists are supposed to solve for them. All human action takes place in an empirical moral reality, where judgements and assessments are constantly made quite regardless of the presence or absence of the moral philosopher.

Subsequently, the philosopher's first task in studying real-life moral dilemmas is to uncover the principles and codes which have been applied previously to the issue in hand. This preliminary work does not always belong to the category of normative ethics, since the moral opinions people hold do not in and by themselves make their actions right or wrong. But if applied ethicists do not know, to some extent at least, what other people think about the problem they are dealing with, they may end up wasting time in search of principles which cannot possibly be accepted by those whose lives and well-being are at stake.

Once the mapping of the relevant rules and beliefs has been completed, the strictly philosophical work can begin, in the form of conceptual and emotional cognitive deprogramming. By cognitive deprogramming I mean here the critical assessment of prevailing ethical views which have their roots in commonsense morality, personal convictions, religious doctrines, professional codes, philosophical theories and in fragments of scientific thinking. The evaluation may or may not result in changes in these views, as philosophers can sometimes but not always make people unlearn specious models of moral reasoning which they have grown up to accept uncritically. The methods by which applied ethicists can try to make other people abandon their previous views are, first, conceptual analysis, and second, the use of idealized or imaginary test cases. Philosophers are not, however, licensed to employ methods like coercion and manipulation, since the deprogramming of people's minds must, ultimately, remain in their own voluntary and autonomous control.[62]

Conceptual cognitive deprogramming consists of the analysis and critical assessment of the terms and arguments which have been used in the formulation of everyday moral rules and principles. If the terminology in use is ambiguous, or if the inferences made are invalid, the rules and principles in question must be either reformulated or rejected. Emotional cognitive deprogramming, in its turn, centres on the use of idealized or imaginary examples. These examples are normally designed to portray how, under particular hypothetical circumstances, apparently reasonable moral rules and principles lead to actions which have intuitively unacceptable consequences. Imaginary cases cannot be employed to establish moral views or to refute them absolutely or objectively, but if they are well chosen, they can in many cases provide good grounds for abandoning certain prima facie approvable ethical rules and principles.

(2) Successful cognitive deprogramming may create a momentary moral vacuum, which must then be refilled with new ideals and new rules of conduct. If called upon at this point, applied philosophers

can continue their work by trying rationally to reconstruct acceptable ethical principles and theories to replace the previous ones. Rationality in this context means that the norms and rules arrived at must be intrinsically consistent, mutually compatible and on the whole reasonably acceptable. But the criteria of consistency and acceptability cannot always be set from outside, or from above. While conceptual consistency and logical soundness may yield to objective criteria, intuitive acceptability is often a function of the deep values which prevail in the community under scrutiny. The conclusions of the applied ethicist are in these cases *ad hominem*, or of the form: 'Since your own basic norms, values and beliefs are this-and-this, and you presumably wish to be consistent, you ought to consider it your duty or right to have or to do that-and-that.' Reconstruction instead of free creation is therefore frequently needed.

Rational reconstruction proceeds in three stages, which are closely analogous to the steps taken in cognitive deprogramming. While the philosophical criticism of prevailing views must be preceded by the mapping of these views, the reconstruction of critical morality ought to be initiated by a survey of at least some of the axiological and normative principles which have been applied to relevantly similar cases in the past. When this survey has been completed, the potential solutions must, once again, undergo the tests of consistency and intuitive acceptability. As these remarks suggest, the destructive and constructive aspects of applied ethics are, in actual academic work, closely related, if not positively indistinguishable. The crux of the matter is, however, that by balancing between critique and theory-building, applied philosophers aim at spelling out moral rules, norms and principles which, taken as a whole, are consistent and reasonably acceptable to those to whom the ethicists in question address their arguments.

The methods of applied philosophical ethics have been presented schematically in Figure 3.

It is not always necessary to employ all the methods described in Figure 3 to solve particular moral or social problems. If it is to be expected that the majority of people are reasonably familiar with the major views regarding the issue in hand, it is often futile to survey these views in any great detail. Furthermore, if a prevailing doctrine or a potential solution can be refuted by an appeal to purely conceptual or logical incongruities, there is normally no need to evoke

	Cognitive deprogramming	Rational reconstruction
Mapping	A survey of some of the prevailing theories and views regarding the issue to be settled.	A survey of some of the potential solutions suggested to analogous issues in the past.
Conceptual and logical critique	The assessment of these theories and views from the conceptual and logical point of view.	The assessment of these potential solutions from the conceptual and logical point of view.
Intuitive and emotional critique	The evaluation of these theories and views in the light of idealized or imaginary examples.	The evaluation of these potential solutions in the light of hypothetical examples.

Figure 3 The methods of applied philosophical ethics

further intuitive responses for or against the doctrine or the solution. If, on the other hand, the logical soundness of an argument is well established, it is often possible to proceed directly to the realm of intuitions and emotional reactions. But complete studies in applied philosophical ethics can always contain all the elements presented in Figure 3.

There are three ways in which the methods of applied philosophical ethics can be employed to solve particular problems concerning the duties and rights of moral agents and moral patients. First, the three techniques of cognitive deprogramming can be applied directly to real-life moral, social, political and legal issues. Assuming that all previously suggested solutions but one can be refuted by logic or by intuitions, the remaining solution is, at least until proven otherwise, the right one. The rights and duties of the individuals involved can in this case be derived from the victorious view by any methods which are compatible with the semantics of liberal utilitarianism. As a matter of fact, if the arguments I have presented in the foregoing chapters are valid, any solution which can evade all known counter-arguments at this level is, in the final analysis, at least implicitly liberal utilitarian.

Second, the methods of applied philosophical ethics can be employed to resolve disputes over axiological issues. It is often difficult to determine where to draw the line between basic and derivative, or hierarchically more basic and less basic needs. When this is the case, the techniques of cognitive deprogramming and rational reconstruction can be used to clarify the value-theoretical distinction which is vital to liberal utilitarianism. Once the axiological entanglements have been sorted out, the duties and rights of individuals can in the majority of cases be defined without further difficulties.

Third, the methods of applied ethics can also be employed to solve conflicts between equally basic needs, or, in other words, to reconcile clashes between moral licences. Since conflicts between basic needs cannot be settled by liberal utilitarianism, nor by any other general moral theory, rational reconstruction is in these cases the moral philosopher's last resort. As regards negative results, or the refutation of proposed solutions by appeals to logic and emotions, the ethicist is on relatively firm ground here. If the suggested solutions are incoherent or clearly unacceptable, they can be quite confidently rejected. But the situation is different when it comes to positive conclusions. Coherence and consistency do not in and by themselves guarantee moral acceptability, and intuitive evaluations concerning the outcomes of alternative courses of action are often as contradictory as the original interests and needs. Despite the lack of universal approval, however, the results achieved by rational reconstruction mostly provide an option which is superior to relapses into defeatism or arbitrary decision-making. It is better to have an inclusive and reasonably coherent, if partly unstable, account of the rights and duties of moral agents and moral patients than to have no complete account of normative ethics at all.

One way to describe the relationship between liberal utilitarianism and applied ethics is to say that the methods of applied ethics can be employed both to justify liberal utilitarianism and to deal with the problems that it cannot solve. According to the foregoing considerations, liberal utilitarianism can be justified by the fact that it is the only version of universal altruism that can survive the process of cognitive deprogramming. This implies that, unless shown otherwise, the doctrine is valid. But since there are moral questions which cannot be answered by the principles of liberal utilitarianism, the methods of applied ethics are also needed to complement and to support the theory in difficult situations. The techniques of cognitive deprogramming can be utilized to show that no other theory can tackle conflicting needs any better than liberal utilitarianism, and rational reconstruction can be used in the search for more focused solutions to the problems in hand.

EQUALITY, LIBERTY AND JUSTICE

When real-life social, legal and political issues are addressed by applied philosophers, the discussion is often centred on concepts like equality, liberty and justice rather than on the liberal utilitarian terminology of needs and their hierarchical ordering.[63] My claim is, however, that the positive features which have been attached to these fundamental concepts of social philosophy can be explained, and indeed explicated, in terms of basic and derivative need satisfaction, awareness and autonomy.

The principle of equality has in one form or another been at the core of universal altruism since the emergence of the doctrine. The early proponents of the view argued that human beings are, as a matter of empirical fact, capable of taking everybody's happiness and misery equally into account in their moral calculations.[64] Abraham Tucker, the advocate of the eighteenth-century theological version of utilitarianism, asserted that God distributes happiness and misery equitably among all human beings, in the afterlife if not in this world.[65] William Godwin urged us to put ourselves in the place of impartial spectators of human concerns[66] and Jeremy Bentham, according to John Stuart Mill at least, emphasized that in moral calculations 'everybody should count for one, and nobody should count for more than one'.[67] And Henry Sidgwick maintained that whatever actions individuals judge to be right for themselves, they implicitly judge to be right for all similar persons in similar circumstances.[68]

The classical utilitarian principles concerning the equal consideration of interests and the equal assessment of actions put forward by Bentham and Sidgwick contained the seeds of egalitarian thinking, but the status of these principles in nineteenth-century universal altruism was undermined by the cumulative hedonism of the doctrine. If, hypothetically speaking, one individual could feel more pleasure than the rest of humanity put together, all possible resources should according to classical utilitarianism be allocated to that individual, regardless of the consequences in terms of equality and justice.[69]

Liberal utilitarianism, in its turn, firmly rejects all forms of inequality which tend to further the derivative need satisfaction of one individual or group at the cost of frustrating the basic need satisfaction of others. Discrimination against individuals or groups on the basis of morally irrelevant features like race, gender, age, religion or species mostly falls within this category. The same applies to many social and political arrangements within which burdens and benefits are distributed unevenly. There are, however, also cases in which an even distribution of burdens and benefits would frustrate the basic needs of one group without furthering the basic need satisfaction of others. In these cases, the liberal utilitarian principle of equality requires an uneven distribution to be enforced. This maxim constitutes the liberal utilitarian justification for affirmative action.

If the basic needs of one group are systematically satisfied by frustrating the basic needs of another, or if there is a clash of derivative needs between rivalling parties, the principles of liberal utilitarianism do not offer the moral guidance expected by typical egalitarian doctrines. When conflicts occur between necessary needs, cognitive deprogramming and rational reconstruction are the only methods by which consistent and intuitively acceptable solutions can be reached, while contingent needs yield to the simple rules of maximization. This apparent shortcoming does not, however, make liberal utilitarianism an inegalitarian theory. If deontological egalitarians come up with a sound principle which can be employed to regulate clashes between basic needs, the principle in question can be incorporated into the combination of liberal utilitarianism and applied ethics. The conflicts which occur between derivative needs, on the other hand, are not intrinsically important except to the firmest proponents of deontological egalitarianism.

The liberal utilitarian view of equality can be employed to define the proper range of benefit-all arguments for inequality, or arguments which defend moves towards an uneven distribution of benefits and burdens in the name of what has been called in the literature 'Pareto-optimality'.[70] Those who find benefit-all arguments appealing believe that it would be fair as well as rational to allow inequalities between individuals and groups on the condition that everybody would, in some concrete and material sense, benefit from the arrangement. According to liberal utilitarianism, it would indeed be right to guarantee one group of people a higher degree of derivative need satisfaction, if this is the only way to secure the basic need satisfaction of another group. Furthermore, the doctrine

would also condone an uneven distribution of derivative need satisfaction, provided that the arrangement would have no influence
upon the basic needs of the individuals involved, and provided that
any alterations in the situation would reduce the overall satisfaction
of needs. The real question is, however, whether these conditions
are ever met in real life. Since inequalities tend to increase need frustration by creating unfavourable comparisons between the lives of
individuals, the burden of proof in these cases is always on those
who defend deviations from an even distribution. Furthermore, in
situations where basic needs are at stake, the proponents of benefit-
all arguments should venture to explain why those who are already
better off should be rewarded by additional benefits for acting in
ways which are morally required of them in any case.

Opponents of egalitarianism have sometimes contended that all
social institutions which aim at the redistribution of benefits and
burdens are morally condemnable because they infringe the individual liberty of those who are originally better off. This contention
is mistaken on two accounts. First, not all redistributive measures
can be said to infringe individual liberty in a morally relevant sense.
Suppose, for instance, that I am extremely well off, and that I happen to live on a planet where thousands of children starve to death
every day. Suppose, further, that one-tenth of my fortune could, if
seized and redistributed by a benevolent and sovereign world government, save hundreds of children from starvation. Although the
world government would, by seizing my fortune, curtail my freedom to control the property that I legally own, it would not do
anything morally dubious, since the basic needs of a number of
individuals would be satisfied without any interference with my
basic need satisfaction.

Second, even if the redistributive measures taken by the world
government did have an effect on my basic need satisfaction, it
would not, according to the principles of liberal utilitarianism, be
clear that one person's need satisfaction ought to be preferred to the
similar need satisfaction of hundreds of others. By seizing my whole
property instead of only one-tenth of it the dominant agency would
presumably frustrate my necessary needs, but by choosing not to
seize my fortune and distribute it among the needy the agency
would let hundreds of other people die of hunger. Liberal utilitarianism does not in and by itself obligate the world government to
interfere with my well-being in order to promote the well-being of

others. The demands of the doctrine can be satisfied by redistributing only that part of my wealth which is not essential to my own welfare and happiness. But if, for some reason, my property cannot be divided in the required manner, the theory does not endow the sovereign with a right to protect me against the demands of those in need, either. The rights and duties of the dominant agency must, in situations like this, be defined by the methods of applied philosophical ethics, not by oblique references to freedom and constraint.

These remarks are not intended to undermine the value and significance of liberty in human life. The principles of liberal utilitarianism dictate that individuals ought to be left free to live their lives according to their own ideals and beliefs, at least as long as their free choices are more likely to benefit than to harm themselves and others, and as long as their actions do not violate the like liberty of other individuals. The value of liberty, understood as freedom of choice and freedom of action, is, however, instrumental rather than intrinsic. Liberty is good because it enables individuals to pursue the goals that they consider important in their lives. Freedom of choice and freedom of action are also valuable insofar as they promote, quite independently of the particular goals that individuals have, the personal autonomy of moral agents.[71] But since liberty has no intrinsic value, it can be quite legitimately restricted when agents threaten to inflict serious harm on others or, if certain additional conditions prevail, on themselves.

The liberal utilitarian principle of autonomy states that need satisfaction which is freely and informedly chosen by competent individuals ought to be preferred, in moral calculations, to the need satisfaction of the same individuals which is not.[72] This axiom implies that the advocates of liberal utilitarianism cannot condone autonomy-violating forms of paternalism, prudentialism or moralism.[73] Actions which are performed by competent agents and are based on free, informed and uncoerced decisions should not be interfered with even if the consequences of those actions would be harmful to the agents themselves, or even if other people think that the decisions made by the agents are irrational or immoral. The degree to which particular choices are free, informed and uncoerced varies, of course, considerably. But the high value liberal utilitarianism places on personal autonomy implies that the burden of proof is, in problematical cases, on those who wish to defend an interventionist policy.

One case in which an interventionist policy can be successfully defended is the circumcision of pre-pubertal girls. The young girls who are subjected to the mutilation of their sexual organs may sometimes express a preference for the operation, and it is frequently the case that they are not fully accepted as members of their communities unless they submit to the procedure. The consent and the expected consequences of the operation may seem to imply that the girls have voluntarily chosen a beneficial treatment which should not be banned because of the adverse attitudes which prevail among outsiders. According to the defenders of the practice, female circumcision can be compared to such widely sanctioned Western rites and habits as male circumcision or the straightening of mis-aligned teeth with braces.

But the morally relevant difference between male and female circumcision is that while the basic need satisfaction of men is not endangered by the operation, the basic need satisfaction of women most certainly is. Procedures like male circumcision and dental correction can be condoned by liberal utilitarianism, because they bring about social benefits without requiring major sacrifices in terms of necessary needs. The relatively harmless nature of male circumcision and cosmetic dental correction can be further elucidated by the fact that competent individuals can subject themselves to these operations for purely personal reasons, quite apart from any enhancement of their social status. This, however, is unfeasible in the case of female circumcision. Although many women who live in traditional communities may prefer clitoridectomy to complete social rejection, similar mutilation can hardly be seen as an option to educated and economically independent women who live in the affluent West. The comparison seems to imply that the supposedly free decisions of the women in the traditional societies are, in fact, made under coercive pressure. The individuals in question would presumably not choose circumcision if their social survival and well-being could be guaranteed in other ways. And given that this is the case, the prohibition of pre-pubertal circumcision cannot genuinely violate the autonomy of young girls who make their decisions in similar circumstances.

Those who cherish traditional ways of life can argue, at this point, that the consent of the girls is immaterial to the legitimacy of female circumcision. The practice can, according to these traditionalists, be justified by appeals to holy scriptures and religious obedience. Seen

162

from the viewpoint of liberal utilitarianism, this moralistic view is flawed on two accounts. First, the religious feelings which prevail in a community do not always constitute an essential part of the happiness and well-being of its members. When they do not, the basic needs of individuals are not frustrated by the prohibition of rites like circumcision. Second, even in cases where religious beliefs and personal welfare are closely intertwined, it would not be right to reinforce one's own faith by inflicting harm on innocent bystanders. Although the principles of liberal utilitarianism do not unequivocally condemn such actions, a judgement to this effect can be easily defended by the methods of applied ethics. We do not, after all, believe that sadistic actions can be justified by referring to the unhappiness of the sadists in cases where their actions are restricted. Why should we think, then, that the harm inflicted on women by circumcision could be legitimized by the feelings of individuals who sanction the mutilation of young girls rather than abandon or modify their own religious beliefs?

The case of female circumcision, as well as many other cases in which liberty and equality are at stake, raises important questions concerning the practical bearing of liberal utilitarianism and applied ethics. Granting, for instance, that clitoridectomy ought to be condemned, what consequences does this condemnation have in terms of law, morality and social policy? Should the practice be legally prohibited? If so, what should be done to those who violate the prohibition? What do people mean by saying that a given practice is morally unacceptable? Should immorality be suppressed? How should we respond to our own immorality?

Individuals learn answers to such questions through moral education and through their own experiences. Those who have been brought up in the spirit of liberal utilitarianism can, psychologically speaking, be expected to experience pangs of conscience if they wantonly inflict harm on others.[74] They can also be expected to feel indignation and disapproval towards similarly unacceptable actions performed by other individuals. Since the remorse and the resentment that these people feel are, by and large, likely to prevent future immorality, liberal utilitarian moral education is clearly justifiable. It should be remembered, however, that the direct application of individual ethics to law and social policy may create problems which cannot always be anticipated by moral education.

At the level of social interaction, the demands of morality become manifest through group pressures, public opinions, professional codes and social-policy regulations. To the extent that these extra-legal modes of social control are based on the principles of liberal utilitarianism, no clashes between individual morality and social ethics should occur. But when it comes to actions which must be justified or rejected by the methods of applied ethics, the situation is different. Suppose, for instance, that individuals are under an obligation to warn other individuals against threats of violence posed to them by malevolent third parties. Such duties cannot be legitimized by liberal utilitarian precepts, since the basic needs of the potential wrongdoers will presumably be frustrated in the process. But let us assume that the methods of cognitive deprogramming and rational reconstruction can be successfully employed to enforce the obligation. The important point here is that even if individuals, as individuals, can be shown to have the duty to warn each other, it does not necessarily follow that they have a similar duty as members of their communities and professional groups. It has been argued, for example, and probably not without justification, that medical professionals should in many cases be licensed to conceal the intentions and tendencies of their patients or clients. If this code of confidentiality is sanctioned in medical matters, then physicians and nurses possess conflicting duties as individuals on the one hand and as members of their profession on the other. The recently invented branch of study called 'professional ethics' mostly consists of attempts to reject, explain away, avoid or reconcile these conflicts, which in the minds of individuals take the form of cognitive dissonances.

When moral education and social pressure, professional codes and administrative decisions fail to prevent immoral actions, legal sanctions provide the public authorities with their last resort. The regulation of human actions by law is, however, a matter which should be considered carefully in each particular case. Individuals who knowingly and voluntarily break the law should, as a rule, be punished, but the utilitarian theory of punishment does not allow purely retributive forms of correction. The aims of the corrective system are, according to the classical Benthamite doctrine, the reformation and temporary disablement of the wrongdoer, the prevention of future crime by the deterrence of prospective wrongdoers, and the gratification of those who have been injured by the criminal act as well as others who feel that vengeance is required.[75]

As Bentham correctly pointed out in his discussion of the role of vengeance and gratification, however, 'no punishment ought to be allotted merely to this purpose, because (setting aside its effect in the way of control) no such pleasure is ever produced by punishment as can be equivalent to the pain'.[76] In liberal utilitarian terms, Bentham's remark can be taken to state that the derivative needs satisfied by revenge and retribution can never outweigh the more basic needs of the wrongdoer which are frustrated by the punishment.

Those legal sanctions which do not interfere with the basic need satisfaction of the wrongdoers can be justified simply by the principles of classical utilitarianism. Fines and short prison sentences, for instance, are morally acceptable if they can be expected to prevent, by deterring potential criminals, more need frustration than they are likely to produce. But more severe forms of punishment are a different matter. Since long prison sentences, dismemberment and death penalties almost always reduce substantially the well-being of the convicts, liberal utilitarianism does not in and by itself condone these modes of correction. There may be cases in which determinate imprisonment can be defended by the methods of applied ethics,[77] but indeterminate sentencing, retributive mutilation and capital punishment are practices which can hardly be regarded as generally acceptable. Whether or not they can be defended by using cognitive deprogramming and rational reconstruction is a question which must be examined separately in each particular class of cases.

The legal rights and duties of individuals can in the majority of cases be defined with relative precision by the methods of liberal utilitarianism and applied ethics. In real life, however, most existing laws have been implemented by non-utilitarian legislators, who have either ignored or deliberately rejected the requirements of liberty, equality and justice as understood by liberal utilitarians. The existence of potentially immoral laws both nationally and internationally raises difficult questions concerning the legitimacy of an array of political activities. These range from democratic political participation and passive resistance through civil disobedience, sabotage and *coups d'état* to revolution, assassination, warfare and terrorism. The moral status of all these practices varies, of course, according to the degree of violence involved in them. In addition, the historical background is often a relevant factor when the rights and wrongs of these activities are assessed.

All non-violent forms of political participation, resistance and civil disobedience can be justified by assessing and comparing the harms and benefits produced by them. Non-violent actions do not, by definition, frustrate the basic needs of individuals or groups, but they can be instrumental in both necessary and contingent need satisfaction. Violent political action, in its turn, does inflict serious harm on individuals and it can therefore be accepted only if two equally important conditions prevail. First, the need satisfaction which is expected to flow from the use of violence must be at least as great as the need-frustration caused by the action. This is the classical utilitarian part of the justification. Second, however, proponents of political violence must also be able to support their view by additional moral reasons which cannot be refuted by logic or intuitions. These additional reasons are implicitly required by the principles of liberal utilitarianism, and the methods by which they ought to be formulated and tested fall within the scope of applied ethics.

It is not easy to justify conclusively violent political activities like revolution, assassination, warfare and terrorism. Revolutions are disorderly occasions during which individuals who are by all accounts innocent may lose their lives and belongings. Assassins and terrorists commit, in ordinary legal terms, murders for political motives, and there are good grounds for morally condemning all kinds of murder. Wars, in their turn, are most often senseless orgies of destruction, which can be expected to benefit only a handful of politicians, bankers and military industrialists. But although explicit political violence is difficult to vindicate, the same applies to the implicit violence that often precedes resorts to the use of force. Unjust laws, corrupt administration, economic exploitation and structural injustice between nations and regions are all factors which should be thoroughly considered in moral calculations regarding the legitimacy of political violence. The threats these factors pose to liberty, equality and justice are as real as the threats presented against general well-being by revolutionary and warlike attitudes and actions. In their admirable attempt to reduce basic need frustration by banning explicit violence between individuals, those who decide about laws and regulations should not forget that unhappiness and ill-being can also be caused by the implicit violence which is built into the social and political structure we live in.

SUMMARY AND
CONCLUSIONS

In the preceding chapters I have shown how the once popular but now generally discredited British doctrine of utilitarianism, or universal altruism, can be reconstructed and defended against the most prominent critiques levelled at the classical and modern formulations of the view. I have also indicated how real-life moral questions concerning duties and rights can be answered by combining my reformed version of universal altruism, or liberal utilitarianism, and the techniques of conceptual and emotional critique that I have called the methods of applied ethics. It is now time to summarize the main arguments presented in the foregoing chapters, and to examine the conclusions that can be drawn from them.

In the subsection entitled 'The justification of liberal utilitarianism' in Chapter 3, my defence of needs-based universal altruism did not prove, nor did it strive to prove, the general validity of the doctrine. My main concern was to show how the principles of classical utilitarianism can be revised in order to meet some of the most important critiques directed against the Benthamite theory. The revision of the principles eventually led, however, to the conclusion that the reformed, intuitively acceptable maxims of liberal utilitarianism cannot solve all the moral problems that the earlier versions of the doctrine had claimed to untangle. This deficiency, which is not necessarily peculiar to liberal utilitarianism, prompted me to introduce, in Chapter 4, the methods of applied ethics. When these methods are added to the revised theory of universal altruism, the duties and rights of individuals and groups can be defined with relative accuracy in all problematical situations.

The need for applied philosophy in normative ethics only arises from the fact that general ethical theories, liberal utilitarianism among others, are unable to resolve certain moral dilemmas. It would therefore have been historically incorrect to present the techniques of applied ethics at the earlier stages of my argument. There would have been no need for these analytical tools in real-life ethical decision-making if one of the classical or modern versions of utilitarianism had proved to be unequivocally valid. As regards the analysis and assessment of ethical theories, however, I have employed the methods of cognitive deprogramming and rational reconstruction throughout the foregoing chapters. From the systematic viewpoint, the entire book can be seen as a defence of liberal utilitarianism by the methods of applied ethics. If this reading is assumed, the argument presented in the book can be summarized as follows.

In Chapters 1 and 2, I undertook to refute two persistent but mistaken notions concerning the history and nature of utilitarianism. The first common assumption among present-day moral philosophers is that Jeremy Bentham was the first to make the doctrine of the greatest happiness of the greatest number the central issue of morality. Due to this assumption, Bentham's theory has been widely regarded as the original and paradigmatic statement of the utilitarian doctrine, and the model for all legitimate attempts to create happiness-based theories of ethics. In Chapter 1 I showed, however, that Bentham's work had been preceded by a century-long tradition of universal altruism in Britain. Before Bentham published his *An Introduction to the Principles of Morals and Legislation* in 1789, the universal happiness of humankind had been the cornerstone of the psychological, theological and philosophical theories of Richard Cumberland (1672), George Berkeley (1712), Francis Hutcheson (1725), John Gay (1731), David Hume (1739–40), John Brown (1751), Abraham Tucker (1768) and William Paley (1785), and the ideas of universal altruism had also formed the basis of the radical views of William Godwin (1793). The theory of aggregative hedonism proposed by Bentham and restated by John Stuart Mill (1861), Henry Sidgwick (1874) and George Edward Moore (1903) cannot, in the light of these historical facts, be seen as the original, or the only natural, statement of the utilitarian doctrine.

The second assumption I set about to refute concerns the legitimacy of the twentieth-century versions of utilitarianism. The majority of contemporary utilitarians, including J.J.C. Smart

(1961), R.B. Brandt (1979) and R.M. Hare (1981), have believed that the doctrine of universal altruism can best be defended by employing the Benthamite ideas of aggregation and strict consequentialism. The findings of the second chapter do not, however, support this belief. On the contrary, it became quite evident that even if one of the modern forms of utilitarianism could evade the conceptual and theoretical problems of justification and axiology, it would not be possible to defend these views against the charges of injustice and intuitive illegitimacy. The sacrifice of the innocent in the name of the general good required by most utilitarian theories is emotionally unacceptable to the vast majority of enlightened individuals, and as the proponents of universal altruism have been unable to provide adequate reasons to ignore this emotional reaction, it must be concluded that their views are refutable by the methods of cognitive deprogramming.

In Chapters 3 and 4, I moved on to the rational reconstruction of utilitarian ethics. In Chapter 3, the principles of happiness, hedonism and impartiality were gradually revised until the modified axioms of liberal utilitarianism ceased to condone the undesired implications of the Benthamite doctrine. The reformed principles conserve the utilitarian spirit in stating that it is always right to promote basic need satisfaction in those situations where the basic needs of individuals or groups are not in conflict. The axioms also state that it is right to maximize non-basic need satisfaction when this does not lead to the frustration of more important needs. But the liberal utilitarian constraint to the direct aggregation of material good is that when the basic needs of individuals are in conflict, the theory does not assign clear-cut duties and rights to moral agents. This constraint is necessary, because unrestricted theories of utilitarianism do not survive the test of intuitive acceptability.

The liberal utilitarian constraint, however, leaves the theory open to another type of criticism. Theories of normative ethics are usually expected to give a complete account of the duties and rights of moral agents and moral patients, but liberal utilitarianism fails to accomplish this task. In Chapter 4, this failure was counteracted by the introduction of the methods of applied philosophical ethics. Moral dilemmas which result from conflicts between basic needs can, given that these methods are employed, be solved by appeals to conceptual coherence and emotional acceptability. The solutions reached by the techniques of cognitive deprogramming and rational reconstruction cannot always be seen as unequivocally valid. But these solutions can in most cases be regarded as well-founded hypotheses which can be interpersonally tested by further appeals to logic and shared emotions.

Although the precepts of liberal utilitarianism cannot be extended to all ethically problematical situations, the theory does provide individuals with certain duties and rights which are both interesting and important. First, according to the liberal utilitarian principles moral agents have a strict duty to promote the basic well-being of sentient beings in cases where the basic needs of other sentient beings are not put in jeopardy. The universal recognition of this duty would, I believe, change life on Earth considerably and beneficially. Second, moral agents (and arguably moral patients) have a claim-right to the satisfaction of their necessary needs, provided that this can be effected without frustrating the similar needs of others. The claim-right in question can be interpreted both as a negative right to non-interference and as a positive right to the assistance of other people. Third, as far as the doctrine of liberal utilitarianism is concerned, moral agents have a licence to protect their own basic well-being, as well as the autonomously chosen basic well-being of others, against the claims presented by third parties. This moral licence guarantees the immunity of individuals against the impending liberal and utilitarian tyrannies of democracy and the general good.

The rights and duties determined by the methods of applied ethics cannot be summarized in a concise form, primarily because different moral principles can and must be employed in different real-life situations. The role of applied moral philosophy is, however, well-defined. Since there are cases in which general ethical theories do not tell individuals what they ought to do or what they are permitted to do, decisions must be made by other methods. The techniques of applied philosophical ethics offer an alternative model of decision-making which is based on the use of reason and logic, but which also takes into account the shared emotions which for their part shape our moral existence.

FURTHER READING

The following selection of works can be recommended to those readers who want to know more about the history and theory of utilitarianism and applied ethics.

1 UTILITARIANISM AND THE BRITISH TRADITION

Albee, E. (1902) *A History of English Utilitarianism*, New York: Macmillan. An engaging account of the history of universal altruism. One of the main attractions of this book is that it was published a year before the appearance of G.E. Moore's *Principia Ethica*, and it is thus free of the influence of twentieth-century linguistic analysis.

Quinton, A. (1989) *Utilitarian Ethics* (first published 1973), second edition, London: Duckworth. A brief accessible account of the history of universalistic hedonism. Written in the early 1970s, Quinton's book is a delightful mixture of normative thinking and analytical philosophy.

2 THE DEVELOPMENT OF MODERN UTILITARIANISM

Glover, J. (ed.) (1990) *Utilitarianism and Its Critics*, New York: Macmillan. A useful collection of essays on the forms and limits of utilitarian thinking.

Griffin, J. (1982) 'Modern utilitarianism', *Review of International*

Philosophy 36: 331–75. A clear and concise account of utilitarianism in the 1970s.

3 FROM CLASSICAL TO LIBERAL UTILITARIANISM

Mill, J.S. (1859) *On Liberty*, many editions. The first attempt to give an account of the relationship and tension between the principles of liberty and utility.

Mill, J.S. (1861) *Utilitarianism*, many editions. A classical statement of the Benthamite view, with an inclination towards the qualitative versions of hedonism.

4 ETHICAL THEORY AND PRACTICE

Rachels, J. (ed.) (1979) *Moral Problems: A Collection of Philosophical Essays*, third edition, New York: Harper & Row, Publishers. A representative American collection of essays on contemporary moral issues.

Singer, P. (ed.) (1986) *Applied Ethics*, Oxford: Oxford University Press. A representative British collection of studies in applied ethics.

NOTES

1 UTILITARIANISM AND THE BRITISH TRADITION

1 J.S. Mill 1987c, 281.
2 J.S. Mill 1975, 15.
3 Dinwiddy 1989, 2. References are to Beccaria 1965 and Helvétius 1758.
4 Hutcheson 1725. Quoted from Raphael 1991a, 284 (italics deleted).
5 Aristippus of Cyrene, founder of the Cyrenaic school, professed hedonism as early as the beginning of the fifth century BC, a century before Epicurus.
6 Bentham 1982, 12.
7 J.S. Mill 1987c, 336.
8 Bentham 1983, 310; 1962, 211.
9 J.S. Mill 1987b, 231–2.
10 Godwin 1985.
11 Sidgwick 1922.
12 Cumberland 1672.
13 Shaftesbury 1711.
14 Hutcheson 1725.
15 Hume 1739–40; Hume 1751.
16 Locke 1977.
17 Hartley 1934.
18 J. Mill 1829.
19 Berkeley 1712.
20 Gay 1731.
21 Brown 1751.
22 Tucker 1805.
23 Paley 1785.
24 Stephen 1967.
25 Godwin 1985.
26 The following historical account is based, when not otherwise indicated, upon the works of Albee 1902, Copleston 1985, Quinton 1989 and P. Singer 1989.

27 Macchiavelli 1983.
28 More 1908.
29 Hobbes 1985; Macpherson 1985, 30-45.
30 The term 'state of nature' is not used in Hobbes 1985, but it is used in Hobbes 1949.
31 Since the contract will lack credibility unless it can be enforced, Hobbes further argued that all individual rights, liberties and powers ought to be transferred to an absolute sovereign, whose task it is to protect people from each other.
32 Cudworth 1731.
33 More 1667. Quoted in P. Singer 1989, 638.
34 Clarke 1706. Quoted from Raphael 1991a, 208. Cf. Matthew 7: 12.
35 Albee 1902, 26-7, 48.
36 Shaftesbury 1711 vol. I, 121. Quoted in Albee 1902, 56.
37 Albee 1902, 58-9.
38 Hutcheson 1725. Quoted from Raphael 1991a, 283-4.
39 Hutcheson (1725) writes: 'Our perception of pleasure is necessary, and nothing is advantageous or naturally good to us, but what is apt to raise pleasure mediately, or immediately.' Quoted from Raphael 1991a, 262.
40 Hutcheson seems to state the principle of impartiality, albeit indirectly, when he recommends that agents are allowed to (and should) regard their own interests as the interests of another person who is in every respect equal to the agent. See Raphael 1991a, 283.
41 Hutcheson 1725. Quoted from Raphael 1991a, 284.
42 Raphael 1991a, 285 ff.
43 Albee 1902, 100 ff.; Broad 1930, 84 ff.; Quinton 1989, 17 ff.
44 Hume 1739-40; Hume 1751.
45 Cf., however, Hume 1751, quoted from Raphael 1991b, 71 n.:
    It is needless to . . . ask, why we have humanity or a fellow-feeling with others. . . . We must stop somewhere in our examination of causes; and there are, in every science, some general principles, beyond which we cannot hope to find any principle more general. No man is absolutely indifferent to the happiness and misery of others. The first has a natural tendency to give pleasure; the second, pain. This every one may find in himself. It is not probable, that these principles can be resolved into principles more simple and universal, whatever attempts may have been made to that purpose.
46 Raphael 1991b, 71-2.
47 Raphael 1991b, 48-9.
48 Raphael 1991b, 74.
49 Raphael 1991b, 73-4; Albee 1902, 101.
50 Cf. Raphael 1991b, 19.
51 E.g., Quinton 1989, 21.
52 Locke 1977, 33 ff. (II.I).
53 Locke 1977, 45 ff. (II.II).
54 Locke 1977, 33, 103 (II.I, II.XX).

55 Locke 1977, 199 (II.XXXIII.5) (italics deleted, numerals in brackets added).
56 Locke 1977, 198, 201, 203 (II.XXXIII.4, 10, 17).
57 Neither of these two ways is directly connected with his ethics. Some theorists and historians have maintained that Locke was the founder of British utilitarianism, on the grounds that his ethical theory is based on the concept of happiness. This, however, is a false interpretation. It is true that Locke's axiology was hedonistic. He asserted that things are good if they tend to cause or increase our pleasure, or remove or decrease our pain; and that things are evil if they tend to cause or increase pain, or remove or decrease pleasure (1977, 103; II.XX). But he did not hold the view that the universal maximization of pleasure should guide human action. Rather, he argued that people should seek their own personal happiness, i.e., the greatest ratio of pleasure over pain in their lives (1977, 120–1; II.XXI.42, 51, 52). In order to achieve this, people must learn to avoid transitory pleasures and desires, and to direct their actions according to their long-term interests, by a mental operation that Locke called 'suspension'. Human freedom depends upon the use of this capacity. As for what is morally good or evil, Locke held the view that this is defined by law, religion and habit (1977, 173-5; II.XXVIII, 5–10).
58 Locke himself did not effectively employ this critique. See Albee 1902, 53–4.
59 Gay 1731; Albee 1902, 74 ff.
60 As described in the account of 'universal altruism' above, David Hume also employed this view.
61 Hartley 1934, part I, proposition x. Quoted from Albee 1902, 116.
62 Albee 1902, 118 ff.
63 It cannot be inferred with confidence from Hartley's text whether his theory was intended in the end to be descriptively or normatively altruistic.
64 Hartley also explains the position of this 'unintellectual' affection in his system. See Albee 1902, 120.
65 Albee 1902, 121–2.
66 Albee 1902, 123–5.
67 Albee 1902, 126–8.
68 If, indeed, Hartley had such beliefs to share.
69 Albee 1902, 135. In fact, Tucker anticipated the later theories concerning 'subconscious motives' by adding that in some cases one can observe that parts of the 'train' are physiological rather than (consciously) mental.
70 Albee 1902, 136–7.
71 The rationality of convictions also depends on the consistency and validity of the train of thought which leads to them. Tucker did not, however, explicitly refer to this requirement.
72 See the account of James Mill's theory below.
73 Albee 1902, 140.
74 Thomas 1985, 23–6.

75 James Mill's idea of 'wide representation', though, seems to have been universal adult male suffrage (where 'adult' stands for 'not less than forty').

76 Thomas 1985, 26.

77 Hume 1739-40; Hume 1751; Smith 1759.

78 Albee 1902, 64 ff.

79 Berkeley 1713.

80 By the use of the male personal pronoun here I am not stating that the divine being referred to by Berkeley is either male or a person. The usage simply reflects the fact that Berkeley – and his fellow theological utilitarians – always referred to their God as 'he'.

81 Albee 1902, 66–7.

82 Gay 1731. Quoted from Raphael 1991a, 411 (italics deleted).

83 It is interesting to note that Gay's only justification for the connection between morality and general happiness is linguistic. He argues that what we usually mean by words like 'virtue' and 'morality' is that aspect of our actions which concerns the well-being of others. This argument has been revived by certain twentieth-century utilitarians as well. Cf. Hare 1981; P. Singer 1979.

84 Gay 1731. Quoted from Raphael 1991a, 411 (italics deleted).

85 Cf. Locke 1977, 174–5 (II.XXVIII.6-10). Gay's list was later on assumed, almost without changes but certainly without any mention of the original source, by Jeremy Bentham. See Bentham 1982, 34–7.

86 Gay 1731. Quoted from Raphael 1991a, 412.

87 Gay was in fact the first to extend explicitly the requirement of normative universal altruism to omissions as well as to positive actions. See Raphael 1991a, 411.

88 Albee 1902, 84–5.

89 Gay and Brown, as well as their followers, can be counted both as theological utilitarians and as associationists. In their theories the greatest happiness principle acquired a double function. On the one hand, both moralists believed that general happiness is the decisive determinant of God's will. God's will, in its turn, is the immediate criterion of what people ought to do, regardless of the reasons behind the will. On the other hand, Gay and Brown also believed that the promotion of general happiness is what human beings naturally mean by virtue and virtuous action, quite apart from any theological considerations. How these two uses of the greatest happiness principle can be consolidated was left open by theological utilitarians. Berkeley, who wrote before Hume and Hartley, was the only theological utilitarian who did not have to face this potential difficulty. He started from the selfish motives of human beings, and proceeded through prudence and God's will to the principle of greatest happiness. As a result, the role of the principle is unambiguous in his theory.

90 Albee 1902, 153.

91 Although opinions may differ concerning the quality of Tucker's philosophy and theology, he did (try to) answer a very real question which had been left unanswered by Berkeley, Gay and Brown. If God is omnipotent and infinitely benevolent, why did he not create a

NOTES

world where everybody is continuously and immeasurably happy? Tucker's assumption that there is only a finite amount of happiness in the 'bank of the universe', while possibly questioning God's original omnipotence in creation, explains at least the fact that not all of us are permanently and incalculably happy.

92 Albee 1902, 168 ff.
93 Paley 1785. Quoted from Albee 1902, 170 (numerals in brackets added).
94 Paley 1785. Quoted from Copleston 1985, 197.
95 It should be noted, at this point, that the term 'utilitarian' was first used as a noun *c.* 1780, and as an adjective in 1802. The name 'utilitarianism' is even more recent: it was first used in 1827. My point is that linguistically Paley was one of the first utilitarians, although the doctrine was not labelled as such until nearly half a century later.
96 Stephen 1967; H. Häyry 1991, 87 ff.
97 Henry Sidgwick, for instance, seems to have shared the belief that the existence of God and afterlife would guarantee the rationality of altruism and benevolence. Sidgwick eventually concluded, contrary to Stephen's view, that lack of evidence prevents us from becoming wholehearted utilitarians. But before reaching this conclusion, Sidgwick had spent years – and founded the Society for Psychical Research – in an attempt to find some truth behind stories of miracles, ghosts, mediums, and the like (Sidgwick 1922; Schneewind 1977, 30–1).
98 See, e.g., Kramnick 1985.
99 I.e., principles 1–3 which were given at the beginning of this chapter.
100 Godwin 1985, 185.
101 Similarly, of course, an act or an omission which is well-intentioned is not virtuous if it does not in fact promote general happiness. But this remark is perfectly utilitarian, so it does not require further comment.
102 Cf. Godwin 1985, 153: 'Virtue demands the active employment of an ardent mind in the promotion of the general good.'
103 Godwin 1985, 75 (paragraphing ignored and italics deleted).
104 The tension between the two readings is visible throughout the book. See, e.g., Godwin 1985, 389 ff.
105 Godwin 1985, 76 (paragraphing ignored).
106 Schneewind 1977, 145 ff.
107 See Ryan 1987, 55.
108 J. S. Mill 1987c, 314 ff.
109 Schneewind 1977, 137 ff.
110 Godwin 1985, 170.
111 Godwin 1985, 170. Apparently Godwin did not mean to offend his readers. In the first edition of the *Enquiry Concerning Political Justice* his example was Fénelon's maid who is the decision-maker's mother or sister. The substitution of male relatives seems to be a concession to popular feeling.
112 Godwin 1985, 171.
113 Godwin 1985, 217 ff.

177

114 Godwin 1985, 228–9.
115 Godwin 1985, 635.
116 Godwin 1985, 635.
117 Godwin 1985, 641 ff., 668-9.
118 Godwin 1985, 663-5.
119 Godwin 1985, 393-5.
120 Godwin 1985, 395.
121 Godwin 1985, 396.
122 Helvétius 1758; Condorcet 1795.
123 Bentham 1982; Hart 1982, xlvii–xlviii.
124 Bentham could be defended here by referring to the Hobbesian idea that even the strongest have to sleep, and while they are asleep, they are vulnerable. But this point applies best only to the tyrants and despots Hobbes wanted to see dethroned. It is quite possible – in fact extremely probable – that there are less sinister individuals and groups in modern societies who cannot be touched by other people, law or no law, because they have been able to build impenetrable defence systems, physical or financial, around themselves. Some of these individuals and groups may need the stable structure of society – and thereby laws for others – to survive, but there may be those who do not. And even the (intelligible) theoretical possibility that some people do not need the support of laws shakes the foundation of Bentham's theory.
125 Bentham did not, indeed, profess anarchism – in fact, even the principles of democracy were alien to his early theory. Before James Mill converted him to democracy during the first decades of the nineteenth century, Bentham firmly thought that the best subject of the changes he had in mind would be an enlightened despot. To a certain degree, this idea was also prominent in later utilitarian reformism. James Mill and John Stuart Mill, too, seemed to think that benevolent philosophers should educate and govern the masses.

2 THE DEVELOPMENT OF MODERN UTILITARIANISM

1 Bentham 1982.
2 Bentham's idiosyncracies in ethics are well described by J.S. Mill in his early essay on Bentham (1987a).
3 J.S. Mill 1987b, 235.
4 Bentham 1982, 38–41; J.S. Mill 1987c, 278–83; Hartley 1934; Godwin 1985. The quantitative version of hedonism, which Bentham assumed, had also been defended by Abraham Tucker 1805 in the 1760s.
5 Huxley 1983.
6 During the twentieth century, this view has come to be called 'ideal utilitarianism'.
7 J.S. Mill 1975.
8 J.S. Mill 1975, 43. See also Bronaugh 1974a; 1974b.

9 This is a view which I have called, in an earlier paper, 'liberal utili-tarianism'. See Häyry and Häyry 1990. Liberal utilitarianism, as I see it, appears in many forms, some of which will be developed in more detail in the next chapter.
10 Stephen 1967. Cf. H. Häyry 1991, 87 ff.
11 See, e.g., Quinton 1989, ch. 4.
12 E.g., Quinton 1989, 37.
13 Grote 1870; Quinton 1989, 85.
14 Holbrook 1988, 83–90.
15 Bradley 1876, ch. 3; Quinton 1989, 93.
16 Albee 1902, 252.
17 Moore 1903.
18 See, e.g., MacIntyre 1967, ch. 18.
19 J.J.C. Smart 1987; Brandt 1979; Hare 1981.
20 For a taste of the diversity, see, e.g., Brock 1973; Griffin 1982.
21 The principle of happiness is nowadays often more generally called the principle of utility (cf. Bentham 1982, 11), and the principle of pleasure may be substituted by principles relating to welfare, prefer-ences or desires.
22 Baker 1987.
23 Nozick 1974.
24 See, e.g., P. Singer 1981; Scottia 1990.
25 Bentham 1982, 13–33; J.S. Mill 1987c, 307–14. Both Bentham and J.S. Mill started by noting that first principles are, by definition, beyond actual demonstrative proof. They cannot be deduced from, nor supported by, some more basic principles, since in that case these latter principles would be the genuine first principles, and the real question would concern their justification.
26 Bentham 1982, 13–16.
27 Bentham 1982, 17–33. The principle of asceticism states that one should always aim at the greatest general misery; the principle of sym-pathy and antipathy asserts that moral rightness and wrongness can be recognized by feelings of approbation and disapprobation, respec-tively.
28 J.S. Mill 1987c, 307–14.
29 In what follows, I shall omit the parenthetical additions which indi-cate that happiness is the only thing which can or ought to be desired. It should be remembered, however, that when I write 'happiness is desirable', the sentence means, in the Millian context, 'happiness and only happiness is desirable'. J.S. Mill in his presentation (1987c, 308) says that happiness is 'a good', but in the passages which immediately follow he proves that happiness is the only good.
30 E.g., Brock 1973, 268; Marshall 1973; Mackie 1977, 140–5; Quinton 1989, 58–71. Brock's article includes further references to the philosophical discussion concerning J.S. Mill's 'proof'.
31 Quinton 1989, 67.
32 It is faintly possible that this individualistic critique is fundamentally mistaken. J.S. Mill may have had in his mind the idea that 'general happiness' is a communitarian term, and that general happiness does

not simply equal the happiness of all individuals. J.S. Mill's romanticism could have led him into this direction. For hints which support this interpretation, see Albee 1902, 416.

33 Sidgwick 1922. My interpretation of Sidgwick's view is based on Schneewind 1977, 267–9, 291–7; Quinton 1989, 89–90. For a slightly different reading, see P. Singer 1974.
34 Sidgwick 1922, 215; Schneewind 1977, 267.
35 Sidgwick 1922, 379; Schneewind 1977, 295.
36 Sidgwick 1922, 381; Schneewind 1977, 296.
37 Sidgwick 1922, 381; Schneewind 1977, 296.
38 Sidgwick 1922, 382; Schneewind 1977, 296.
39 Sidgwick 1922, 382; Schneewind 1977, 296.
40 Cf. note 97 to Chapter 1 above.
41 It is not self-evident that Sidgwick meant his arguments to be understood in this way. His main aims in the *Methods of Ethics* may have been methodological rather than substantial. See P. Singer 1974.
42 Moore 1903; 1912.
43 E.g., in the *Encyclopedia of Philosophy* in 1967 J.J.C. Smart defined utilitarianism as 'the doctrine which states that the rightness or wrongness of actions is determined by the goodness and badness of their consequences' (p. 206).
44 Moore himself (1903) was the first to develop this possibility of objectivist ideal utilitarianism.
45 This is the spirit, e.g., in many of the contributions in Sen and Williams 1982.
46 See, e.g., J.J.C. Smart 1967, 207.
47 See, e.g., Hare 1981; 1982; Narveson 1967; P. Singer 1979; 1988.
48 I shall return to all the corresponding axiological positions in the following subsection.
49 Matthew 7: 12; Luke 6: 31.
50 Brandt 1979, 6–10.
51 Brandt 1979; Harsanyi 1982a; J.J.C. Smart 1987.
52 J.J.C. Smart 1987.
53 J.J.C. Smart 1987, 3.
54 J.J.C. Smart 1987, 5.
55 Rawls 1972.
56 Nozick 1974; Narveson 1988.
57 Cumberland 1672; Albee 1902, 32–3.
58 Hartley 1934; Albee 1902, 118 ff.
59 Tucker 1805; Albee 1902, 140.
60 Godwin 1985, 395.
61 Bentham 1982, 11.
62 Bentham 1982, 88–9.
63 Bentham 1982, 12.
64 Cf. Bentham 1982, 42–50; Bentham 1817.
65 Bentham stated, in conformity with Gay (see the subsection entitled 'Theological utilitarianism' in Chapter 1 above) but without any reference to him, that there are four sources from which pleasures and pains usually proceed: the physical, the political, the moral and the

religious. The origins of any given experience can, according to Bentham, be traced, but pleasures and pains which belong to one category 'differ not ultimately in kind from those which belong to any one of the other three: the only difference there is among them lies in the circumstances that accompany their production' (Bentham 1982, 36). Thus people who claim that virtue and vice are more fundamental to morality than pleasure and pain have simply confused the intrinsic quality of pleasures and pains related to virtue and vice (which is similar to all other experiences) with the external sources of these pleasures and pains (which are 'moral', and unique to these experiences).

66 Bentham 1982, 35. Cf. Gay 1731 – see Chapter 1, note 85 and the adjoining text, above.
67 Bentham 1982, 36.
68 Bentham 1982, 38.
69 Bentham 1982, 39.
70 Bentham 1982, 39 (italics deleted).
71 Bentham 1982, 39.
72 Bentham 1982, 40.
73 J.S. Mill 1987c, 278–9.
74 On the futility of the distinction between mental and bodily pleasures, see Ossowska 1961.
75 J.S. Mill 1987c, 279.
76 J.S. Mill 1987c, 279.
77 J.S. Mill 1987c, 280.
78 J.S. Mill 1987c, 281.
79 J.S. Mill 1987c, 281–2.
80 Patten 1980, 279–80.
81 Holbrook 1988, 83–90; Moore 1903, 78–80.
82 Sidgwick 1922; Bradley 1876; Moore 1903; J.J.C. Smart 1987; Narveson 1967; Brandt 1979. Cf. Holbrook 1988, 89 ff.
83 Moore 1903, 6 ff.
84 Moore 1903, 16.
85 Moore 1903, 16 ff.
86 Moore 1903, 146–7.
87 Moore 1903, 188.
88 For Moore's early influence, see Levy 1981.
89 For more modern versions of ideal utilitarianism, see Crisp 1988.
90 Godwin 1985, 393 ff.
91 Holbrook 1988, 55–67.
92 Holbrook 1988, 60, 63; Narveson 1967, 75–6.
93 E.g., Harsanyi 1982a, 54–6.
94 One of the main forums for these 'mathematical utilitarian' studies is the journal *Erkenntnis*.
95 These, in fact, were the uses for which J.S. Mill (1987c, 279–83, 307–8) introduced the concepts of 'desire' and 'preference'.
96 Those who put their faith in the 'exact' methods usually evade this problem simply by stipulating that anti-social preferences will be excluded from the moral calculus. But unless they explain how this

exclusion can be reconciled with the underlying ideas of preference utilitarianism, the stipulation remains an intuitionist *ad hoc* addition to the theory.

97 Brandt 1979, 11–12.
98 Brandt 1979, 11.
99 Hare 1982, 170 ff.
100 Hare 1981, 170–1.
101 Hare 1981, ch. 6.
102 One possible response to this problem would be to state that all desires and preferences are equal, but that the fulfilment of immoral wishes will be checked by the universal calculation of consequences at the next level of the theory. But critics have argued that it would then be morally right to condone sadistic acts and attitudes if the pleasure received by the sadist is greater than the pain suffered by the victims.
103 E.g., Braybrooke 1968 (on needs); P. Singer 1979 (on interests).
104 R.N. Smart 1958; Acton 1963; Watkins 1963; Walker 1974; Edwards 1986.
105 An example would be the offended party in a criminal case.
106 See, e.g., Ewing 1953; Urmson 1953; Stout 1954; J.J.C. Smart 1956; 1960; 1967; 1987; Rawls 1958; Strang 1960; Brandt 1963; Ezorsky 1965; Lyons 1965; Braybrooke 1967; Barnes 1971; Brock 1973; Emmons 1973; Feinberg 1973; Flathman 1966; Griffin 1982; Harsanyi 1982b; Kupperman 1982; Quinton 1989, 108–9.
107 See the subsection entitled 'Theological utilitarianism' in Chapter 1 above.
108 Godwin 1985, 170.
109 J.S. Mill 1987c, 278.
110 Godwin 1985. See also the subsection entitled 'Radical utilitarianism' in Chapter 1 above.
111 Bentham 1982.
112 J. Mill 1829; J.S. Mill 1987c.
113 Moore 1912, 97 (italics deleted).
114 Moore 1912, 34–5.
115 Quinton 1989, 108.
116 Harrod 1936, 147–8.
117 Harrod 1936, 149 (italics added).
118 Harrod 1936, 149.
119 E.g., Ewing 1953; Toulmin 1953; Nowell-Smith 1954; Stout 1954.
120 J.J.C. Smart 1956; 1960; 1967. Cf. Brandt 1959; Kaplan 1960.
121 J.J.C. Smart 1956, 346.
122 J.J.C. Smart 1956, 348–9.
123 Brandt 1963; Harsanyi 1982b.
124 I shall return to the questions of justice and fairness in the following subsection.
125 Lyons 1965.
126 E.g., Sumner 1979; Kupperman 1982. This idea may also be implicit in Brandt 1979.
127 Hare 1981; 1982.
128 Hare 1982, 31. Hare builds his theory in *Moral Thinking* on ideas

which have been developed in many earlier articles and books, and his two-level theory reaches its culmination in the book. But, probably due to avoidance of repetition, the descriptions of the different elements of the theory are often more precise in his previous work.

129 Hare 1982, 31.
130 Another way of expressing this is to say that actions are right if, and only if, relevantly similar actions in relevantly similar situations would produce the greatest utility. Cf. Lyons 1965.
131 People act according to their own intuitive principles, and can be trusted to act according to them, since deviation would cause remorse and mental distress. Due to this descriptive moral fact, individuals can in many cases predict the behaviour of others, and plan their own actions accordingly.
132 Griffin 1982, 352–3.
133 Rawls 1972; Dworkin 1981a; 1981b; Griffin 1986.
134 E.g., Rawls 1972; Nozick 1974; Donagan 1977; Dworkin 1977; Mackie 1977; Foot 1978.
135 On these critiques and on the utilitarian answers to them, see, e.g., Narveson 1967; Brandt 1968; Sprigge 1968; Rawls 1972; Brock 1973; Marshall 1973; Williams 1987 (first published 1973); J.J.C. Smart 1977; 1978; Primorac 1978; Berger 1978; 1979; Hart 1979; Narveson 1979; Griffin 1981; 1982; McDermott 1982; Foot 1985; Brink 1986; Mulholland 1986; Ball 1990.
136 Baker 1987.
137 Campbell 1988.
138 Nozick 1974.
139 If, however, libertarianism ought to be reconciled with a Millian type of 'liberal utilitarianism', which contains the deontological distinction between self-regarding and other-regarding actions, other solutions may become theoretically possible. See Häyry and Häyry 1990, 151–2.
140 See, e.g., Ball 1990.
141 See, e.g., Marshall 1973; Bronaugh 1974a; 1974b; Berger 1978; 1979.
142 See, e.g., Mendola 1990; Trapp 1990.
143 This is why, for instance, John Rawls (1972) and Ronald Dworkin (1977) are clearly non-utilitarian, even anti-utilitarian, theorists despite the fact that their implicit goals include the elimination of misery and the promotion of human happiness. Rawls, of course, started his career as a utilitarian.
144 Rawls 1972, 187.
145 Quoted by Rawls (1972, 188 n. 37) from the original version of J.J.C. Smart's *An Outline of a System of Utilitarian Ethics*.
146 J.J.C. Smart 1987, 67.
147 Rawls 1972, 22–4, 27, 181, 183, 187.
148 Parfit 1986.
149 Rand 1961; Nozick 1974; Narveson 1988.
150 Hart 1979; Griffin 1982.
151 The best defence of negative responsibility by far is Harris 1980.

152 Williams 1987, 116; Williams 1976, 209 (the citations are originally in the singular form, where only 'he' has projects and commitments). See also Griffin 1982, 358–9.
153 Williams 1987, 116–18.
154 Griffin 1982, 358–9.
155 One way to express one's resentment against calculations in morality is that employed by Noam Chomsky. He felt that 'by entering into the arena of argument and counter-argument, of technical feasibility and tactics, of foot-notes and citations, one has already lost one's humanity' (Chomsky 1969 – cited from Harris 1980, 112.) For a critique of this and related views, see Harris 1980, 111–13; Griffin 1982, 359–61.
156 E.g., McCloskey 1963; 1965; 1967; Primorac 1978. Cf. Sprigge 1965; J.J.C. Smart 1987; Ten 1987.
157 McCloskey 1963.
158 Primorac 1978.
159 Sprigge 1965; Hare 1981; J.J.C. Smart 1987, 69–72. Cf. Ten 1987, 13 ff.
160 McCloskey 1965; J.J.C. Smart 1987, 70.
161 Sprigge 1965.
162 Hare 1981; Ten 1987, 27 ff.
163 Griffin 1982, 352–3.

3 FROM CLASSICAL TO LIBERAL UTILITARIANISM

1 See the subsection entitled 'The greatest happiness principle defended' in Chapter 2 above.
2 Häyry and Häyry 1990.
3 This subsection is partly based on Häyry and Häyry 1990.
4 See especially the subsection entitled 'The greatest happiness principle defended' in Chapter 2 above.
5 *Webster's* 1983, s.v. *liberalism* (2c).
6 I have borrowed this example from Lagerspetz *et al.* 1985, 127–8.
7 The fact that only one of the listed practices, homosexuality, has actually been restricted by law exemplifies the arbitrariness of the real-life implications of this axiology.
8 For a critique of moralism, see H. Häyry 1991, 95 ff.
9 Given that there are more than two categories of needs (e.g., needs related to survival, health and pleasure), those needs which are more important should be referred to as 'more basic' and 'more primary', while those needs which are less important should be referred to as 'less basic' or 'more derivative' and 'less primary' or 'more secondary'. For the sake of linguistic economy, however, I have occasionally also used the terms 'basic' and 'primary' to refer to 'more basic' and 'more primary', and the terms 'derivative' and 'secondary' to refer to 'less basic' and 'less primary'.
10 For a fuller account of medical paternalism, see H. Häyry 1991.

11 J.S. Mill 1975, 15.
12 J.S. Mill 1975, 15.
13 J.S. Mill 1975, 18.
14 J.S. Mill 1975, 17.
15 J.S. Mill 1975, 17.
16 Moore 1912. The term 'action' here is intended to refer to acts, omissions, rules, policies and reforms alike.
17 For detailed studies of this case, see Foot 1978, 19 ff.; Thomson 1986, chs 6 and 7.
18 Thomson 1986, 94.
19 This point cropped up in a philosophical family discussion, and I owe it to Heta Häyry.
20 To verify these claims, see Thomson 1986, chs 6 and 7, and 'Afterword'.
21 This claim must, for practical reasons, remain essentially unsubstantiated here. It would take hundreds of pages to show how all moralists since Socrates have failed to present a theory which could solve all the problems that can confront human beings. Besides, even this historical account would not prove my thesis correct, since negative statements of this kind cannot be conclusively verified.
22 The account given in the following paragraphs is partly based on ideas presented by von Wright in his 1963, 1984, 1986 and undated manuscript 'Values and needs'. Since there has been an exchange of books and papers between Prof. von Wright and the Häyry family (including Heta and myself) for some years now, I have no way of telling to what extent his ideas have influenced the rough-and-ready axiology presented in the subsection entitled 'The derivation of liberal utilitarianism'. I presume that his influence has been considerable. On needs and desires, cf. Griffin 1986, 40 ff.
23 The following distinctions are in many important respects similar to those made by Michael Tooley (1972, 44–9), Peter Singer (1979, 82–3) and John Harris (1985, 16–17).
24 For an adverse, biocentric, view see Taylor 1986.
25 See, e.g., Bentham 1982; Glover 1977; P. Singer 1979; Tooley 1983; Harris 1985.
26 For an adverse view see Taylor 1986.
27 E.g. M. Häyry 1990, ch. 2; Häyry and Häyry 1993; Cavalieri and Singer 1993.
28 On the complex questions of who is reasonably autonomous and which decisions are sufficiently voluntary, see H. Häyry 1991.
29 For a more detailed analysis of these circumstances which may justify paternalistic interventions, see H. Häyry 1991, 68 ff.
30 Roses, for instance, can hardly be said to suffer from their inability to feel pleasure or pain, and it would be absurd to state that oysters suffer from not being fully aware of themselves.
31 On the intrinsic value of autonomy as an ingredient of happiness, see H. Häyry 1991, 47–9.
32 By 'negative respect' I mean a policy of non-interference with the already existent autonomy of autonomous persons. By 'positive

enhancement' I mean support which enables non-autonomous persons to become autonomous.

33 See the subsections entitled 'Acts or rules?' and 'Justice, integrity and rights' in Chapter 2 above.

34 See the subsection entitled 'Theological utilitarianism' in Chapter 1 above.

35 There can, of course, be circumstances which would change the situation. If, for example, Alice would for some obscure reason die without ice cream, the choice would have to be made between her basic needs and the basic needs of the other person. Under these circumstances it would no longer be uncle Edward's obvious duty to rescue the other person.

36 Gay 1731. Quoted from Raphael 1991a, 411 (italics deleted).

37 J.S. Mill 1975, 16–17.

38 Glover 1977; P. Singer 1979; Harris 1980. The last-mentioned contribution, John Harris's *Violence and Responsibility* could easily be nominated as the Bible of the doctrine of negative responsibility.

39 Harris 1980, 145.

40 J.S. Mill 1975, 17.

41 Harris 1980, 151.

42 Sidgwick 1922; Moore 1903; J.J.C. Smart 1987; Lyons 1965; Bergström 1966; Rawls 1972; Quinton 1989: Temkin 1978.

43 J.J.C. Smart 1987, 49.

44 M. Singer 1977; 1983; Gruzalski 1981.

45 Russell, 'The elements of ethics', in *Philosophical Essays* – quoted in Gruzalski 1981, 163.

46 M. Singer 1977; 1983.

47 Gruzalski 1981, 166–7.

48 In theory, of course, the question concerns the optimum amount of human and other sentient beings everywhere in the universe. But since we do not have any evidence concerning sentient life-forms in other solar systems, and since our own capacity even to inhabit other planets in our own solar system does not seem particularly promising for the time being, the restriction to Earth's population can, I trust, be considered reasonably realistic.

49 The example is derived from P. Singer 1979, 86–7.

50 See, e.g., Anglin 1977, 746, 748.

51 P. Singer 1979, 87. Cf. Narveson 1990.

52 By 'liberal' I refer here to classical liberalism and modern libertarianism, not to the social democratic liberalism which I myself prefer and which recognizes the values of equality and justice within the family.

53 The example is derived from P. Singer 1979, 87.

54 Peter Singer presents the following indirect argument which is intended to condemn the creation of unhappy children while defending the prior existence thesis. Since the children produced by the other couple would be miserable and die in a couple of years, it would be the parents' duty to consider active euthanasia for the infant as soon as it exists. But this would be psychologically and socially rougher than early abortion, or the use of contraceptives. Therefore, a decision not

to have the suffering babies would benefit all those concerned. As Singer himself notes, however, this argument is not very impressive. See P. Singer 1979, 87–8.

55 See, e.g., Sikora 1975; Anglin 1977; Hurka 1982a; 1982b; Hudson 1987.

56 There is no need to become existent.

57 Popper 1966, 304 n. 62.

58 On negative utilitarianism, see, e.g., R.N. Smart 1958; Acton 1963; Watkins 1963; Walker 1974; Edwards 1986.

59 Harris 1980; Quinton 1989, x–xii, 47, 69. Quinton comes close to confusing in his readers' minds negative utilitarianism, i.e., the view that only the elimination of suffering falls within the scope of morality, and another view, namely the view that the only duty we have is to abstain from causing suffering to others by our positive actions. Harris, who opposes the latter view fervently, seems to hold the original negative utilitarian view that the prevention of suffering is more important to morality than the promotion of happiness.

60 See the end of the subsection entitled 'The varieties of utility' in Chapter 2 above.

4 ETHICAL THEORY AND PRACTICE

1 The universal human right to life is a case in point. Suppose that a sleepwalker poses a threat to another person's life, and the threat can only be removed by killing the sleepwalker. Does the other person have a right to self-defence, and if so, what about the sleepwalker's right to life? The theory of natural rights does not without auxiliary considerations provide answers to questions like these.

2 The Kantian maxim sanctions, for instance, the principles of universal truth-telling and universal promise-keeping. But what is a person supposed to do when another person asks her to disclose a secret she has promised not to disclose to anybody? The categorical imperative does not provide the answer to this question.

3 Holy scriptures typically postulate several commandments and prohibitions which ought to be obeyed. But when these commandments and prohibitions conflict with one another, the resolution must be sought from interpretations which are not directly based on the original scriptures.

4 See the subsection entitled 'Justice, integrity and rights' in Chapter 2 and the subsection entitled 'The derivation of liberal utilitarianism' in Chapter 3.

5 E.g., Williams 1985.

6 Williams 1985, 104.

7 Furthermore, as Max Charlesworth (1989, 13) has pointed out, the acceptance of oppressive and unjust folkways would be against the current Western folkway which has prevailed for two millennia.

8 The labels 'practical ethics' and 'applied philosophy' have also been

used, but it seems that 'applied ethics' is gradually becoming the most popular choice.

9 The Sophists of the fifth century BC were perhaps the first Western thinkers to address systematically practical moral problems, although the great thinkers of the Orient and the Middle East at least had preceded the Sophists by centuries.

10 Rachels 1979 and P. Singer 1986 are representative collections of applied ethical studies. A comparison of the selections used in these works elucidates the subtle differences between the American (Rachels) and Anglo-Australian (Singer) approaches to the discipline.

11 E.g., Armour 1983; Rescher 1983; Nielsen 1984; Young 1986.

12 This point has been argued for and against in the case of bioethics in Altman 1983, Caplan 1983, M. Häyry 1990; and Wikler 1991.

13 This formulation is part of the principle called 'The essence of liberal utilitarianism', stated in Chapter 3 above. I am employing this shortened principle purely for the sake of convenience: it would be cumbersome to repeat all the seven basic principles of liberal utilitarianism every time I want to refer to the doctrine. It is to be understood, however, that the concise formula is a shorthand expression for the entire theory of liberal utilitarianism.

14 For authoritative and detailed statements of this view, see Moore 1903 and 1912.

15 By 'moral agents' I mean autonomous persons who are aware of their own capacity to make ethical judgements and moral choices.

16 Urmson 1969, 63.

17 Urmson 1969, 63.

18 Quinton 1989, xi.

19 Moore 1912, 15.

20 Quinton 1989, x-xi.

21 Urmson 1969, 72–3.

22 Quinton would not accept this conclusion, as he believes that there is a morally significant difference between causing suffering and failing to relieve suffering (1989, xi). But the ethical legitimacy of this distinction has been questioned in the subsection entitled 'Acts, rules, consequences and responsibilities' in Chapter 3 above.

23 Urmson 1969, 72.

24 Urmson 1969, 70.

25 J.S. Mill 1987c, 322.

26 J.S. Mill 1987c, 321.

27 Urmson 1969, 72.

28 The conditions on which paternalistic interventions are legitimate are well explained in H. Häyry 1991, ch. 3.

29 The duty in question will, of course, be a prima facie duty, since the needs of others can in many cases override the agent's derivative or basic needs.

30 On the relationship between rights, duties and obligations see, e.g., White 1984, ch. 5.

31 The nature and scope of legal rights has been analysed, for instance, in Corbin 1919; Hohfeld 1923; Feinberg 1973; Waldron 1984.

32 Hohfeld 1923; Feinberg 1973, 56; Waldron 1984, 6.
33 White 1984, ch. 11. White extends his criticism to attempts to identify privileges with other types of right as well.
34 *Webster's* 1983, s.v. *liberty.*
35 Feinberg 1973, 59–60.
36 On Good Samaritan laws, see Feinberg 1984, 126 ff. and 256 n. 2.
37 Feinberg 1973, 59.
38 Thomson 1986, 94. See the subsection entitled 'The justification of
liberal utilitarianism' above.
39 This subsection is partly based on the introduction to my *Critical
Studies in Philosophical Medical Ethics* (M. Häyry 1990).
40 De Beauvoir 1963a. The ideas of this article have been analysed in
Häyry and Häyry 1987.
41 De Beauvoir 1963b, 100–1.
42 De Beauvoir 1981; 1979.
43 Other French post-war philosophers who studied and wrote about
practical moral issues included Albert Camus, whose interest ranged
from suicide to capital punishment, assassination and terrorism (see
Glover 1977, 316–17). Simone de Beauvoir later made a contribution
to the euthanasia discussion with her novel *A Very Easy Death* (1964).
44 Wasserstrom 1979, 7.
45 See, e.g., the articles reprinted in Rachels 1979.
46 Hare 1972; 1975.
47 P. Singer 1973a; 1972; 1973b; 1975.
48 Harris 1974; 1975.
49 The third edition of James Rachels's influential American collection
Moral Problems (1979) contains three articles by Singer, while nobody
else is represented by more than two contributions.
50 Richard Brandt was the exception who confirmed the rule.
51 Chapters 2 and 3 of Foot 1978. With her article 'Moral arguments'
(Chapter 7 of the book) Foot had in 1958 been among the first to
argue against ethical emotivism (see, e.g., MacIntyre 1967, 262 ff.).
52 A major attempt toward an ethical theory based on virtues has, though,
been made by Alistair MacIntyre in his *After Virtue* (1981).
53 E.g., Chadwick 1989.
54 Rawls gives his theory of justice a 'Kantian interpretation' in 1972,
251–7.
55 'Practical philosophy' is the term used for the study of moral, social,
legal and political philosophy in the Scandinavian countries.
56 The dissolution of American applied ethics into pure philosophy on
the one hand and casuistry on the other is well evidenced in the vol-
umes of *Philosophy & Public Affairs.*
57 All quotations in this paragraph are from Caplan 1983, 313.
58 See, e.g., von Wright 1971, 11 ff.
59 Caplan 1983, 317–18.
60 Glover 1977, 22–35. John Harris (1980; 1985) and Peter Singer
(1975; 1979) employ this more scientific view, but they do not formulate it explicitly.
61 M. Häyry 1990, 11.

62 This norm can be derived, on certain factual conditions, from the principles of liberal utilitarianism.
63 When distinctly *moral* issues are discussed, the terms most commonly in use are presumably 'right' (as an adjective), 'wrong', 'right' (as a noun) and 'duty'. I have explained in the first and second subsections of this chapter how these concepts are related to needs and their satisfaction. The concepts employed in virtue ethics cannot be completely explained by liberal utilitarian terms, as they contain factual psychological elements. Individuals who have *courage*, for instance, probably perform duties and supererogatory actions even under dangerous circumstances which would discourage the majority of agents.
64 See the subsection entitled 'Universal altruism' in Chapter 1 above.
65 See the subsection entitled 'Theological utilitarianism' in Chapter 1 above.
66 See the subsection entitled 'Radical utilitarianism' in Chapter 1 above.
67 J.S. Mill 1987c, 336.
68 Sidgwick 1922, 379.
69 The idea of a 'utility monster' in whose maw we all ought to be sacrificed was introduced by Nozick 1974, 41.
70 Rawls 1972, 66 ff.; Baker 1987, 93 ff.; Campbell 1988, 128–9.
71 See, e.g., H. Häyry 1991, 46–9.
72 See the subsections entitled 'The axiology of liberal utilitarianism' and 'The principles of liberal utilitarianism' in Chapter 3 above.
73 On the definitions and relationships of paternalism, prudentialism and moralism, see H. Häyry 1991, esp. 76–7.
74 This does not, of course, necessarily imply that the term 'liberal utilitarianism' has ever been mentioned to these individuals.
75 Bentham 1982, 158–9 n. a.
76 Bentham 1982, 159 n. a.
77 I have sketched some lines of argument to this effect in M. Häyry 1992.

BIBLIOGRAPHY

Acton, H.B. (1963) 'Negative utilitarianism', *Aristotelian Society* Supp. 37: 83–94.

Albee, E. (1902) *A History of English Utilitarianism*, New York: Macmillan.

Altman, A. (1983) 'Pragmatism and applied ethics', *American Philosophical Quarterly* 20: 227–35.

Anglin, B. (1977) 'The repugnant conclusion', *Canadian Journal of Philosophy* 7: 745–54.

Armour, L. (1983) 'Should we have pure philosophy?', *Philosophy in Context* 13: 17–30.

Baker, J. (1987) *Arguing for Equality*, London and New York: Verso.

Ball, S.W. (1990) 'Uncertainty in moral theory: an epistemic defence of rule-utilitarian liberties', *Theory and Decision* 29: 133–60.

Barnes, G.W. (1971) 'Utilitarianisms', *Ethics* 82: 56–64.

Beccaria, C. (1965) *Dei delitti e delle pene* (first published 1764), Turin.

Bentham, J. (1817) *A Table of the Springs of Action*, London: R. Hunter.

—— (1962) *The Works of Jeremy Bentham*, vol. III, ed. by J. Bowring, New York: Russell.

—— (1982) *An Introduction to the Principles of Morals and Legislation* (first published 1789), ed. by J.H. Burns and H.L.A. Hart. Reprinted with new introduction, London and New York: Methuen.

—— (1983) *Deontology together with a Table of the Springs of Action and Article on Utilitarianism*, ed. by A. Goldworth, Oxford: Clarendon Press.

Berger, F.R. (1978) 'Mill's concept of happiness', *Interpretation* 7: 95–117.

—— (1979) 'John Stuart Mill on justice and fairness', *Canadian Journal of Philosophy* Supp. 5: 115–36.

Bergström, L. (1966) *The Alternatives and Consequences of Actions*, Stockholm: Almqvist and Wiksell.

Berkeley, G. (1712) *Passive Obedience*. Reprinted in *The Works of George Berkeley*, vol. 3, second edition 1901, ed. by A.C. Fraser, Oxford.

—— (1713) *Three Dialogues between Hylas and Philonous*. Reprinted in

191

The Works of George Berkeley, Bishop of Cloyne, vol. 2, critical edition 1948, ed. by A.A. Luce and T. Jessop, London.

Bradley, F.H. (1876) *Ethical Studies*, Oxford: Oxford University Press.

Brandt, R.B. (1959) *Ethical Theory*, Englewood Cliffs, New Jersey: Prentice-Hall.

—— (1963) 'Towards a credible form of utilitarianism', in H.-N. Castañeda and G. Nakhnikian (eds), *Morality and the Language of Conduct*, Detroit: Wayne University Press.

—— (1968) 'Review of "Morality and Utility" by Jan Narveson', *Journal of Philosophy* 65: 544–50.

—— (1979) *A Theory of the Good and the Right*, Oxford: Clarendon Press.

Braybrooke, D. (1967) 'The choice between utilitarianisms', *American Philosophical Quarterly* 4: 28–38.

—— (1968) 'Let needs diminish that preferences may prosper', in N. Rescher (ed.), *Studies in Moral Philosophy*, Oxford: Oxford University Press.

Brink, D.O. (1986) 'Utilitarian morality and the personal point of view', *Journal of Philosophy* 83: 417–38.

Broad, C.D. (1930) *Five Types of Ethical Theory*, London: Routledge & Kegan Paul.

Brock, D.W. (1973) 'Recent work on utilitarianism', *American Philosophical Quarterly* 10: 241–76.

Bronaugh, R. (1974a) 'The quality in pleasures', *Philosophy* 49: 320–2.

—— (1974b) 'The quality of utility: an understanding of Mill', *Canadian Journal of Philosophy* 4: 317–25.

Brown, J. (1751) *Essays on the Characteristics*, London.

Campbell, T. (1988) *Justice*, London: Macmillan.

Caplan, A.L. (1983) 'Can applied ethics be effective in health care and should it strive to be?', *Ethics* 93: 311–19.

Cavalieri, P. and Singer, P. (1993) *The Great Ape Project: Equality Beyond Humanity*, London: Fourth Estate.

Chadwick, R. (1989) 'The market for bodily parts: Kant and duties to oneself', *Journal of Applied Philosophy* 6: 129–39.

Charlesworth, M. (1989) 'Bioethics and the limits of philosophy', *Bioethics News* 9 (1): 9–25.

Chomsky, N. (1969) *American Power and the New Mandarins*, Harmondsworth, Middlesex: Penguin Books.

Clarke, S. (1706) *A Discourse Concerning the Unchangeable Obligations of Natural Religion, and the Truth and Certainty of the Christian Revelation*. Partly reprinted in D.D. Raphael (ed.) (1991) *British Moralists 1650–1800 I. Hobbes–Gay* (first published 1969), Indianapolis and Cambridge: Hackett Publishing Company.

Condorcet, Marie-Jean-Antoine-Nicolas de Caritat, Marquis de (1795) *Esquisse d'un tableau historique des progrès de l'esprit humain*. Reprinted in *Oeuvres*, 1847–9, ed. by A. Condorcet O'Connor and M.F. Arago, Paris.

Cooper, Anthony Ashley, *see* Shaftesbury.

Copleston, F. (1985) *A History of Philosophy*, vols IV-VI (first published in 1960, 1959 and 1960), New York: Image Book/Doubleday.

Corbin, A.L. (1919) 'Legal analysis and terminology', *Yale Law Journal* 29: 163–73.

Crisp, R. (1988) 'Ideal utilitarianism: theory and practice', unpublished doctoral thesis, St Anne's College, Oxford University.

Cudworth, R. (1731) *A Treatise Concerning Eternal and Immutable Morality.* Partly reprinted in D.D. Raphael (ed.) (1991) *British Moralists 1650–1800 I. Hobbes–Gay* (first published 1969), Indianapolis and Cambridge: Hackett Publishing Company.

Cumberland, R. (1672) *De Legibus Naturae.* Trans. by D.D. Raphael and partly reprinted in D.D. Raphael (ed.) (1991) *British Moralists 1650–1800 I. Hobbes–Gay* (first published 1969), Indianapolis and Cambridge: Hackett Publishing Company.

de Beauvoir, S. (1963a) *L'existentialisme et la sagesse des nations*, fifth edition, Paris: Gallimard.

—— (1963b) *La force des choses I*, Paris: Gallimard.

—— (1964) *Une mort très douce*, Paris: Gallimard.

—— (1979) *Le deuxième sexe 2* (first published 1949), Paris: Gallimard.

—— (1981) *Le deuxième sexe 1* (first published 1949), Paris: Gallimard.

Dinwiddy, J. (1989) *Bentham*, Oxford and New York: Oxford University Press.

Donagan, A. (1977) *The Theory of Morality*, Chicago and London: University of Chicago Press.

Dworkin, R. (1977) *Taking Rights Seriously*, London: Duckworth.

—— (1981a) 'What is equality? Part 1: Equality of welfare', *Philosophy & Public Affairs* 10: 185–246.

—— (1981b) 'What is equality? Part 2: Equality of resources', *Philosophy & Public Affairs* 10: 283–345.

Edwards, R.B. (1986) 'The principle of utility and Mill's minimizing utilitarianism', *Journal of Value Inquiry* 20: 125–36.

Emmons, D.C. (1973) 'Act vs. rule-utilitarianism', *Mind* 82: 226–33.

Ewing, A.C. (1953) 'Suppose everybody acted like me', *Philosophy* 28: 16–29.

Ezorsky, G. (1965) 'Utilitarianism and rules', *Australasian Journal of Philosophy* 43: 225–9.

Feinberg, J. (1967) 'The forms and limits of utilitarianism', *Philosophical Review* 76: 368–81.

—— (1973) *Social Philosophy*, Englewood Cliffs, New Jersey: Prentice-Hall.

—— (1984) *Harm to Others*, New York and Oxford: Oxford University Press.

Flathman, R. (1966) 'Forms and limits of utilitarianism', *Ethics* 76: 309–17.

Foot, P. (1978) *Virtues and Vices and Other Essays in Moral Philosophy*, Berkeley and Los Angeles: University of California Press.

—— (1985) 'Utilitarianism and the virtues', *Mind* 94: 196–209.

Gay, J. (1731) 'Preliminary dissertation concerning the fundamental principle of virtue or morality', in W. King, *Essay on the Origin of Evil.* Partly reprinted in D.D. Raphael (ed.) (1991) *British Moralists 1650–1800 I.*

Hobbes–Gay (first published 1969), Indianapolis and Cambridge: Hackett Publishing Company.

Geach, P. (1977) *The Virtues*, Cambridge: Cambridge University Press.

Glover, J. (1977) *Causing Death and Saving Lives*, Harmondsworth, Middlesex: Penguin Books.

Godwin, W. (1985) *Enquiry Concerning Political Justice and its Influence on Modern Morals and Happiness* (first published 1793, third edition first published 1798), ed. by I. Kramnick, Harmondsworth, Middlesex: Penguin Books.

Griffin, J. (1981) 'Equality: on Sen's weak equity axiom', *Mind* 90: 280–6.

—— (1982) 'Modern utilitarianism', *Review of International Philosophy* 36: 331–75.

—— (1986) *Well-Being*, Oxford: Clarendon Press.

Grote, J. (1870) *Examination of the Utilitarian Philosophy*, ed. by J.B. Mayor, Cambridge: Deighton Bell & Co.

Gruzalski, B. (1981) 'Foreseeable consequence utilitarianism', *Australasian Journal of Philosophy* 59: 163–76.

Hare, R.M. (1972) 'Rules of war and moral reasoning', *Philosophy & Public Affairs* 1: 166–81.

Hare, R.M. (1975) 'Abortion and the Golden Rule', *Philosophy & Public Affairs* 4: 201–22.

—— (1981) *Moral Thinking: Its Levels, Method and Point*, Oxford: Clarendon Press.

—— (1982) 'Ethical theory and utilitarianism', in A. Sen and B. Williams (eds), *Utilitarianism and Beyond*, Cambridge: Cambridge University Press.

Harris, J. (1974) 'The Marxist conception of violence', *Philosophy & Public Affairs* 3: 192–220.

—— (1975) 'The survival lottery' *Philosophy* 50: 81–7.

—— (1980) *Violence and Responsibility*, London, Boston and Henley: Routledge & Kegan Paul.

—— (1985) *The Value of Life*, London, Boston, Melbourne and Henley: Routledge & Kegan Paul.

Harrod, R.F. (1936) 'Utilitarianism revised', *Mind* 45: 137–56.

Harsanyi, J.C. (1982a) 'Morality and the theory of rational behaviour', in A. Sen and B. Williams (eds), *Utilitarianism and Beyond*, Cambridge: Cambridge University Press.

—— (1982b) 'Some epistemological advantages of a rule-utilitarian position in ethics', *Midwest Studies in Philosophy* 7: 389–402.

Hart, H.L.A. (1979) 'Between utility and rights', *Columbia Law Review* 79: 828–46.

—— (1982) 'Introduction', in J. Bentham, *An Introduction to the Principles of Morals and Legislation* (first published 1789), ed. by J.H. Burns and H.L.A. Hart, London and New York: Methuen.

Hartley, D. (1934) *Observations on Man, his Frame, his Duty, and his Expectations* (first published 1749), third edition, ed. by J.B. Priestley, London.

Häyry, H. (1991) *The Limits of Medical Paternalism*, London and New York: Routledge.

—— and Häyry, M. (1987) 'Revenge and punishment, common morality and the law', in Å. Frändberg and M. Van Hoecke (eds), *The Structure of Law*, Uppsala: Iustus Förlag.

—— and Häyry, M. (1990) 'Liberty, equality, utility – Classical to liberal utilitarianism', in T.D. Campbell (ed.), *Law and Enlightenment in Britain*, Aberdeen: Aberdeen University Press.

—— and Häyry, M. (1993) 'Who's like us?', in P. Cavalieri and P. Singer (eds), *The Great Ape Project: Equality Beyond Humanity*, London: Fourth Estate.

Häyry, M. (1990) *Critical Studies in Philosophical Medical Ethics*, Helsinki: Department of Philosophy, University of Helsinki.

—— (1992) 'A defence of the utilitarian theory of punishment', in W. Gragg (ed.), *Retributivism and Its Critics*, Stuttgart: Franz Steiner Verlag.

Helvétius, C.-A. (1758) *De l'esprit*. Reprinted in *Oeuvres*, 1792, Paris.

Hobbes, T. (1949) *De Cive or the Citizen*, ed. by S.P. Lamprecht, New York.

—— (1985) *Leviathan* (first published 1651), ed. by C.B. Macpherson, Harmondsworth, Middlesex: Penguin Books.

Hohfeld, W. (1923) *Fundamental Legal Conceptions*, New Haven: Yale University Press.

Holbrook, D. (1988) *Qualitative Utilitarianism*, Lanham, New York and London: University Press of America.

Hudson, J.L. (1987) 'The diminishing marginal value of happy people', *Philosophical Studies* 51: 123–37.

Hume, D. (1739–40) *A Treatise of Human Nature*. Partly reprinted in D.D. Raphael (ed.) (1991) *British Moralists 1650–1800 II. Hume–Bentham* (first published 1969), Indianapolis and Cambridge: Hackett Publishing Company.

—— (1751) *An Enquiry Concerning the Principles of Morals*. Partly reprinted in D.D. Raphael (ed.) (1991) *British Moralists 1650–1800 II. Hume–Bentham* (first published 1969), Indianapolis and Cambridge: Hackett Publishing Company.

Hurka, T. (1982a) 'Average utilitarianisms', *Analysis* 42: 65–9.

—— (1982b) 'More average utilitarianisms', *Analysis* 42: 115–19.

Hutcheson, F. (1725) *An Inquiry into the Original of our Ideas of Beauty and Virtue*, Treatise II. Partly reprinted in D.D. Raphael (ed.) (1991) *British Moralists 1650–1800 I. Hobbes–Gay* (first published 1969), Indianapolis and Cambridge: Hackett Publishing Company.

Huxley, A. (1983) *Brave New World* (first published 1932), ed. by M.S. Ellis, Harlow, Essex: Longman.

Kaplan, M.A. (1960) 'Some problems of the extreme utilitarian position', *Ethics* 70: 228–32.

Kramnick, I. (1985) 'Introduction', in W. Godwin, *Enquiry Concerning Political Justice and its Influence on Modern Morals and Happiness* (first published 1793, third edition first published 1798), ed. by I. Kramnick, Harmondsworth, Middlesex: Penguin Books.

Kupperman, J.J. (1982) 'Utilitarianism today', *Review of International Philosophy* 36: 318–30.

Lagerspetz, E., Talja, J. and Vihjanen, S. (1985) *Problems and Paradoxes of*

Philosophy (in Finnish), Turku: Department of Philosophy and Statistics, University of Turku.

Levy, P. (1981) *Moore: G.E. Moore and the Cambridge Apostles*, Oxford: Oxford University Press.

Locke, J. (1924) *Two Treatises of Government* (first published 1690). Reprinted 1988, Everyman's Library, London: J.M. Dent & Sons Ltd.

—— (1977) *An Essay Concerning Human Understanding* (first published 1690), ed. and abridged by J.W. Yolton, London: J.M. Dent & Sons Ltd.

Lyons, D. (1965) *Forms and Limits of Utilitarianism*, Oxford: Clarendon Press.

Macchiavelli, N. (1983) *The Discourses*, ed. by B. Crick, using the translation of L.J. Walker, with revisions by B. Richardson, Harmondsworth, Middlesex: Penguin Books.

McCloskey, H.J. (1963) 'A note on utilitarian punishment', *Mind* 72: 599.

—— (1965) 'A non-utilitarian approach to punishment', *Inquiry* 8: 249–63.

—— (1967) 'Utilitarian and retributive punishment', *Journal of Philosophy* 64: 91–110.

McDermott, M. (1982) 'Utility and distribution', *Mind* 91: 572–8.

MacIntyre, A. (1967) *A Short History of Ethics*, London: Routledge & Kegan Paul.

—— (1981) *After Virtue*, Notre Dame, Indiana: Indiana University Press.

Mackie, J.L. (1977) *Ethics: Inventing Right and Wrong*, Harmondsworth, Middlesex: Penguin Books.

Macpherson, C.B. (1985) 'Introduction', in T. Hobbes, *Leviathan* (first published 1651), ed. by C.B. Macpherson, Harmondsworth, Middlesex: Penguin Books.

Marshall, J. (1973) 'The proof of utility and equity in Mill's Utilitarianism', *Canadian Journal of Philosophy* 3: 13–26.

Mendola, J. (1990) 'An ordinal modification of classical utilitarianism', *Erkenntnis* 33: 73–88.

Mill, J. (1829) *Analysis of the Phenomena of the Human Mind*, London.

Mill, J.S. (1975) *On Liberty* (first published 1859), in J.S. Mill, *Three Essays*, ed. by R. Wollheim, Oxford and New York: Oxford University Press.

—— (1987a) 'Bentham' (first published 1838), in J.S. Mill and J. Bentham, *Utilitarianism and Other Essays*, ed. by A. Ryan, Harmondsworth, Middlesex: Penguin Books.

—— (1987b) 'Whewell on moral philosophy' (first published 1852), in J.S. Mill and J. Bentham, *Utilitarianism and Other Essays*, ed. by A. Ryan, Harmondsworth, Middlesex: Penguin Books.

—— (1987c) *Utilitarianism* (first published 1861), in J.S. Mill and J. Bentham, *Utilitarianism and Other Essays*, ed. by A. Ryan, Harmondsworth, Middlesex: Penguin Books.

Moore, G.E. (1903) *Principia Ethica*, Cambridge: Cambridge University Press.

—— (1912) *Ethics*, London, Oxford and New York: Oxford University

Press.

More, H. (1667) *Enchiridion ethicum*, London.

More, T. (1908) *Utopia* (first published 1516), London: Chatto & Windus Publishers.

Mulholland, L.A. (1986) 'Rights, utilitarianism, and the conflation of persons', *Journal of Philosophy* 83: 323–40.

Narveson, J. (1967) *Morality and Utility*, Baltimore, Maryland: Johns Hopkins Press.

—— (1979) 'Rights and utilitarianism', *Canadian Journal of Philosophy* Supp. 5: 137–60.

—— (1988) *The Libertarian Idea*, Philadelphia: Temple University Press.

—— (1990) 'Utilitarianism and new generations' (first published 1967), in J. Glover (ed.), *Utilitarianism and Its Critics*, New York: Macmillan.

Nielsen, K. (1984) 'On the need for "moral experts": A test case for practical ethics', *The International Journal of Applied Philosophy* 2: 69–73.

Nowell-Smith, P. (1954) *Ethics*, Harmondsworth, Middlesex: Pelican Books.

Nozick, R. (1974) *Anarchy, State and Utopia*, Oxford and New York: Basil Blackwell.

Ossowska, M. (1961) 'Remarks on the ancient distinction between bodily and mental pleasures', *Inquiry* 4: 123–7.

Paley, W. (1785) *Principles of Moral and Political Philosophy*. Partly reprinted in D.D. Raphael (ed.) (1991) *British Moralists 1650–1800 II. Hume–Bentham* (first published 1969), Indianapolis and Cambridge: Hackett Publishing Company.

Parfit, D. (1986) *Reasons and Persons*, Oxford and New York: Oxford University Press.

Patten, S.C. (1980) 'Some are base, some are sublime: a defence of hedonistic utilitarianism', *Journal of Value Inquiry* 14: 275–86.

Popper, K.R. (1966) *The Open Society and Its Enemies* (first published 1945), vol. II, fifth revised edition, London: Routledge & Kegan Paul.

Primorac, I. (1978) 'Utilitarianism and self-sacrifice of the innocent', *Analysis* 38: 194–9.

Quinton, A. (1989) *Utilitarian Ethics* (first published 1973), second edition, London: Duckworth.

Rachels, J. (ed.) (1979) *Moral Problems: A Collection of Philosophical Essays*, third edition, New York: Harper & Row, Publishers.

Rand, A. (1961) *The Virtue of Selfishness: A New Concept of Egoism*, New York: New American Library.

Raphael, D.D. (ed.) (1991a) *British Moralists 1650–1800 I. Hobbes–Gay* (first published 1969), Indianapolis and Cambridge: Hackett Publishing Company.

—— (ed.) (1991b) *British Moralists 1650–1800 II. Hume–Bentham* (first published 1969), Indianapolis and Cambridge: Hackett Publishing Company.

Rawls, J. (1958) 'Justice as fairness', *Philosophical Review* 67: 164–94.

—— (1972) *A Theory of Justice*, Oxford: Oxford University Press.

Rescher, N. (1983) 'Problems in applying philosophy', in M. Bradie, T. Attig and N. Rescher (eds), *The Applied Turn in Contemporary*

Philosophy, Bowling Green: The Applied Philosophy Program, Bowling Green State University.

Ryan, A. (1987) 'Introduction', in J.S. Mill and J. Bentham, *Utilitarianism and Other Essays*, ed. by A. Ryan, Harmondsworth, Middlesex: Penguin Books.

Schneewind, J.B. (1977) *Sidgwick's Ethics and Victorian Moral Philosophy*, Oxford: Clarendon Press.

Scottia, D. (1990) 'Utilitarianism, sociobiology, and the limits of benevolence', *The Journal of Philosophy* 87: 329–45.

Sen, A. and Williams, B. (1982) (eds) *Utilitarianism and Beyond*, Cambridge: Cambridge University Press.

Shaftesbury, the third Earl of (1711) *Characteristics of Men, Manners, Opinions, Times*, vol. II. Partly reprinted in D.D. Raphael (ed.) (1991) *British Moralists 1650–1800 I. Hobbes–Gay* (first published 1969), Indianapolis and Cambridge: Hackett Publishing Company.

Sidgwick, H. (1922) *The Methods of Ethics* (first published 1874, seventh edition first published 1907), London: Macmillan.

Sikora, R.I. (1975) 'Utilitarianism: the classical principle and the average principle', *Canadian Journal of Philosophy* 5: 409–19.

Singer, M. (1977) 'Actual consequence utilitarianism', *Mind* 86: 67–77.

—— (1983) 'Further on actual consequence utilitarianism', *Mind* 92: 270–4.

Singer, P. (1972) 'Famine, affluence, and morality', *Philosophy & Public Affairs* 1: 229–43.

—— (1973a) *Democracy and Disobedience*, Oxford: Oxford University Press.

—— (1973b) 'Animal liberation', *The New York Review of Books*, April 5. Reprinted in J. Rachels (ed.) (1979) *Moral Problems: A Collection of Philosophical Essays*, third edition, New York: Harper & Row, Publishers.

—— (1974) 'Sidgwick and reflective equilibrium', *Monist* 58: 490–517.

—— (1975) *Animal Liberation*, New York: a New York Review Book.

—— (1979) *Practical Ethics*, Cambridge: Cambridge University Press.

—— (1981) *The Expanding Circle*, New York: Harper & Row, Publishers.

—— (1988) 'Reasoning towards utilitarianism', in D. Seanor (ed.), *Hare and Critics*, Oxford: Clarendon Press.

—— (1989) 'Ethics', in *The New Encyclopaedia Britannica*, Vol. 18, Chicago: Encyclopaedia Britannica, Inc.

—— (ed.) (1986) *Applied Ethics*, Oxford: Oxford University Press.

Smart, J.J.C. (1956) 'Extreme and restricted utilitarianism', *Philosophical Quarterly* 6: 344–54.

—— (1960) 'Extreme utilitarianism: a reply to M.A. Kaplan', *Ethics* 71: 133–4.

—— (1967) 'Utilitarianism', in *The Encyclopedia of Philosophy*, New York.

—— (1977) 'Benevolence as an over-riding attitude', *Australasian Journal of Philosophy* 55: 127–35.

—— (1978) 'Utilitarianism and justice', *Journal of Chinese Philosophy* 5: 287–99.

—— (1987) *An Outline of a System of Utilitarian Ethics* (first published

1961), in J.J.C. Smart and B. Williams, *Utilitarianism: For and Against*, Cambridge: Cambridge University Press.

Smart, R.N. (1958) 'Negative utilitarianism', *Mind* 67: 542–3.

Smith, A. (1759) *The Theory of Moral Sentiments*, London.

Sprigge, T.L.S. (1965) 'A utilitarian reply to McCloskey', *Inquiry* 8: 264–91.

—— (1968) 'Professor Narveson's utilitarianism', *Inquiry* 11: 332–46.

Stephen, J.F. (1967) *Liberty, Equality, Fraternity* (first published 1873, second edition first published 1874), ed. by R.J. White, Cambridge: Cambridge University Press.

Stout, A.K. (1954) 'Suppose everybody did the same', *Australasian Journal of Philosophy* 32: 1–29.

Strang, C. (1960) 'What if everyone did that?', *Durham University Journal* 23: 5–10.

Sumner, L.W. (1979) 'The good and the right', in W. Cooper, K. Nielsen and S.C. Patten (eds), *New Essays on John Stuart Mill and Utilitarianism*, *Canadian Journal of Philosophy* Supp. 5: 99–114.

Taylor, P.W. (1986) *Respect for Nature: A Theory of Environmental Ethics*, Princeton, New Jersey: Princeton University Press.

Temkin, J. (1978) 'Actual consequence utilitarianism: A reply to Professor Singer', *Mind* 87: 412–14.

Ten, C.L. (1987) *Crime, Guilt, and Punishment*, Oxford: Clarendon Press.

Thomas, W. (1985) *Mill*, Oxford and New York: Oxford University Press.

Thomson, J. (1986) *Rights, Restitution, and Risk: Essays in Moral Theory*, Cambridge, Massachusetts and London: Harvard University Press.

Tooley, M. (1972) 'Abortion and infanticide', *Philosophy and Public Affairs* 2: 37–65.

—— (1983) *Abortion and Infanticide*, London: Oxford University Press.

Toulmin, S. (1953) *The Place of Reason in Ethics*, New York: Cambridge University Press.

Trapp, R. (1990) 'Utilitarianism incorporating justice – a decentralized model of ethical decision making', *Erkenntnis* 32: 341–81.

Tucker, A. (1805) *The Light of Nature Pursued* (first published 1768–77), ed. by H.P. St John Mildmay, London.

Urmson, J.O. (1953) 'The interpretation of the philosophy of J.S. Mill', *Philosophical Quarterly* 3: 33–9.

—— (1969) 'Saints and heroes', in J. Feinberg (ed.), *Moral Concepts*, Oxford: Oxford University Press.

von Wright, G.H. (1963) *The Varieties of Goodness*, London: Routledge & Kegan Paul.

—— (1971) *Explanation and Understanding*, London: Routledge & Kegan Paul.

—— (1984) 'On need' (in Finnish), *Ajatus – The Journal of the Philosophical Society of Finland* 41: 25–38.

—— (1986) 'Rationality: means and ends', *Epistemologia* 9 (1986): 57–72.

—— (undated) 'Values and needs' (in Finnish), undated manuscript.

Waldron, J. (ed.) (1984) *Theories of Rights*, Oxford: Oxford University Press.

Walker, A.D.M. (1974) 'Negative utilitarianism', *Mind* 83: 424–8.

Wasserstrom, R. (1979) 'Rights, human rights, and racial discrimination' (first published 1964), in J. Rachels (ed.), *Moral Problems: A Collection of Philosophical Essays*, third edition, New York: Harper & Row.

Watkins, J.W.N. (1963) 'Negative utilitarianism', *Aristotelian Society* Supp. 37: 95–114.

Webster's Ninth New Collegiate Dictionary (1983), Springfield, Massachusetts: Merriam-Webster Inc.

White, A.R. (1984) *Rights*, Oxford: Clarendon Press.

Wikler, D. (1991) 'What has bioethics to offer health policy?', *The Milbank Memorial Quarterly* 69: 233–51.

Williams, B. (1976) 'Persons, character and morality', in A. Rorty (ed.), *The Identities of Persons*, Berkeley: University of California Press.

—— (1985) *Ethics and the Limits of Philosophy*, Cambridge, Massachusetts: Harvard University Press.

—— (1987) 'A critique of utilitarianism' (first published 1973), in J.J.C. Smart and B. Williams, *Utilitarianism: For and Against*, Cambridge: Cambridge University Press.

Young, J.O. (1986) 'The immorality of applied ethics', *The International Journal of Applied Philosophy* 3 (2): 37–43.

INDEX